Propaganda and Aesthetics

The Literary Politics of Afro-American Magazines

in the Twentieth Century

Abby Arthur Johnson & Ronald Maberry Johnson

The University of Massachusetts Press   Amherst, 1979

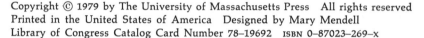
Copyright © 1979 by The University of Massachusetts Press   All rights reserved
Printed in the United States of America   Designed by Mary Mendell
Library of Congress Catalog Card Number 78–19692   ISBN 0–87023–269–x

Grateful acknowledgment is extended to the following for permission to reprint copyrighted material:
North Dakota Quarterly, for material from Abby Arthur Johnson and Ronald Maberry Johnson, "Reform and Reaction: Black Literary Magazines in the 1930s," in *North Dakota Quarterly* 46 (Winter 1978), 5–18.
Journal of American Studies, for material from Abby Arthur Johnson and Ronald Maberry Johnson, "Forgotten Pages: Black Literary Magazines of the 1920s," in *Journal of American Studies* 8 (December 1974), 363–82.
The Sterling Lord Agency, Inc., for material from LeRoi Jones, "Black Art," in *Black Magic Poetry*, published by Bobbs-Merrill, copyright © 1969 by LeRoi Jones. Reprinted by permission of The Sterling Lord Agency, Inc.
The Association for the Study of Afro-American Life and History, Inc., for material from Abby Arthur Johnson and Ronald Maberry Johnson, "Away from Accommodation: Radical Editors and Protest Journalism, 1900–1910," in *Journal of Negro History* 62, no. 4 (1977).

Grateful acknowledgment for permission to publish is also extended to: Dorothy West, for quotations from her correspondence; Mrs. James Weldon Johnson, for the letters exchanged between Claude McKay, Dorothy West, and James Weldon Johnson; The James Weldon Johnson Memorial Collection, for the letters of James Weldon Johnson; The Estate of Claude McKay, for the correspondence of Claude McKay; Hope McKay Virtue, for her kind permission to publish previously unpublished correspondence; Mrs. Frederick Douglass III, for the letters of Booker T. Washington.

Library of Congress Cataloging in Publication Data
Johnson, Abby Arthur.
Propaganda and aesthetics.
Bibliography: p.
Includes index.
1. American literature—Afro-American authors—Periodicals—History. 2. Afro-American periodicals—History. 3. American literature—20th century—History and criticism. 4. Afro-Americans—Race identity. 5. Little magazines—United States.
I. Johnson, Ronald Maberry, joint author. II. Title.
PS153.N5J6   810'.8'0052   78–19692
ISBN 0–87023–269–X

Contents

Preface

The literary materials in Afro-American magazines of the twentieth century weave into a rich narrative. The journals provide insight, not available in a comparable manner elsewhere, into the evolution of Afro-American literature. They trace the contributions made by major figures, including W. E. B. Du Bois, Langston Hughes, Charles S. Johnson, Alain Locke, and Richard Wright, among several others. They record the discussions over art and propaganda which have been long prominent in black literature. Decade by decade, black artists and intellectuals have debated the function of Afro-American literature: should it serve the aesthetic tastes of the individual writer, or should it advance the interests of Afro-Americans as a group. Some writers favored art-for-art's sake, or approximations of that emphasis; others articulated the need for art-for-people's sake, as they termed it.

Little work has been done on individual Afro-American periodicals and nothing, up to this point, has been published on twentieth-century black journals as a group. Studies of magazines in general are relatively rare, with only *The Little Magazine*, by Frederick Hoffman, Charles Allen, and Carolyn P. Ulrich, attempting a survey of small journals in this century. With the exception of Afro-American publications, the book provides valuable insight into numerous journals predating 1946, when the volume was published. It includes a brief note on *Fire* and *Challenge*, but excludes reference altogether to many other notable black small journals, such as *Black Opals*, *Harlem*, *Saturday Evening Quill*, and *Stylus*. We have attempted, with our study, to fill a considerable gap in literary history by detailing the development of Afro-American magazines in this century.

We limited our study to journals generally owned, managed, and read by Afro-Americans. Some publications tried to be exclusively black, as were those of the 1960s and early 1970s. Others allowed white participation to a greater or lesser extent, as did *Voice of the Negro, Crisis, Opportunity, Negro Story,* and *Phylon.* All of the journals, whether involving whites or not, focused primarily on Afro-American concerns, including the proper direction for an evolving black literature. We could not examine each Afro-American magazine, since there have been so many. Instead, we focused on the publications most significant to the course of black literature.

These publications include large cultural and political journals as well as little literary magazines. In the former category are *Colored American Magazine, Voice of the Negro,* and especially *Crisis* and *Opportunity,* which served important literary purposes. The black little magazines were more numerous, appearing originally in embryonic form in the first decade of the century. The magazines were designated little not because of publication size or contents but because of a limited readership, usually numbering below 1,000 for each journal. The audience was small since the publications were so controversial, both in the subjects and styles of the material included. The poems and stories frequently highlighted characters—prostitutes, gamblers, and con men—and language—obscenities and slang terms like "nigger" and "cracker"—which offended the bourgeoisie on both sides of the color line. As controversial publications, the little magazines could not, as a rule, attract well-heeled benefactors or advertisers, who usually were conservative in their tastes and gifts. As a result, many of the small journals died with pride in their beginnings, some after only one issue, such as *Fire* and *Harlem,* others after a valiant struggle sustained over three or four years, such as *Challenge* and *Negro Story.*

This book follows a chronological plan, with each chapter focusing on a significant period in Afro-American history and letters. Chapter one discusses magazines and literature in the first decade of the century, in relation to the Booker T. Washington-W. E. B. Du Bois controversy. Chapters two and three trace the careers of the large journals and the little magazines as they prepared for and contributed to the black renaissance of the 1920s. Chapter four examines publications of the 1930s, in their response to the Depression and contemporary emphases on proletarian literature; and chapter five considers the impact of World War II on the journals of the 1940s and 1950s, as they developed a literary aesthetic based on integration. Chapter six views the revolutionary little magazines of the 1960s and early 1970s in their attempts to reject western culture and to establish a viable black aesthetic.

This book originated five years ago, when Professor Arthur P. Davis of Howard University suggested that we look at *Fire* and *Harlem*, copies of which are located in the Moorland-Spingarn Research Center at the university. After reading the journals, along with other black magazines prominent in the 1920s, we saw the basis for an article which could best be done in collaboration. The joint involvement proved a successful blending of our scholarly backgrounds and interests and led to plans for a larger study. In the larger effort, Ron provided insights as an American social and cultural historian and Abby as a literary historian, with a specialty in little magazines. Abby drafted the manuscript, drawing on our joint research, several position papers, and innumerable and often interminable discussions. At the beginning of the study, neither of us thought that an adequate presentation of the material could be done without the considerable help of the other. We feel the same way now. Throughout our labors, we have shared some memorable experiences: the discovery of lively magazines and charismatic individuals, the unexpected locating of revealing correspondence, the unfolding of a dramatic story.

We remain grateful to numerous persons. We are, of course, especially thankful for the advice and support that Professor Davis has given us. The staff of the Moorland-Spingarn Research Center proved most helpful, particularly Michael R. Winston, Director, in giving us access to the material; Denise D. Gletten, Senior Manuscript Librarian and Esme Bhan, Manuscript Research Associate, in assisting our use of archival collections; and Cornelia Stokes, Coordinator of Reader Services, in gathering the large number of magazines used for this study. We were helped as well by the responsive personnel at the Library of Congress Manuscript Division, Beinicke Library of Yale University, and the Schomburg Center for Research in Black Culture. In developing the last chapter of our study, we gained valuable insights through conversations with Larry P. Neal, E. Ethelbert Miller, and Edward S. Spriggs. We are also indebted to Professor Mary McHenry of Mount Holyoke College for a critical, as well as encouraging, assessment of our effort as we brought the manuscript into final shape. Finally, we want to state our appreciation to the hardworking members of the University of Massachusetts Press: Richard Martin, Editor; Carol Schoen, Production Editor; Elsie Landstrom, Copy Editor; and Don Strandberg, Marketing Manager.

Washington, D.C.   A.A.J.

December 1978   R.M.J.

1. Away from Accommodation

Colored American Magazine,
Voice of the Negro, and *Horizon,*
1900–1910

J. Max Barber, editor of *Voice of the Negro,* understood the importance of black magazines. In his first editorial, published in January 1904, he shared his insight with readers in words that deserve remembrance. "To the casual observer," he declared, "there is nothing interesting in the launching of a Negro magazine; but to the careful observer, to the philosopher of history, to him who is a reader of the signs of the times it means much. It means that culture is taking a deep hold upon our people. It is an indication that our people are becoming an educated, a reading people, and this is a thing of which to be proud." Black journals supply indices to Afro-American culture and thereby provide rich resources for future generations, as Barber explained in connection with his publication: "We want it to be more than a mere magazine. We expect of it current and sociological history so accurately given and so vividly portrayed that it will become a kind of documentation for the coming generations." [1]

The journals at the beginning of the twentieth century—*Colored American Magazine* and *Horizon,* along with *Voice of the Negro*—documented a stage in Afro-American culture. They were race periodicals, involved first in political and social occurrences and then in black literature. In their literary function, they published the work of young poets and fiction writers, most of whom had no other outlets for their efforts. Concerned with politics, the editors favored creative work which harmonized with the broader emphases of their publications. They occasionally made comments suggesting that they were searching for a black literary aesthetic which would meet the needs of the day. The editors disagreed in their political assessments, and thus they differed as well in their understanding of Afro-American literature.

Black journals in the first several decades of the nineteenth century had been more unified in approach, although less literary in emphasis. They were all involved in abolitionism, from the first black magazine, *Freedom's Journal*, published in 1827 in New York City; through subsequent periodicals which also emerged in New York, including the *National Reformer* (1833), an early *Colored American Magazine* (1837–41), and *Mirror of Liberty* (1837); to the *Douglass' Monthly* (1858–61), a publication originating in Rochester, New York. Stressing the evils of slavery and racial discrimination, they became an essential part of the black protest tradition. Such involvement, imperative as it was, deflected attention from purely literary endeavors, as Charles S. Johnson later observed: "The immediate personal concern of the educated Negroes in the abolition of slavery and their necessary abolition activities, precluded the calm, deliberate creative writing of *belles lettres.*" [2]

Johnson reserved compliments for the *Anglo-African Magazine*, a journal reaching its fullest development just before the outbreak of the Civil War. He declared that the periodical had "a kinship to none of the Negro publications that preceded it and to few that followed. Its standards were clear-cut and high, its articles scholarly and superior." *Colored American Magazine* lauded the journal in a similar manner, saying that "no periodical we have to-day has as brilliant a staff of contributors as the *Anglo-African* had." [3] Edited by Thomas Hamilton and published in New York under various titles from 1859 to 1862, the *Anglo-African* was diversified in approach, including protest pieces along with nonpolitical literature. It featured scholarly articles, short fiction, and poems from persons who had concerned themselves with abolitionism: Martin Delany, Frederick Douglass, John Langston, Daniel A. Payne, Charles Lenox Remond, George Vashon, Frances Ellen Watkins Harper and, with others, William Whipper. William Wells Brown with "Miralda, or the Beautiful Quadroon," a serialized story, and Martin Delany, in his twenty-six chapters of "Blake or the Huts of America," score the practice of slavery, with Delany being the more successful of the two. Sterling Brown claimed, in the *Negro Caravan*, that "*Blake* contains some pictures of slavery more convincing than anything in *Uncle Tom's Cabin* or *Clotel.*" Frances Harper, a frequent contributor of poems, stories, and essays to the journal, stated the essential goal that the *Anglo-African* advanced time and again: "We need men and women whose hearts are the homes of a high and lofty enthusiasm, and a noble devotion to the cause of emancipation, who are ready and willing to lay time, talent and money on the altar of universal freedom." [4]

The expectation of greater opportunity and participation became pronounced as the Civil War drew to a close. Along with countless others, William Wells Brown thought the future held much promise, for the formerly oppressed as well as for their oppressors. Eyeing freedom for all, he declared the black American had "that intellectual genius which God has planted in the mind of man, that distinguishes him from the rest of creation, and which needs only cultivation to make it bring forth fruit." [5] The optimism behind Brown's comment, the feeling that liberty and opportunity were at hand, expired as the last federal troops left the South in 1877 and as the failure of Radical Reconstruction became clearly evident.

Black literary magazines, along with occasional emphases on *belles lettres*, also disappeared in the remaining years of the century. As new forms of oppression developed, different expressions and involvements appeared in black communities. With the emergence of Booker T. Washington, accommodationism increasingly supplanted the earlier protest tradition. Washington, a prominent educator, speaker, and writer, had achieved a national reputation even before his famous 1895 address at the Atlanta Cotton Exposition. After the speech, in which he asserted that Afro-Americans must work within the system of Southern segregation, Washington expanded his influence in Northern as well as Southern communities. He concentrated particularly on black newspapers and magazines, hoping to use them to spread the gospel of accommodationism. By 1900, he essentially controlled *Alexander's Magazine* and *Colored Citizen* of Boston, the *Colored American* of Washington and, among others, the New York *Age*, all of which propagandized his own approach to race relations.

To a small group of Afro-Americans, however, Washington did not have the answers. Southern segregation was becoming more intolerable, as blacks experienced political disfranchisement and continued manifestations of white violence, especially in the increased numbers of lynchings. Such conditions encouraged the formation of a radical black perspective. In Boston, Cleveland, Chicago, and other Northern cities, a growing minority of influential Afro-Americans began to oppose accommodationism. The opposition included important creative writers, among whom were Charles Chesnutt and Paul Laurence Dunbar, and outspoken newspaper editors, including Harry C. Smith of the Cleveland *Gazette* and especially the controversial William Monroe Trotter of the Boston *Guardian*. Editors of Afro-American magazines also joined in the rejection of accommodationism. Pauline Hopkins, Max Barber, and William E. B. Du Bois after he finally broke with Washington in 1904, did much to reassert the protest tradition in black journalism. Through this effort, they brought a measure of freedom to Afro-American editors and provided a basis for the eventual development of black little magazines.

Colored American Magazine was the first significant Afro-American journal to emerge in the twentieth century. The idea for the publication originated with Walter Wallace, a native Virginian in his twenties who had come to Boston. In the early spring of 1900, he met with three other young men also in their twenties who had been born in Virginia but had migrated to Boston. With Jesse W. Watkins, Harper S. Fortune, and Walter Alexander Johnson, he founded the Colored Co-operative Publishing Company and the *Colored American Magazine*, first issued in May 1900. Wallace became president of the company and managing editor of the journal, while Watkins served as secretary and assistant treasurer, Fortune as treasurer, and Johnson as advertising manager. Wallace and the others attracted a talented staff, foremost of whom was Pauline Hopkins, who served as editor from 1902 until 1904. Hopkins had been born in Portland, Maine, in 1859, but had been raised as "a Boston girl," in the full sense of that expression.[6] Proud of her heritage, and hoping to revive protest literature, Hopkins wrote frequently in the periodical about the abolitionist tradition in New England, thereby gaining a secure following among black Bostonians. At the same time, though, she and the others worked to make the magazine a quality national journal.

They spoke forthrightly from the first, saying they intended to fill a great need: "American citizens of color, have long realized that for them there exists no monthly magazine, distinctively devoted to their interests and to the development of Afro-American art and literature." White folks, they indicated, could not be counted upon, for "as a rule, the Anglo Saxon race, fails to sufficiently recognize our efforts, hopes and aspirations." Since only a few exceptional writers, such as Chesnutt, ever appeared in journals owned by whites, they believed it essential to provide a medium for black creative and scholarly writers involved in all aspects of race. Most of all, they wanted to encourage black consciousness, believing that advancement lay primarily in group solidarity. "Above all," the editors wrote, the magazine "aspires to develop and intensify the bonds of that racial brotherhood, which alone can enable a people, to assert their racial rights as men, and demand their privileges as citizens."[7]

Under the leadership of Hopkins, each issue of the magazine was varied. There were articles by various writers on politics—"An Answer to 'Mr. Roosevelt's Negro Policy' "—business—"Catering, and Chas. H. Smiley of Chicago"—education—"An Appeal for the Colored Schools in the State of Georgia"—and religion—a series called "Fascinating Bible Stories." Hopkins's heart, however, was in history and fiction, and her enthusiasms bear examination, since they set the tone for the magazine during its first two years.

She was outspoken on the value of black history, believing that "the true romance of American life and customs is to be found in the history of the Negro upon this continent." She stated that the time was ripe for the dissemination of information on the Afro-American past, so long excluded from conventional texts: "History has recorded these deeds, and they shall be known; God intends it so!" For Hopkins, the discipline revolved not around military or political battles, but around the deeds of charismatic individuals. Time and again, she claimed that history is biography, "an account of the deeds of men who have been the models aand patterns for the great mass of humanity in past centuries even from the beginning of the world." [8] She stressed the importance of biography in the *Colored American Magazine* because she believed that the lives of powerful blacks could be strong incentives to Afro-American youth. In the introduction to her biographical essay on Robert Morris, she made this point with the emotional language customary to her character sketches: "We delight to honor the great men of our race because the lives of these noble Negroes are tongues of living flame speaking in the powerful silence of example, and sent to baptize the race with heaven's holy fire into the noble heritage of perfected manhood." [9]

She had no trouble finding exemplary lives for sketches or persons to do the writing. She published a section called "Here and Now," which included biographical commentary on blacks prominent in various localities, and she featured biographical essays by contributors. She also wrote her own series of character studies which appeared, with a few exceptions, every month for two years. One of the series, "Famous Men of the Negro Race," carried essays on, among many others, William Wells Brown, Frederick Douglass, Robert Brown Elliott, and Toussaint L'Overture. Another, "Famous Women of the Negro Race," featured articles on educators, musicians, artists, and on abolitionists, including Harriet Tubman and Sojourner Truth.

For subjects, she generally chose individuals like Robert Morris who had achieved in the face of great odds: "His life comes to us as a lesson of accomplishment from the barest possibilities." She generally preferred those who had lived in or near Boston, as had Robert Elliott, Lewis Hayden, Charles Remond, and several of the women educators. In considering the latter, she ended one essay: "May my tongue cleave to the roof of my mouth and my right hand forget its cunning when I forget the benefits bestowed upon my persecuted race by noble-hearted New England." [10] She believed in the lessons of biography so much that she often became didactic, even preachy, in her characteristically long introductions and conclusions. As a creative writer, though, she knew how to offset these passages with moving dialogue and dramatic incidents.

Under Hopkins's direction, the *Colored American Magazine* did much to encourage black writers. Editorial statements praised the creative work, describing it as a harbinger of new developments in Afro-American literature: "Our short stories, by our Race writers, are becoming more and more literary in style, and we shall soon see an era of strong competition in the field of letters." Regular contributors followed the lead, with William Braithwaite proclaiming that "we are at the commencement of a 'Negroid' renaissance . . . that will have in time as much importance in literary history as the much spoken of and much praised Celtic and Canadian renaissance." [11]

More and better fiction and poetry was published by the *Colored American Magazine* during the years Pauline Hopkins was editor than at any other time in its history. Each issue of the journal included three or four poems and one or two short stories. Conventional verses, on love and the changing of the seasons, came from Benjamin Brawley, Braithwaite and, occasionally, from T. Thomas Fortune. D. Webster Davis contributed some amusing stanzas in dialect. The most memorable poems, written variously in dialect and in standard English, were from James D. Corrothers. He could be humorous, as he was in "Me 'N' Dunbar," when he described the literary rivalry between himself and Paul Dunbar: "A debblish notion tuck me 't Paul wuz gittin' on too fast." He could also be angry, as he was in "Juny at the Gate," which is a portrait of a black family wrenched apart during slavery; in "An Awful Problem Solved," a satire of "Uncle Sammy Yankee" and his "school for witty boys," staffed by "Professor Prejudice" and "Dr. Degradation"; and in "The Gift of the Greatest God," a portrayal of white bigotry in the face of black heroism, such as that exhibited by James Parker, who captured the assassin of President William McKinley.[12]

Much of the fiction was in the protest tradition. In "Black Is, As Black Does," by Angelina Grimke, God condemns the white racist, covered with blood, to hell: "Begone!" he thunders. Braithwaite ex-

plored the tragedies of separation and death experienced by an interracial couple in a racist society.[13] Pauline Hopkins used similar material in the fiction she wrote monthly for the magazine. Her output was
prodigious, including ten short stories and three serialized novels:
Hagar's Daughters (March 1901–March 1902), *Winona* (May 1902–
October 1902), and *Of One Blood* (November 1902–November 1903).
Several of the pieces bore a pseudonym, Sarah Allen, which was the
name of Hopkins's mother.[14] As editor, she did not want her own
signature to appear more than two or at most three times in each
number.

The motivation behind her fiction deserves commentary, for she
held ideas which would be stressed for decades, especially during
the 1920s. In the preface to her first novel, *Contending Forces*, which
was issued by the Colored Co-operative Publishing Company in 1900,
she emphasized the "great value" of fiction "as a preserver of man-
ners and customs—religious, political and social. It is a record of
growth and development from generation to generation." She claimed
that the race must encourage black writers, because they only could
preserve the rich Afro-American heritage: "*No one will do this for us;
we must ourselves develop the men and women who will faithfully
portray the inmost thoughts and feelings of the Negro with all the
fire and romance which lie dormant in our history, and, as yet, un-
recognized by writers of the Anglo-Saxon race.*" [15]

Throughout her short stories and novels, Hopkins explored the
color line, as Charles Chesnutt was doing, and as Jessie Fauset and
Nella Larsen, among others, would do two or three decades later.
Over and again, she asserted that the boundary separating black and
white was blurred. *Winona* begins in a "mixed community of Anglo-
Saxons, Indians and Negroes . . . the world [would] stand aghast and
try in vain to find the dividing line supposed to be a natural barrier
between the white and the dark-skinned races." The beautiful Susan,
an octoroon in "A Dash for Liberty," carries the blood of slave and
slaver, "representative of two races, to which did she belong?" [16]

Typically, Hopkins's light blacks marry whites. The results are
commonly tragic, particularly when both partners believe they are
white, which is often the case in her fiction. The initial shock of racial
discovery is devastating, as in *Hagar's Daughters*: "The sense of her
bitter shame overpowered her, and she shrank before him, cower-
ing. . . . Twice he essayed to speak, and twice a groan issued from
his white lips. How could he bear it! She stood before him with
clasped hands and hanging head as became a slave before her master." [17] Usually, the marriage is shattered, with a long and agonizing

separation following the discovery, or with illness and death visiting one or both of the parties. The relationship most likely to avoid these difficulties in Hopkins's fiction is that between an octoroon and an Englishman, whom she considered essentially free of racial prejudices. Such a match occurs in *Winona.*

In a letter to the editor, Cornelia A. Condict, an indignant white reader, dropped her subscription to the magazine and questioned the persistent use of interracial themes: "The stories of these tragic mixed loves will not commend themselves to your white readers and will not elevate the colored readers." Hopkins responded publicly in the journal. "My stories are definitely planned to show the obstacles persistently placed in our paths by a dominant race to subjugate us spiritually," she countered. By her stories, she hoped among other matters to educate white readers: "I sing of the *wrongs* of a race that ignorance of their pitiful condition may be changed to intelligence and must awaken compassion in the hearts of the just." She believed that Condict's very protest justified such emphases: "I am glad to receive this criticism for it shows more clearly than ever that white people don't understand *what pleases Negroes.*" [18]

Wallace and other members of the staff praised Hopkins for her fiction, as well as her other work. They offered *Contending Forces* as a gift to each new subscriber. They praised the novel as a challenge to Southern bigotry: "The book will certainly create a sensation among a certain class of 'whites' at the South. . . ." In one page of "Announcements," the publishers lauded not only *Contending Forces* as a "powerful race book," but the "popular serial story" just concluding, which was *Hagar's Daughters,* and the "thrilling story" waiting in the wings, *Winona.*[19]

These plaudits could not save Hopkins, however, who lost her editorship in 1904 soon after the magazine came under the control of persons sympathetic to Booker T. Washington. The new management found her embarrassingly outspoken. In her short stories and serialized novels, she romanticized abolitionists and damned Southern racists, especially old-style politicians and lynch mobs. With her essays and editorials, she surveyed the scene of rape, lynching, disfranchisement, and generally "wicked laws," and she concluded that "the South needs nothing less than a new moral code." [20]

The new management did not discuss the reasons for Hopkins's dismissal. Instead, it dismissed her with brevity and faint praise in the "Publishers' Announcements" for November 1904, two months after her resignation: "On account of ill-health Miss Pauline Hopkins has found it necessary to sever her relations with this Magazine and has returned to her home in Boston. Miss Hopkins was a faithful and conscientious worker, and did much toward the building up the Magazine. We take this means of expressing our appreciation of her services, and wish for her a speedy return to complete health." No more was said, beyond a similar announcement in the May 1905 issue.[21] Meanwhile, Hopkins turned up in the December 1904 number of *Voice of the Negro*, with a commissioned article on "The New York Subway." One of her series immediately followed, from February to July 1905, on "The Dark Races of the Twentieth Century."

Explicit commentary on her resignation came from outsiders. A revealing statement appeared in *Crisis*, November 1912: "It was suggested to the editor . . . that her attitude was not conciliatory enough. As a white friend said: 'If you are going to take up the wrongs of your race then you must depend for support absolutely upon your race. For the colored man to-day to attempt to stand up to fight would be like a canary bird facing a bulldog, and an angry one at that.' The final result was that the magazine was bought by friends favorable to the conciliatory attitude. . . ." Charles S. Johnson substantiated the claim years later. Hopkins lost financial support for the magazine and ultimately her editorship because, he summarized, she "made no attempt to modify the magazine's expressions out of consideration for the white persons from whom most of the support was obtained." [22]

Spring 1903 to spring 1904 had been a transitional period for the magazine. Some specifics of that year are not made clear in the magazine itself, in the correspondence among key figures, or in subsequent scholarly works. One fact, however, is certain. On May 15, 1903, William H. Dupree, a postal superintendent and businessman, and two other black Bostonians, William O. West and Jesse W. Watkins, purchased both the Colored Co-operative Publishing Company and the *Colored American Magazine*. Apparently, they wanted to redeem the magazine financially and to secure its location in Boston, with Hopkins as editor. In the May–June issue, the new owners sketched transactions which have remained vague to the present, even though they hoped "at some future day . . . to tell our true story to our readers, who will then give us the full sympathy of their warm hearts." There had been a struggle for control of the magazine: "Envy and covetousness have sat with us in council." Representing the triumphant party, Dupree and the others were grateful, saying that "God has permitted us to save this enterprise to our race." They pledged their best "to restore public confidence in this enterprise and satisfy the demands of all those who have honored us with their patronage." [23] With the best of intentions, they failed, and the magazine succumbed to serious financial difficulties.

In the spring of 1904, the journal continued only by the benevolence of John C. Freund, a New York publisher. Meanwhile, Freund was corresponding with Booker T. Washington, who was once again interested in the publication. In 1901, Washington had owned a few shares of stock in the company, only to dispose of them when the charge circulated that he was attempting to control the magazine, along with other Afro-American publications. Washington proceeded more cautiously in 1904. Rather than approach the owners directly, he commissioned Fred R. Moore, the national organizer and recording secretary of the National Negro Business League, to do the work. After hearing about the company and journal from Washington, Moore made several business trips to Boston, after which he decided to buy the combined enterprise. Sometime in the spring of 1904, he paid the management $8,000, $5,000 of which came from his own pocket and $3,000 from the coffers of Washington.[24] The change in ownership was not specifically announced in the magazine. Readers learned about the transfer first in the June 1904 number, which included congratulatory letters from Freund and Thomas Fortune to Moore as the new owner and general manager.

Nothing was said about Washington's part in the transaction. It cannot be determined, from the existing record, if Dupree and the others suspected that $3,000 had come from Washington. It can be established, from the magazine and from private correspondence, that readers were kept ignorant of the Tuskegean's involvement. In the September 1904 issue, for example, Moore countered an assertion which had appeared in the Dallas *Express* as follows: "Dr. Booker T. Washington has purchased *The Colored American Magazine* and made Emmett J. Scott [Washington's secretary] editor." Moore flatly denied the claim: "We desire to state that Dr. Washington has not purchased *The Colored American Magazine,* neither is Mr. Scott connected with its editorial department. Both gentlemen are friends of the publisher and their only interest is that of friendly support in wishing the Magazine success." [25]

The rumors persisted, and Moore continued to disavow Washington's support of the journal. In his editorial for November 1904, he claimed that he remained in sole control of the publication: "The writer desires . . . to have it thoroughly understood that he alone is responsible for the Magazine." He then felt free to say, in the next paragraph, that the journal would endorse Washington as "the greatest living Negro" and as a strong leader "in behalf of the race":

"We desire to have it emphatically understood in this connection that we are proud and feel honored in having the friendship of Dr. Booker T. Washington and we shall always take pleasure in publishing in the Magazine any matter in which he is interested, or which he desires us to publish." He went so far as to repeat the denials in personal letters. To James W. Woodlee, he stated that Washington "has no financial interest in the Magazine." [26]

Meanwhile, Moore was asking for and receiving financial aid from Washington. He tried to be delicate, avoiding bold requests for assistance. He began one characteristic letter outlining the financial position of the magazine: "Note of $500. due at State Bank on the 11th, with interest; also, Dupree note on the 15th, $230. The $500. note, I think by payment of $125. can renew for four more months. Kindly let me hear from you beforehand." In the next paragraph, he apologized for even this degree of forwardness: "Even though I am burdened I do not like the idea of burdening you, and I never want to have the reputation of being a 'grafter'. However, as you understand the conditions, I am quite sure you will appreciate my position." [27]

In the summer of 1904, Moore moved the company and magazine to New York. The apparent reason was that the city needed and could support a race journal. The move could also have been calculated to break the influence which could have been exerted by Bostonians had the journal remained in its first location. If such was part of the intention, the end was certainly reached. Moore spoke obliquely, in the May 1905 issue, about the New England constituency: "Some criticism was expressed by a certain class because of the removal of the Magazine from Boston to New York. This particular class gave small support when the property was in Boston and its success is certainly not now dependent upon them—a more broadminded clientele has come to us and we are of the opinion that we shall continue the publication, notwithstanding the withdrawal of the support of this class of people." In a letter to Emmett Scott, he gave his candid estimate of the Bostonians: "We had 150 Boston subscription to drop out [sic]—They are a queer lot—Some new ones will however come along—and we wont [sic] die on their account." [28] New subscribers, generally those favoring accommodationist policies, did come along. At its best, the *Colored American Magazine* reached a circulation of 15,000 copies, which was a sizeable number when compared with some of the smaller magazines, both in that day and later. [29]

Situated in New York, Moore could give full attention to Washington and his emissaries, who included Emmett Scott and Roscoe Conkling Simmons, a favorite nephew. Scott gave Moore advice on matters relating to the appearance of the periodical. Simmons, who served as associate editor from November 1904 to the spring of 1906, wrote "The Way of the World," a regular column in the journal, and generally watched out for the interests of his uncle. Conversant about several publications in New York, Simmons had assured his uncle that "I should be able to do much work for the school and the cause you speak for . . . I have always tried to do this; I shall try harder now." [30] When he resigned from the journal, because he felt his talents were not being appreciated, Simmons established an independent newspaper in New York, called the *Review*.

Directed by Moore and Washington, *Colored American Magazine* shifted dramatically in tone. A conciliatory approach was discernible as early as May 1904. The editorial for the issue, which was either written or influenced by Moore, contained statements at opposition with the ringing denunciations formerly penned by Hopkins. The introduction, for example, de-emphasized the importance of black franchisement: "What the nation desires to know about the Southern Negro is not how many votes he casts so much as whether he is bringing himself into such a position that he can discharge his social and personal duties as an American citizen." The tone became most accommodating toward the conclusion: "We implore the white men of the North and the white men of the South to deal with the Negro question soberly, tenderly, discerningly; and throw their strong arms about the Negro, and protect and counsel him, and be his elder brother, and help him get education. . . ." Moore elaborated in a letter to James Woodlee that "the policy is things done for colored people and things done by colored people: without whacking all white people, but to discriminate in our criticism of them." [31]

The emphasis was decidedly pragmatic. In the November 1904 issue, Moore outlined his intentions, which were clearly different from those of Hopkins. "The Magazine," he explained, "seeks to publish articles showing the advancement of our people along material lines, believing that the people generally are more interested in having information of the doings of the members of the race, rather [than] the writings of dreamers or theorists." [32] Influenced by Washington, with his concern for the "material" advancement of Afro-Americans, Moore did not consider literature of prime importance. As editor, he did not develop literary theories as had his predecessor, nor did he attract the best black creative writers of the day. As for quantity, Moore paralleled Hopkins's inclusions, often using two or three poems and one story in a single issue. In quality, however, he fell short. The angry poems of Corrothers and the outspoken stories of Hopkins gave way to conventional verses by the prominent journalist and friend of Washington, T. Thomas Fortune, and by persons of much lesser reputation, such as Louise Cass Evans, Charles Bertram Johnson, and Dora Lawrence. Fiction came from others, like Gertrude Brown and Osceola Madden, whose literary reputations did not survive the collapse of the journal. The creative work was generally inoffensive, as it included descriptions of the seasons, celebrations of holidays, and nostalgic reminiscences of days gone by. The magazine did feature reprints of Dunbar's poems, but the reprints were posthumous, when the poet was being lauded in many publications. The only newcomer introduced who would be important in later literature was Alain Locke, the first black recipient of a Rhodes scholarship. The April 1907 issue included a biographical sketch of young Locke, and the September 1909 number featured his well-written essay on life as a Rhodes scholar.

Moore dreamed of making the journal into the most influential black magazine. To accomplish this, he followed Washington's lead and stressed the positive rather than the negative, the successes achieved by particular Afro-Americans, rather than the crying needs of the race. Echoing a phrase made famous by Washington, he announced his predeliction for "the stories of the men and women who have struggled up from slavery, the stories of our school teachers, their sacrifices and their successes, the stories of our business men." [33] "Stories" meant articles and biographical essays on leaders in education and business. Foremost among these figures was Washington, and the magazine accordingly included as many as two or three articles in a single issue on his life and work, particularly at Tuskegee. There was much talk of "Industrial Education," with a series of articles on the subject written by Washington, Kelly Miller and, among others, T. Thomas Fortune. Business received much attention, as Moore published essays on the Business League; the Afro-American Building Loan and Investment Company, of which he was president; and the Afro-American Realty Company, of which he was secretary and treasurer. The journal boomed as well the achievements of black businessmen in New York, Boston, and other metropolitan centers.

Washington kept a watchful eye on the magazine. He recommended in several letters that Moore be careful to keep both his own and Washington's profile low. "I hope," he wrote Moore on September 14, 1905, that "for the next two or three months there will not be much in your magazine regarding myself or the Business League.

It will be hurtful for the public to get the idea that your magazine is the special organ of the League." [34] Primarily, it would be harmful for Washington if the public knew with certainty the extent of his control over the *Colored American Magazine* and other Afro-American publications. Support for Washington was most influential if it derived from seemingly independent sources.

Because Moore provided a good cover, Washington felt free to shape the course of the journal with discreet praise and specific advice given confidentially. He commended the editor for work complementing Washington's own emphases, as did an article boosting the black community of Pensacola: "It sets the pace for the kind of thing that your magazine ought to be continually engaged in. That is the kind of reading our people want and the kind that really helps them." [35] He proposed new directions when Moore seemed headed astray. "I beg to suggest," he offered in a letter of April 28, 1906, "that in the way of toning up the magazine, a symposium on the subject, 'What the Negro Race Can do to Help Itself in Constructive Directions', might be a good thing. I attach herewith a list of names of men whom I think should be asked to contribute towards the symposium. An article of say, five hundred to one thousand words would be a good thing." Such counsel seemed necessary because the *Colored American Magazine* was, Washington thought, running second to its main competitor: "In magazine breadth, dignity and form, your best friends will tell you that it does not come up to the Voice of the Negro." [36]

Moore and Washington were very conscious of their rivals, who were gathering around Du Bois. To undermine his support, they went on the offensive, using ridicule as their primary weapon. In the editorial for March 1905, Moore suggested that Du Bois was a pawn of William Monroe Trotter and no leader at all. He had best turn to literature: "With not one element of leadership about him, but a master with his pen, a poet, will he be led astray by the ravings of one who is not responsible, when he could so well defend the race with his songs?" [37]

When Du Bois established his first periodical, *Moon,* Moore laughed derisively again, saying that Du Bois was motivated by personal ambition, that he would sell out to the highest bidder, and that his only abundance lay in meaningless words. "Some of the Afro-American newspapers have been unkind enough to intimate that the 'Moon' is a subsidized organ," he went on. "Some people do not believe this. For if such were true, the subsidizers would demand that the mechanical appearance measure to the literary front—that is, if the subsidizers knew anything about the making of a paper. At this writing the 'Moon' shines. May its brilliance increase." [38] Metaphors predominated in later articles, as Moore characterized Du Bois and his associates in the Niagara Movement as "hot air artists," "fire-eating speech makers," and "professional wind-jammers." Moore had told Woodlee that he would not knock all white heads. As he testified later, he would, though, "continue to whack the heads of wind-jammers and pretenders, false prophets and holders of perpetual indignation meetings who are constantly yelling for manhood rights but who do not support their own people." [39]

Moore remained loyal to Washington, but Washington eventually lost faith in the capacity of Moore and the potential of the *Colored American Magazine*. As enthusiasm for the journal diminished and the relationship between Moore and Washington became strained, the last issue appeared in November 1909. Moore wrote from his heart to Washington on March 23, 1910. Lest the Tuskegean forget, he enumerated the work he had undertaken on Washington's behest, both as editor of the *Colored American Magazine* and as national organizer of the Negro Business League. The journal had not become a paying enterprise, which was the case of many white publications as well, but it had served a valuable purpose: "You have been protected, you have been able to say whatever you pleased without being known and I think that this is a valuable asset to you, for I have stood sponsor and there never has been a time or will be a time when my loyalty in this particular will ever be questioned." Moore had, he related, sacrificed the interests of himself and his family on Washington's behalf: "Your enemies were my enemies." To purchase the *Colored American Magazine*, he had mortgaged his house and his insurance policy. To maintain the journal he had worked for next to nothing and sometimes for no pay at all: "I have not drawn any salary for over a year." For all this, he had received little. "I have served but have not been served," he protested. In retrospect, his relationship with Washington over the past several years seemed unpleasant: "I feel that I have been nagged rather than encouraged, for what I have done and have tried to do." [40]

None of these complaints surfaced publicly, which was in keeping with the habits of Moore and Washington. Instead, the *Colored American Magazine* quietly slipped from view. *Crisis* was one of the few publications to acknowledge its passing. In 1912, an unidentified writer claimed that the journal, under Moore, became "so conciliatory, innocuous and uninteresting that it died a peaceful death almost unnoticed by the public." [41] From a literary standpoint, the magazine certainly did depreciate after Hopkins's resignation. Controlled by Moore and Washington, the *Colored American Magazine* has interest for the literary historian because it suggests an incompatibility between accommodationism and the development of a healthy minority literature. If a primary emphasis for a creative writer is cooperation, getting along with those opposing his ways, he loses the freedom of individual expression. He mutes some of his deepest emotions because they might confuse or antagonize readers of another race. He may even forego creative literature because it can lead into potentially explosive situations. The best creative writers were not inspired to propaganda for accommodationism, as the *Colored American Magazine* under Moore shows. The journal illustrates, too, the type of control Washington exerted over many contemporary Afro-American journals. Little and independent magazines could not flourish until alternate positions were clearly possible. The *Voice of the Negro* provided encouragement by showing that a black periodical could survive in opposition to Washington.

A. N. Jenkins, a white publisher, established *Voice of the Negro* in Atlanta in January 1904. The magazine remained in the city even when he sold his firm, J. L. Nichols and Company, to a Chicago-based organization, which became known as Hertel, Jenkins and Company. John A. Hertel, also white, shared Jenkins's enthusiasm over the new black journal. The two publishers engaged a competent editorial staff, which was headed by J. W. E. Bowen, a respected black professor at Atlanta University. The bulk of the editorial work was done, however, by J. Max Barber, who joined the staff immediately upon his graduation from Virginia Union University in Richmond. Barber had made his way on "ability" and "pluck," according to Du Bois. His rise had been rapid. He was born in 1878 in Blackstock, South Carolina, of poor but respectable folk, who had themselves been born slaves. Twenty-six years later he became editor of *Voice of the Negro* and "immediately" wrote Du Bois, "the name of J. Max Barber became known throughout the colored race." [42]

The journal established a precedent, being the first magazine ever edited in the South by blacks. In his initial editorial, "The Morning Cometh," Barber stressed the importance of the location: "The launching of a magazine for colored people in the South ought to stand out as a mile-post in the history of our upward march." Such a publication revealed, he explained, the values of a people: "Newspapers, magazines and books are the products of civilization." As a significant part of an evolving black culture, the journal both needed and deserved the backing of Afro-Americans. "The hearty support of such a venture will be conclusive proof," he reminded prospective readers, "that those who sacrificed all for our freedom and education did not die in vain." [43] The audience responded, and Barber later approximated the highest circulation figures attained by the *Colored American Magazine*. In 1912, he wrote to Du Bois that *Voice of the Negro* reached its maximum circulation in May 1906, with a sale of 15,000 copies.[44]

Barber, along with Bowen, apparently believed that *Voice of the Negro* had a role different from that of the *Colored American Magazine*, although he did not say this explicitly. In his early comments, Barber used temperate language in describing the purpose of the journal. *Voice of the Negro* "shall stand as the vanguard of a higher culture and a new literature," he wrote in "The Morning Cometh." "It shall," he continued, "be our object to keep the magazine abreast with the progress of the times. We want to make it a force of race elevation." As opposition developed, his comments became more forthright, as in the May 1907 issue: *"The Voice . . . openly avows itself to be a sentiment-shaping periodical. It is devoted to the unraveling of the snarl of the Color Problem and is published to the end that justice may prevail in the land, that lawlessness and bigotry may be wiped out and that the fetish of color prejudice may pass away forever."* [45]

According to Barber and many of his associates, no other magazine was willing to take a like stand. White journals customarily shut their pages to black writers and opened their editorials to denunciations of the entire race. "It was evident," declared Barber, "that the Negro writers could not appear except as a rarity in the other standard magazines. The attacks upon the race have increased in number and bitterness." Black periodicals established earlier had not been able or willing to redress the balance, as one of Barber's admirers explained: "Of the Negro periodicals that existed before the day of *The Voice*, a few were clean, some were respectable and too many were venal in the extreme." [46]

The climate was little better at the turn of the century, Barber concluded. Most editors of Afro-American journals would sell their opinions, he was convinced, to the highest bidder. Barber and his colleagues would not, as they testified over and again in *Voice of the Negro*: "We wish to have it well understood that the editorial and business management of the *Voice* have consciences and convictions that are not in the market for sale." [47] To attack the offenders, they published bold accusations from Du Bois, who by then had sufficient influence to draw attention to the problem. In his controversial "Debit and Credit" columns included in the January 1905 issue, he listed among the losses of the race some "$3000 of 'hush money' used to subsidize the Negro press in five leading cities." He repeated the claim in "The Niagara Movement," an article he contributed to the September 1905 number: "There has been a determined effort in this country to stop the free expression of opinion among black men; money has been and is being distributed in considerable sums to influence the attitude of certain Negro papers." [48]

Barber lent validity to the statement by saying, in the same number, that Du Bois "is not a man to make reckless assertions." [49] Du Bois would not, though, substantiate his comments with specifics published in the journal, presumably to avoid washing "our dirty linen in public." He reserved names for private correspondence. In a letter to William Hayes Ward, editor of the *Independent*, he pointed an indignant finger at the Boston *Citizen*, Chicago *Conservator*, Indianapolis *Freeman*, and New York *Age*, along with the *Colored American Magazine*. The payments had continued for so long, "three or four years," that they had become "notorious among well-informed Negroes and subject of frequent comment." He had ample "documentary evidence," he noted, although he never proved his case. The correspondence between Washington and Moore, along with other materials now available for study, indicate that Du Bois was generally correct in his assessment.[50]

Barber impressed Du Bois and other radicals because he resisted the pressures exerted by Washington. Du Bois attributed his stand to his idealism, his strength, and possibly to the "arrogance" of his youth.[51] Surely Barber deserves credit for his independence. It must also be remembered, however, that in the early years of his editorship he was supported by a solvent business and thus did not have to moderate his position in order to gain financial backing. Feeling free to speak his mind, even though some members of Hertel, Jenkins and Company increasingly disagreed with his approach, Barber wrote frankly to those in the Washington camp. He carried on a heated exchange with Emmett Scott, who served briefly as associate editor.

Scott had reported, on April 14, 1904, that while Washington endorsed the journal, he disapproved of the regular political column, "The Monthly Review." The comment annoyed Barber because, as he told Scott on April 18, 1904, "there is so much talk of Mr. Washington trying to get a hold on and dictate the policy of every colored interest in the country. . . ." With understatement, Barber indicated that his own position was "not thoroughly in sympathy" with Washington, and suggested the older man's limitations: "No man can be a genius at everything." He could not work with interference, he confessed to Scott in a letter dated April 27, 1904: "Mr. Washington ought to let The Voice of the Negro severely alone and let us run it, or we could get out and let him run it." [52]

Scott could not brook such intransigence, as his subsequent correspondence indicates. In a July 23, 1904 letter to Washington, he talked of leaving the journal and cited Barber as the cause: "He is out of sympathy with you and Tuskegee, and as I explain in the letter to him, is more like a baby than a man." The letter to Barber bore the same date, July 23, and the same simile. "As a matter of fact," he told Barber, "I have been much annoyed by having to deal with you as a baby, not as a man." [53] He thereby tendered his resignation.

Scott and Washington were not ready, despite the resignation, to give up the journal. They began to court Hertel, Jenkins, and Bowen, who seemed to be more pliable than Barber. Scott had the primary task of denying both his and Washington's involvement in other Afro-American publications, particularly in the *Colored American Magazine*. In an August 4, 1904 letter to the publishers, he both abused Barber and denied the editor's earlier allegation of complicity: "His gratituitous [sic] statement that I am connected, directly or indirectly, with a competitor of 'The Voice of the Negro,' is without foundation —is false absolutely and completely." Repeated denials convinced the publishers, who had begun to believe several claims, including the one that "Doubleday-Page and Prof. Booker Washington practically own The Colored American." [54] On August 10, the very day he had received a letter from Tuskegee, a somewhat chastened Jenkins confessed to Washington: "Your letter of the 10th, which denies all connection with the Magazine, is perfectly sufficient to me to warrant me to say that the person who informed us so wrongfully was mistaken." [55]

In the months and years following, Scott essentially discontinued his letters to the editors and publishers. Washington, however, remained an active correspondent as long as the journal seemed a threat to his own interests, which it did until the Atlanta race riot of 1906. A discernible pattern ensued. When an issue of the magazine attacked him and advanced Du Bois, he sent protests, first to Bowen, and then when he seemed unresponsive, to the publishers. Generally, he wrote to Barber only in answer to Barber's occasional letters.

Some of the most intriguing exchanges followed the March 1905 issue. Entitled "Shall We Materialize the Negro," an editorial in that number had gone on at length about the "downright soulless materialism" of Washington's policies.[56] On March 12, 1905, Washington fired off a missive to Jenkins in which he accused Bowen of "hypocrisy" and described the intolerable awkwardness of his own position, "with your firm praising and selling my books on the one hand and your magazine doing all it can to destroy the effect of my books on the other hand." Three days later he made the same complaint to Hertel, who subsequently distinguished between his own interests and those of Barber. "I cannot," he noted, "understand why the editors of our magazine are not in sympathy with your work." Encouraged by the response, Washington tried to warn Hertel of subversion from within, particularly that which would emerge after the August 1905 Niagara Conference: "You will find that they will attempt to use your magazine as a propaganda, and if permitted, you will find that Barbour [sic] will show his hand more fully in the September number." [57]

Hertel replied on August 9 that the situation was delicate. "I must . . . handle our young editor very carefully and very diplomatically," he wrote, but added that he would protect Washington's position by keeping "an eye on the magazine, and you can count on me to always stand for fair play." [58] Hertel could not, however, control his editor. The September issue featured three essays supporting the Niagara Movement, one written by Du Bois and the others by Barber. Through the movement, Barber saw the death of accommodationism and the "beginning of a new epoch in the history of Negro-Americans." He noted that "the signs of the times for the last few years have indicated a growing discontent among Negroes not only with the treatment accorded them by white people but also with certain pernicious and subservient ideals that were fast taking root in the minds of our young people." [59]

Veiled hostility characterized the tone of subsequent communication between Barber and Washington. They exchanged letters when Barber invited Washington to contribute to the January 1906 issue, and Washington refused politely, and after Barber visited Tuskegee in April 1906. In the correspondence following the visit, both men couched criticisms of each other's policies within effusive compliments. On April 6, Barber praised Tuskegee and hoped Washington would not abuse his power. Washington thanked Barber for the "kind letter" on April 14, and said his work would proceed if his contemporaries acted judiciously: "In this critical period we shall have to be very careful to guard against expressions that might prove harmful, by placing the race in a false position, and making its upward march the more difficult." On April 23, Barber thanked him "very much for your favor of April 14th," and noted that he had not felt neglected at Tuskegee: "Everyone was very courteous and I did not suffer at all for lack of attention. I understood that the great crowds prevented you from showing anyone any personal attention." [60]

The Atlanta race riot of September 22, 1906, interrupted further exchanges and began the end of Barber as editor and of the journal itself. The riot became embroiled in issues concerning freedom of the press and as such influenced the evolution of black magazines and newspapers in the South. In the November issue of his journal, Barber discussed the riot and its aftermath in a style which had become intolerable to black accommodationists and to many Southern whites. That same style had, however, become a rallying point for black radicals. Du Bois, for one, praised "The Atlanta Tragedy," one of Barber's controversial articles included in the number. "It is in his most vigorous style," declared Du Bois, "and he wields a [*sic*] exceedingly trenchant pen." Barber attributed the riot, in "The Atlanta Tragedy," to two causes: "Dishonest, unscrupulous, ambitious politicians and conscientiousless newspaper editors." The latter, John Temple Graves of the Atlanta *Georgian* and, especially, Charles Daniel of the Atlanta *News*, had terrorized the white community with frequent and fabricated reports of rapes accomplished by burly, vicious Negroes. Hoke Smith had ridden to the governorship, Barber continued, by playing to those fears: "White politicians in the South will stoop to any dirt against the Negro to get into office." [61]

"Why Mr. Barber Left Atlanta," another Barber essay in the November issue, traced the aftermath of the riot. On the morning of the twenty-third, John Graves, "one of the most vitriolic enemies of the Negro race," had wired a statement to the New York *World* in which he laid the entire responsibility for the riot on black Atlanta. Barber vigorously countered the accusation with a letter to the editor of the *World*, signed "A Colored Citizen." Prominent whites in Atlanta discovered the identity of the author, Barber explained in his essay, and gave him two choices: either to leave town or to expiate his wrongdoing on the chain gang. Barber and his staff hurriedly left for Chicago, saying they had been driven from town because they stood for the truth.[62] Barber's career in the South became an exemplum to later black editors of independent mind, many of whom chose to issue their journals from either New York or Chicago.

In the North, Barber tried to gather his forces. He shortened the name of the magazine to the *Voice*, partly because he wanted to emphasize a new beginning and partly because he hoped to attract advertisements from white firms. "In many instances," he admitted sadly, "the name 'Negro' is as much a handicap as the dark color of the skin." He asked former subscribers to rally to the cause. They responded with money, with enthusiastic praise for Barber, and with barbed criticisms of the South. "I hate the South," confessed Carrie Clifford, "with all the fury of my being. I pray God to smite it with all the curses of perdition." [63]

The support came too late. To the publishers, the removal of the magazine to Chicago had seemed an inglorious retreat, caused by Barber's improvident policies. In the spring of 1907, without telling Barber, they negotiated through Emmett Scott to sell the magazine to Washington. Hertel sent Scott a series of letters he considered "strictly confidential": "You have got to be mighty careful who you take into your confidence so that this matter will not come to the ear of Mr. Barber, otherwise the transfer might not be made in a pleasant, amicable and equitable manner." There was need for secrecy, as Hertel told Scott that Washington "is on the right track" and Barber on the "wrong": "The present management does not seem to have sufficient strength and influence to successfully handle the proposition." Washington was initially interested. In correspondence with Hertel, Scott outlined a new policy for the magazine—"more can be accomplished in race building by actually doing something than by merely whining and complaining"—and even mentioned the possibility of retaining Barber as one of the editors.[64] Washington decided against the purchase, though, presumably because he already had considerable control over the black press.

As the magazine came to an end, in late 1907, Barber enrolled in a Philadelphia dental college, from which he graduated four years later and then withdrew into private life. In tribute to Barber, "as some slight token of appreciation for a plucky man," Du Bois listed him as a contributing editor to *Crisis* in 1910 and 1911, even though he did not take an active part in the new journal.[65]

The politics of *Voice of the Negro* provide background important to understanding the literature published in the magazine. As a supporter of Du Bois and the Niagara Movement, Barber used creative literature to advance radical causes, when such literature was available. In an editorial statement, for example, he explained the political significance of an episode in *The Welding of the Link*, a story by Gardner Goldsby which was serialized in the magazine: "In this chapter he proves that there can never be any permanent and lasting peace between the white North and the white South, if the civil and political rights of the Negro are not guaranteed and maintained by the so-called superior race. The bug-bear of social equality is touched upon and waved aside with a master's hand. Be sure to get the

November number of *The Voice of The Negro* and read this interesting expose [*sic*] of the folly of the American white people." [66]

Barber liked fiction which attacked those he opposed, biased white Southerners and black accommodationists. He accordingly published "The Southern Conspiracy," a story by "H" which claimed that the press was not free, that white Southerners paid Northern editors and publishers to circulate "anti-Negro" propaganda. A piece by John Henry Adams fit into his scheme because it criticized the concept of industrial education by following the career of Simon Elijah Constant, who had undergone such training: "Where is that far-reaching, independent thinking that would make Simon's every effort tend toward the ownership of land, the accumulation of wealth, and the right-shaping of his personal career for the weighty responsibilities of honorable citizenship? Alas, Simon the serf." [67]

Some of the poems followed suit, particularly in the period just preceding and following the Atlanta race riot, when Barber served radical causes most effectively. In a verse published in the November 1905 issue, James French lauded the defiant power of the Niagara Movement, which "bursts with . . . thunder on the world." The November 1906 number featured two poems harmonizing with the mood of Barber's essays on the Atlanta race riot: one was a "Requiem Dirge for Atlanta's Slain" and the other, a satire of the "white man's burden"—"to plunder, kill, deflower." [68]

The radical pieces stressed the basic tone of the magazine, although they did not comprise the bulk of the creative expressions. Barber was limited in his use of like materials partly because poems and stories of this emphasis were not always available and partly because the publishers would not approve of too many outspoken pieces. The *belles lettres* in each issue—often two or three poems and one story along with an occasional essay—included, as a result, contributions which examined racial issues with a more temperate tone or which explored nonracial topics altogether. There were scholarly articles by Kelly Miller, to mention just one writer, on topics like "The Artistic Gifts of the Negro"; literary essays on the importance of Paul Dunbar; entertaining verses and short stories in a regular section by Silas Floyd, called "Wayside"; and conventional poems by some of the rising young writers of the day, Benjamin Brawley, W. S. Braithwaite, and others.[69] Among the newcomers was Georgia Douglas Johnson. Her short love lyrics began a publishing career that was to span six decades and include participation in most subsequent black literary magazines.

Voice of the Negro, as a supporter of Du Bois, looked ahead to the next decade. An early attempt at a race journal, it laid a basis for *Crisis,* which Du Bois considered a successor to Barber's publication. In enunciating a clear political position, it encouraged a "new generation" of writers, as Charles Johnson noted later. It even provided a label for the foremost figures in that generation. In an essay, John Henry Adams described Max Barber, among others, as a "new Negro" and thereby introduced the term which would be applied to black writers emerging in the 1920s.[70]

The other important magazines in the first decade of the twentieth century were those founded and edited by Du Bois. *Moon Illustrated Weekly,* the initial journal, focused primarily on politics and thereby served as a testing ground for ideas which Du Bois would develop further in *Crisis.* Founded in Memphis, *Moon* had all the problems which would be associated with little magazines in that it existed for a brief time—December 1905 to the summer of 1906—and for a small audience—approximately 250 to 500 subscribers. It drove away many potential readers because it seemed too controversial. The journal became a platform for Du Bois to discuss the political climate of the times, at home and abroad, and specific issues relating to equal rights for blacks. Financial problems plagued this small publication, as would be the case with many of its successors. Du Bois and his two partners, Edward Simon and Harry Pace, launched the journal on $3,000, which represented their combined resources.[71] Such a sum could not keep the venture solvent, particularly when more substantial funds were not forthcoming.

For several years Du Bois had sought support for an independent black magazine. He had been considered for the editorship of a journal to be published at Hampton. His name was withdrawn from the project, however, because he insisted on being his own man, beholden to none. "I had written them," he recalled later, "saying plainly that any magazine which I might edit would express my thought and be under my editorial control. This, of course, must have been absolutely inconceivable from their point of view."[72] In an exchange of letters, he pursued the idea with Charles Chesnutt, who also saw the need for a national black magazine. "There are already many 'colored' papers," he wrote to Du Bois on June 27, 1903; "how they support themselves may be guessed at from the contents—most of them are mediums for hair straightening advertisements and the personal laudation of 'self-made man,' most of whom are not so well made that they really ought to brag much about it." Chesnutt agreed with Du Bois that the primary problem with the type of publication they envisioned lay in finances: "The question of support would be the vital one for such a journal." [73]

Du Bois sought financial backing for *Moon* from influential whites, some of whom were sympathetic to the views of Booker T. Washington. Jacob Schiff, a wealthy Jewish banker, politely refused to provide the $10,000 Du Bois had requested in a letter dated April 14, 1905. Neither would Isaac Seligman give him the $5,000 he had asked for in a letter sent during January 1906, several months after the magazine had first appeared.[74] The accommodationist journals also refused to give Du Bois any quarter. They hooted at his attempts to raise funds, and they cheered when the journal collapsed from financial malnutrition. T. Thomas Fortune, editor of the New York *Age,* was one of the most vociferous spectators. "The *Age* is prepared to say today," he wrote in an editorial of February 1, 1906, "that Editor Du Bois is still writing letters to white people in New York asking them to subsidize a paper of which he is editor. Will he deny the allegation and defy the allegator? He will not." [75]

Fortune and the others had clear memories. In the January 1905 issue of *Voice of the Negro,* Du Bois had criticized contemporaries for taking subsidies. Only three months later, he went after money himself, in the letter to Schiff. It should be stressed here that Du Bois lost *Moon* because he would not accept "hush money," or any subsidy limiting his independence. He would take funds only if no strings were attached. Such money was hard to find, as Du Bois indicated in the first issue of *Horizon* when he talked about *Moon*: "We needed capital. I sought it. 'Subsidy' yelled the Cheerful Idiot, who knows what subsidy is. No, Tom and Jerry, it was precisely that which we refused. Well, we started, we had our little feverish trial and failed. It was a good, honest failure without frills and excuses and without dishonor." [76] *Moon* brings into focus the dilemma which would be experienced by many a little magazine editor, who would see his magazine doomed regardless of his actions. If he accepted subsidy, he would lose his independence, the very reason for his magazine's existence. If he refused subsidy, he could not meet his bills and would lose his journal.

As his first journal succumbed to the inevitable, Du Bois established *Horizon,* a monthly magazine published in Washington, D.C., from January 1907 to May 1910. The new journal showed Du Bois to be a more mature editor, one who had profited from his experience with *Moon.* Increasingly aware of limits on the time he had available, Du Bois shared responsibilities for every aspect of the magazine with his new partners, F. H. M. Murray and L. M. Hershaw. Together, the three did all the typing and printing for each issue. More important, they shared in the writing, with Hershaw contributing "The Out-Look," Murray "The In-Look," and Du Bois "The Over-Look," which was the lead section.

With the burden of responsibility divided, Du Bois could concentrate more than he had previously on the stylistic quality of his editorials. As the journal developed, "Over-Look" became increasingly controversial and memorable, with specific challenges and accusations voiced in the concise and lucid manner that would become characteristic of his *Crisis* statements. As in the past, Du Bois devoted much of his attention to politics. He attacked the status quo: "The Negro who votes for Theodore Roosevelt or any of his ilk is worse than a traitor to his race—he is a fool"; and he posed alternatives: "I am a Socialist-of-the-Path. I do not believe in the complete socialization of the means of production . . . but the Path of Progress and common sense certainly leads to a far greater ownership of the public wealth for the public good than is now the case. . . ." [77]

He indicated, as well, an understanding of the politics of literature. With indirect statements, he suggested that his rival, Booker T. Washington, had impeded the evolution of Afro-American literature: "Why aspire and delve for Art's sake and Truth's when you can make MONEY? What is literature compared with bricks? This devilish materialistic philosophy which is rife among us is killing ambition, destroying merit and manufacturing thieves, liars and flunkeys." He concluded with an invocation: "How long, O Lord, how long shall we bow tongue-tied or double-tongued before our enemies?" [78]

As a creative writer, Du Bois maintained his militant posture. He regularly included his poems and short stories in "Over-Look." The stories, some told by a railroad porter to a black traveler, were commonly entertainment pieces, although they had social overtones. The poems were a different matter. In his verse, Du Bois was developing the idea which he would voice later in *Crisis*, to the effect that "all art is propaganda." He wanted to encourage black pride with his poetry. He accordingly wrote boldly, in a way that would shock readers into attention. At the same time, he wanted to relieve his own frustration, to make statements that were occasionally so angry they were difficult to include in his editorials. The most outspoken poems have been the ones most frequently remembered and most commonly anthologized.

In such poems, Du Bois used first person to communicate directly with his readers. The persona in "The Song of the Smoke" celebrates blackness by reiterating two lines: "I am the Smoke King / I am black." The speaker in "The Burden of Black Woman" employs personal reference selectively, for dramatic emphasis. In no uncertain terms, he first criticizes the larger culture:

> The White World's vermin and filth:
> All the dirt of London.
> All the scum of New York;
> Valiant spoilers of women
> And conquerors of unarmed men;
> Shameless breeders of bastards
> Drunk with the greed of gold. . . .

The speaker then summarizes his response in first person:

> I hate them, Oh!
> I hate them well,
> I hate them, Christ!
> As I hate Hell.

In a lesser-known poem, "A Day in Africa," the speaker adopts first person to romanticize his life in the bush, as a hunter.[79]
Du Bois tried to establish a direct relationship with his readers. When a poem did not lend itself to first person, he sometimes appended an editorial note in which he used the pronouns "you" and "I." In one particular instance, he told readers how to act when "America" was announced and questioning eyes turned to black faces. "Now, then," he wrote, "I have thought of a way out," a version which could be sung by blacks and which would probably go unnoticed by the white audience: "They'll hardly note the little changes and their feelings and your conscience will thus be saved." The first stanza reads:

> My country tis of thee,
> Late land of slavery,
> Of thee I sing.
> Land where my father's pride
> Slept where my mother died,
> From every mountain side
> Let freedom ring! [80]

One of the most significant emphases in *Horizon* was Du Bois's discussion of the press, both black and white. In trying to educate readers about periodicals, Du Bois showed a broad understanding of contemporary magazines and newspapers and a particular sensitivity to the challenges faced by black journals. In general, he exhibited an insight which was unmatched by the other editors of the day.

He encouraged readers to subscribe to "a number" of periodicals, beginning with "race" publications. He recommended *Voice* and the Boston *Guardian*, as well as more popular magazines, such as *McGirt's* of Philadelphia—"Not a 'yellow' line in it"—and *Alexander's Magazine* of Boston—"The literary viands are not so bone-building as one might wish but are served in fine style." He also recommended dailies and weeklies published "outside our own race": New York *Evening Post*—"happy is the black man who can take" such a daily; New York *Independent*—"It is the bravest and fairest in its stand on the Negro problem"; and *Literary Digest*—"The Negro has always received fair treatment in this paper."

He told readers to "steer clear of" weekly and monthly periodicals biased against blacks. The former category included *Colliers*, which "tries to be as unfair as it reasonably can be," and *Outlook*, "which represents militant hypocrisy in ethics and literature" and "is doubly unfair to the Negro because it pretends friendship." The most hostile monthlies were, he advised, *Scribner's* and *Century*.[81]

In later issues of *Horizon*, Du Bois began to say less about his contemporaries and more about the problems of editing a black magazine. He talked first about a national journal, because that was the type of publication he wanted to establish. As one issue succeeded another, he indicated the difficulties of black little magazines, which was the category best suiting *Horizon*. Throughout, his comments were both explicit and astute. Du Bois could articulate the frustrations other editors would feel for decades to follow, but either would or could not express so clearly.

The problem was always money, how to sustain an expensive operation on the empty coffers of a "poor people," as Du Bois termed his audience. Because black readers often had limited resources, the editors of Afro-American publications could not charge high subscription rates or secure "multitudinous advertisements," as did many of their white counterparts. Neither could they depend on subsidy, which was "degrading and dangerous" and which "implies the secret buying of a paper's policy by persons unknown and often unsuspected by the readers." Black editors could only, Du Bois claimed, depend on themselves and their readers. He and his partners at *Horizon* not only worked without salaries, but they made up the annual deficit out of their own pockets. In July 1908, Du Bois told his readers that the editors' pockets were bare and contributions were very much in order. He also indicated, in a prophetic statement, that financial difficulties would postpone the emergence of a national black magazine for another five or ten years.[82]

In the following issues, he continued to call for more donations and additional subscribers. He asserted, in the "Over-Look" for November 1909, that an independent black magazine could not pay its way: "No periodical that advocates unpopular or partially popular causes, can be a self-supporting business operation." In the last issue of the magazine, May 1910, he said that the magazine needed 500 additional subscribers by June and 1,000 by September. He threw down the gauntlet: "These are parlous times, friends; if you are not interested in yourselves, who will be interested?" [83] The challenge was not met, and *Horizon* went the way of other contemporary black magazines.

An editorial in the *Colored American Magazine* once stated that "the sea of negro race periodicals has had washed up on its shore many and many a wreck...." [84] The metaphor is dramatic but unduly derogatory in emphasis, both when applied to magazines of the nineteenth century and to those in the first decade of the twentieth century. The most significant magazines in the latter period—*Colored American Magazine, Voice of the Negro, Moon,* and *Horizon*—developed on the traditions established by earlier journals but were no more successful than their predecessors in surviving the "parlous times." Before expiring, though, they achieved noteworthy careers. The magazines became a primary battleground for the struggles between the Bookerites and the Du Bois loyalists. The rival groups used the publications to articulate key positions of the day regarding social and political issues. In so doing, they also initiated tentative discussions on an aesthetic for black literature. The editors and major contributors generally saw literature as propaganda. They disagreed, however, over the type of propaganda, whether it should favor the emphases of accommodationists or radicals. By the end of the decade the radicals were in ascendancy. Booker T. Washington, while still powerful, could not control black periodicals as he had in the past. Along with Du Bois, Pauline Hopkins and Max Barber had done much to effect the change. They had, in the process, published a new generation of black writers and had established a basis for the larger and smaller Afro-American magazines that were to emerge in the next decades.

2. Toward the Renaissance

Crisis, Opportunity, and Messenger,

1910–1928

When *Crisis* began in 1910, the metaphors shifted to the graveyard. W. E. B. Du Bois reported that his "friends" would talk about "the graveyard of ambitious and worthy ventures—the *Colored American* and the *Voice of the Negro* to name the latest—and say the American Negro has not yet reached the place where he appreciates a magazine enough to pay for its support." Du Bois would counter such speculation with confident statements. "We doubt this assertion," he told the naysayers.[1] He had good reason for confidence since *Crisis*, sponsored by the National Association for the Advancement of Colored People, had a base of support broader than that claimed by any previous black magazines. Two other publications emerged in the next several years which also had organizational backing. In 1917, A. Philip Randolph with Chandler Owen started the socialistic *Messenger*, which eventually became a platform for the Brotherhood of Sleeping Car Porters. The Urban League journal, *Opportunity*, began in 1923 with Charles S. Johnson as editor. Advanced by nationally based groups, involving white as well as black members, these monthly journals achieved notable longevity, *Crisis* surviving from 1910 to the present, *Opportunity* from 1923 to 1949, and *Messenger* from 1917 to 1928.

Engaged in the politics of race relations, none of the magazines was involved exclusively in Afro-American literature. All three, however, played an important part in the black renaissance of the 1920s. Under the leadership of Du Bois, *Crisis* laid a foundation in the second decade of the century for the flowering of Afro-American culture in the next decade. *Opportunity*, with the editorship of Charles S. Johnson, reached the height of its literary involvement in the years from 1923 to 1928. During the same period, especially when Wallace Thurman served as acting editor, *Messenger* managed a lesser but nevertheless significant role in relation to the arts.

Gwendolyn Bennett, one of the young writers emerging in the 1920s, acknowledged the importance of the larger journals to the evolution of Afro-American literature. "The magazine situation with regards to the Negro has been," she noted in *Opportunity*, "most encouraging. *Opportunity* and the *Crisis* have gone on record as fosterparents of the young Negro writer.... *The Messenger* too has had its place in the literary tendencies of the race." She then turned immediately to smaller black magazines, commenting, for example, on Wallace Thurman's *Fire* (1926).[2] The progression in Bennett's thought suggests a relationship between the larger and the little magazines. By promoting new tendencies in Afro-American literature, the organizational journals encouraged the development of small magazines devoted exclusively to the arts. Then, too, the journals, by their records of longevity, showed aspiring young editors that a black magazine could find a loyal audience, that the graveyard need not be the immediate fate of an Afro-American periodical.

In 1909, as Mary White Ovington recalled, the NAACP "was born in a little room of a New York apartment" in a meeting attended by herself, a social worker, William English Walling, a journalist, and Henry Moskowitz, a prominent member of the reform administration of John Mitchel, then mayor of New York. The three desired an interracial organization, a group which would revive the spirit of the abolitionists to meet the needs of a new day.[3] Their continuing efforts, along with those of many others who became involved, led to an interracial conference in May 1909 and another in May 1910, at which time the NAACP was established. Officers of the organization included Moorfield Storey as National President, Walling as Chairman of the Executive Committee, John E. Milholland as Treasurer, and W. E. B. Du Bois as Director of Publicity and Research.

Du Bois joined the staff with the understanding that he would continue the research he had been pursuing at Atlanta University on "the Negro problem," as he called it, and that he would eventually become secretary of the NAACP. Upon coming to New York, however, Du Bois immediately developed other plans, primarily because there was no money available for research and because he did not want to become engaged in fund-raising. He began laying the foundation for a monthly magazine which would be sponsored by the NAACP. Such a journal seemed necessary, he recalled later, because Booker T. Washington "had tight hold of most" of the black press, including the most influential Afro-American weekly, the New York *Age*. "The result was," he explained further, "that the NAACP got a pretty raw deal from the colored press and none at all from the white papers." [4]

A magazine did not seem so essential to the Executive Committee of the NAACP, which "hesitated" before succumbing to the persuasiveness of Du Bois. With undue modesty, given the financial records of *Moon* and *Horizon*, Du Bois wrote that the Committee, headed by Oswald Garrison Villard, "knew far better than the editor that magazines cost money, and despite legends to the contrary, they had almost no money." They finally did authorize fifty dollars monthly for a "small" journal but they experienced, according to Du Bois, "many misgivings" in so doing.[5]

Permission granted, the journal proceeded apace. William Walling suggested the name, after a comment of Ovington's at an organizational meeting which had involved a discussion of the magazine. "There is a poem of Lowell's," Ovington had noted, "that means more to me to-day than any other poem in the world—'The Present Crisis.'" Walling immediately interjected, "There is the name for your magazine, *The Crisis*." [6] Substantial contributions came from Mary Dunlop Maclean, who helped Du Bois with the makeup of the journal, and Robert N. Wood, who took charge of the printing, a matter of which "I knew nothing," said Du Bois. Ever the main force behind the magazine was Du Bois, who relished his position and described his decisions involving the first issue with much drama: "It was the editor alone, looking out on the forest of roofs of lower Broadway, who asked and asked again the momentous question: 'Dare I order 500 copies—or 1,000?' And when in a fit of wild adventure he ordered 1,000 copies printed he felt like Wellington before Waterloo." [7]

In his initial editorial, Du Bois elaborated on the approach he had used in *Moon* and *Horizon*: "The object of this publication is to set forth those facts and arguments which show the danger of race prejudice, particularly as manifested to-day toward colored people." To accomplish this he would publish, in addition to his editorials, news and news analysis, reviews of literature bearing on racial matters, and short articles. To quiet former critics, especially the Bookerites, Du Bois concluded by saying that the magazine would be free from any clique and all "personal rancor." [8]

Problems developed from the first issue. Du Bois, in his editorials, eschewed objectivity and engaged in personal commentary, so pointed at times that he embarrassed the NAACP Board of Directors. Thus in the early years, Du Bois and his colleagues struggled over whether *Crisis* should be a house journal, expressing NAACP policies, or a personal magazine, voicing the editor's own views. In his autobiography, Du Bois gave his understanding of the situation, which he believed involved a "delicate matter of policy": "From first to last I thought strongly, and I still think rightly, to make the opinion expressed in *The Crisis* a personal opinion; because as I argued, no organization can express definite and clear-cut opinions." An organization, he continued, could produce only "the dry kind of organ that so many societies support for purposes of reference and not for reading." [9] As chairman of the Executive Committee and as editor of the *Nation*, Villard, who was white, thought he should control both the editor and the fledgling magazine. In the ensuing controversy, Villard charged Du Bois with insubordination and resigned his position in protest late in 1913.

In a letter to Mary Ovington, Du Bois interpreted the confrontation in racial terms, saying essentially that Villard was too white to work on equal terms with a man so dark. He asserted that during the past three and a half years every effort, "conscious, half-conscious, unconscious," had been exerted to force him into a subordinate position. He wondered if the NAACP could successfully combat racial prejudice on the larger scene if it could not put its own house in order. A few months later he expressed similar opinions to his friend Joel Spingarn, who had succeeded Villard to the chairmanship. He spoke of his dream that *Crisis* would become "one of the great journals of the world," and called for editorial freedom: "I demand a full man's chance to complete a work without chains and petty hampering." [10]

Du Bois proved stronger than his opposition and developed, in the words of Elliott Rudwick, "near-absolute control of the magazine." The *Crisis*, a separate department in the NAACP, became known as "Du Bois's Domain." [11] As such, it became one of the "great journals of the world." Roy Wilkins, editor of *Crisis* from 1934 to 1949, said that "the brilliant, bitter and poetic writing of Du Bois" accounted for much of the magazine's success. Never shy about his own accomplishments, Du Bois made a similar claim in his autobiography: "If ... *The Crisis* had not been in a sense a personal organ and the expression of myself, it could not possibly have attained its popularity and effectiveness." [12]

By expressing the opinions of a most articulate and persuasive editor, *Crisis* reached an audience larger than that approximated by any preceding black journal. As Du Bois wrested his periodical from control by the Executive Committee, circulation figures climbed rapidly, from 1,000 copies in November 1910, to 9,000 in 1911, and 35,000 in late 1915. Du Bois, bolstered by such success, publicly declared his independence in the November 1915 editorial, entitled "We Come of Age." With the January 1916 number, the magazine would be completely self-supporting, he stated, its assets sufficient to meet all expenses of publication and the full salary of the editor, which had been paid in the past by the NAACP. He then included comments that embarrassed the committee, saying that the association "has never expended a single cent for publication of *The Crisis*" and that he had used his own salary and borrowed money to meet financial emergencies in the past. "In not a single case," he revealed to his readers, "has the Association or anybody connected with the Association, except the editor, assumed the slightest responsibility or risk or advanced a single cent."[13]

The circulation peaked in 1919, with issues of about 95,000 copies. From then on the statistics declined, to less than 65,000 copies in 1920, and under 30,000 in 1930. The reasons for the decline were "clear," Du Bois explained, for they involved a matter of finances rather than a disaffection of the readers. *Crisis* was too controversial to attract the "Big" advertisers, and thus Du Bois had to raise the price of the magazine from ten to fifteen cents a copy to meet expenses. His audience, which he defined primarily as "Negro workers of low income," could not pay the extra charge for *Crisis* because they were meeting additional expenses everywhere. The Depression which affected the entire nation in 1929 started among black workers as early as 1926, he added.[14]

Du Bois's discussion has merit, particularly in reference to advertising, but it is somewhat misleading. More of the *Crisis* audience was probably middle rather than working class, and some readers were lured away by competing periodicals. As Roy Wilkins noted later, *Crisis* had appealed to a large Afro-American readership primarily because it offered news about blacks not available elsewhere. When Afro-American newspapers expanded in the 1920s, they were able to cover the news more completely, more frequently, and with more pictures and illustrations than could *Crisis*.[15]

Some members of the Board of Trustees were not equally objective about the loss of readers. They had tolerated Du Bois while circulation figures continued to rise, but as circulation fell they withdrew their support, tentative as it was, and tried to secure control of the journal once again. In board meetings, they talked at length about ways to increase the readership of *Crisis*. One trustee went as far as to say, in 1926, that the journal should cater to a mass audience. Two years later, a leader in the NAACP claimed that Du Bois had offended many readers by his personal and often pointed comments in the journal.[16]

In the early part of the decade, Du Bois could defend himself by simply citing the record, as he did in a report to the board in 1924: "*The Crisis* is still preeminently the leading Negro magazine, its nearest competitor [probably *Opportunity*] having about one fifth of its circulation." One word, "still," indicated the qualified nature of Du Bois's defense. Within the year, he had to adopt a new approach to critics on the board. As in the past, he refused any posture smacking of subordination. He would not agree that *Crisis* should seek a larger audience than it had. The drop in circulation proved, he asserted, the very strength of the magazine. "*The Crisis* must be an *Unpopular* magazine," he declared in one draft of a report. "If the cause which we espouse and the means by which we defend it were popular, then there would be no call for this periodical. . . ." He wanted to convince his colleagues that the organization needed a magazine which would be "a sort of spiritual watchman on the walls," not a mere receptacle for NAACP minutes.[17]

The situation came to a head by the end of the decade. On April 11, 1929, a somewhat chastened Du Bois asked the board for $5,000, to be payable to *Crisis* during April 1929 and January 1930. He asked for a "gift," suggesting thereby that the funds should come with no strings attached. He suggested, too, that the stipend might be needed annually, if *Crisis* were to meet its projected deficit. Such a step, he admitted, necessitated that the future course of *Crisis* be considered carefully. Later in 1929, he indicated a similar concern in *Crisis*. "During the 18 years in which *The Crisis* has been published," he wrote to a young reader, "the number of new Negro magazines which have been born, flourished and died, have averaged one a year— eighteen in all. The Editor, therefore, grows cautious." [18]

Du Bois's long-time friends also grew cautious. In a letter of December 20, 1930, Mary Ovington wrote Du Bois explicitly about *Crisis* and the NAACP: "As time has gone on the organization has become increasingly important, and the *Crisis* less important, not just in relation to the Negro world. It is not unique as it once was." As a result, Du Bois could no longer maintain his privileged position. "You will have less and less control" of *Crisis*, she declared, "and it cannot belong to you as it has in the past. You won't enjoy it in the way you have." [19]

After vainly trying to re-establish his former independence, Du Bois finally resigned from the journal and returned to Atlanta University. At his resignation, in 1934, the circulation had dropped to a new low of 8,500 copies a month.[20] Comments from letters, from his article of 1951, and from his autobiography spell out the reasons for his departure. He would be, as he said in his proud way, "Free Lance or nothing." He could no longer control *Crisis* since it had become dependent on NAACP funding. Thus, he no longer had the liberty to develop his own political, economic, and cultural programs. He saw very clearly the differences between an organizational periodical, which the magazine was becoming, and a literary journal, which he said *Crisis* had been at its best. The former was dull and ineffective, filled with unread minutes and routine reports, whereas the latter was worthy of a man's attention, being "free and uncontrolled," "virile, creative, and individual." His emotions upon resigning contained much personal regret, as he conveyed later: "I was leaving my dream and brainchild; my garden of hope and highway to high emprise." [21]

Most commentators recognize that Du Bois had substantial reason for calling *Crisis* a literary journal, since it carried a major role in the cultural renaissance of the 1920s. They disagree, however, over the respective importance of Du Bois and Charles S. Johnson during that time. Many contemporaries and perhaps a majority of the influential scholars to follow have considered Johnson's artistic endeavors to have been far more significant than Du Bois's. Most persuasive are statements by Zora Neale Hurston, who valued Johnson as "the root of the so-called Negro Renaissance"; Langston Hughes, who believed Johnson "did more to encourage and develop Negro writers during the 1920s than anyone else in America"; and Arna Bontemps, who considered Johnson, not Du Bois, a "nursemaid" of the renaissance.[22]

A close examination of *Crisis* shows the vital role Du Bois assumed in the literary renaissance. With *Crisis* and throughout the second decade of the twentieth century, he did more than anyone else to prepare for the flourishing of Afro-American culture in the 1920s. He led the way, first, by his own writing. Nowhere in his poetry or fiction does his writing style appear to better advantage than in his *Crisis* editorials and essays, which contemporaries valued as artistic achievements. A representative comment came from William Stanley Braithwaite, who considered Du Bois the best among Afro-American writers living and dead: "Du Bois is the most variously gifted writer which the Race has produced . . . in many of Dr. Du Bois's essays [it] . . . is often my personal feeling that I am witnessing the birth of a poet, phoenix-like, out of a scholar." Many since have seen the artistry of Du Bois's essays in *Crisis*, but no one has expended more than a few lines in analysis.[23]

In his editorials, Du Bois assumed many roles. First, he wrote as a personal journalist, using techniques he had experimented with in *Horizon*. He seemed on many occasions to be on intimate terms with his readers, treating his audience as he would a confidant, exposing feelings in *Crisis* that were more private than those revealed by other black editors. In so doing, he developed a style which contrasted, sometimes dramatically, with the behavior he often exhibited in social situations. Whereas he could appear reserved, even haughty, in public, Du Bois bore an open countenance before the readers of *Crisis*. He told them in the journal that he often preferred to communicate through his essays rather than face-to-face. He had been bothered, he explained, by visitors bursting unannounced into his office, frequently interrupting "a carefully arranged morning or a happy thought surging to be born." Feeling an urgency about his work, he confessed: "I often discount human facts in comparison with divine thoughts. I cannot jump readily from the understanding mind to the glad hand." [24]

Du Bois saved himself for the written page. There he surprised readers, who had been accustomed to his sometimes acerbic tone, by announcing that "few have more joy in life than I." In a retrospective mood, he evaluated an earlier effort: "I have been reading that old novel of mine—it has points." He discussed his lineage, in an editorial called "The House of the Black Burghardts," and, in "The Shadow of Years," he traced his own development through four stages: "the Age of Miracles, the Days of Disillusion, the Discipline of Work and Play, the Second Miracle Age." [25] The latter piece, written during the time in which he was composing *Darkwater*, was undoubtedly one of his first efforts at synthesizing his past experience.

Du Bois wrote as a propagandist, so convinced of his own views that he penned exceedingly explicit criticisms of individuals and institutions. He did this even though he had stated, in *Crisis*, that "one of the besetting sins of colored journals is the exploitation of personal animosity in their editorial columns." [26] Forgetting or disregarding such a statement, he prided himself on his editorials, which he characterized on several occasions as "fearless and frank," "blazing," and as "stinging hammer blows." [27] No better adjectives could be found, for Du Bois hurled epithets at contemporaries, calling Robert Moton a "pussy footer" and Issac Fisher a " 'white folks' Nigger." He commented frequently on the press, praising William Hayes Ward's *Independent*, the Boston *Guardian*, and the Cleveland *Gazette*, and attacking "Copperheads like the New York *Times*" and *Harper's*, "whose relation to black folks resembles that of the Devil to Holy Water." [28] He became angrier over Southern periodicals: "*Vardaman's*

Weekly, Jim Jam Jems, The Anderson, S.C., *Tribune,* the Jackson, Miss., *Clarion,* the Texas *Harpoon,* and a score of other dirty Southern sheets have been pouring their filth and lies against Negroes into the mails for ten, twenty, and thirty years. . . ." [29]

He often made his points with sarcasm, satire, and irony. The sarcasm predominated more in the latter stages of his editorship, especially in one of his last regular columns in *Crisis,* called "As the Crow Flies." "The Crow is not interested in fools and illiterates," he wrote in 1929. "It fixes its calm gaze upon the Truth and particularly upon the unpleasant truth. It is cynical, sarcastic, mean and low . . . The Crow concentrates its attention mainly on Hell." [30]

Du Bois also used the prophetic mode in his editorials. By 1910, he had refined the mythology begun as early as 1890, when he wove the image of a black Christ into a commencement address at Harvard University. The developed mythology, consisting of a chosen Afro-American people, a barbarian white race, and a black savior, appears in Du Bois's editorials, as well as in his poetry and fiction. To inspire the Afro-American readers of *Crisis,* he commonly adopted biblical language. "Can anyone," he proclaimed to his audience, "doubt the ripeness of the time? Awake, put on thy strength, O Zion!" [31] In some ten editorials, he wrote of the holy family, characterizing them as ragged, unkempt, and black. He described the birth of the black Christ in a ghetto; the coming of the wise men, one black, one yellow, and one white; the crucifixion, commonly in the form of a lynching; and the second coming.

"The Gospel According to Mary Brown," an editorial published in December 1919, has the elements of the other pieces. Mary Brown, "very small and pretty and black," brings forth "her first-born son," called Joshua, in "the cabin beyond the Big Road." Joshua, with skin of "black velvet," essentially follows the career of the historical Jesus. At the age of twelve, he asks the church deacons such questions as: "Why were colored folk poor? Why were they afraid?" He becomes a carpenter and a preacher. The "White Folk" in the area fear his words, form a mob—"Kill the nigger," they yell—and lynch him in the jail yard. The dying man prays for them: "Father, forgive them, for they know not what they do." The risen Joshua reappears before his mother and echoes the words of the resurrected Jesus. [32]

Some of the gospel-editorials, as they might best be described, take unexpected turns. In "Easter," published in April 1911, the lynched black man rises to a radically reordered social structure, "a new literature and the faint glimmering of a new Art." Du Bois did not insist that Christ be a man. In "The Gospel According to St. John,

Chapter 12," Christ is a black woman, identified as the President of the State Federation of Colored Women's Clubs. In another editorial, the savior is a "strong and mighty, golden and beautiful" dog named Steve. His story is told by a "Seer," who must "always, beneath the hand of fate, write—and write—and write." [33]

Du Bois included, in his editorials, more than ten other stories which were not based on biblical themes but which considered the past and present of black peoples. He also penned travelogues, in which he described in much detail his journeys in the United States, Europe, and Africa. He developed excellent character portraits of people he encountered in trains and along the sidewalks of busy cities. He created emotion and suspense in his presentation by using parallelism, repetition of key phrases, periodic and loose sentences, and memorable images.[34] In general, he provided both materials and methods helpful to young contemporary black writers.

Long before the 1920s, Du Bois promoted a renaissance of black literature in his editorials. He envisioned and repeatedly called for the New Negro years before *Opportunity* emerged to publish the same. As early as 1911, he bemoaned the scarcity of Afro-American novelists, poets, and essayists and asserted that "here is a tremendous field for improvement." In 1915, he announced that the magazine should be enlarged to make way for more creative work: "The magazine is far below the ideal and plan of its founder. . . . Its space . . . for the two great departments of serious essays and literature has been hitherto straitly, almost dishearteningly, curtailed." Before the renaissance became associated with Harlem, Du Bois tried to interest young writers in the rich literary resources available in that area. He praised Claude McKay, in 1918, for recognizing the "artistic possibilities" and excelling in "the interpretation of life in Harlem." As the decade concluded, Du Bois reiterated the idea he had stressed from the beginning of *Crisis*: "A renaissance of American Negro literature is due; the material about us in the strange, heart-rending race tangle is rich beyond dream and only we can tell the tale and sing the song from the heart." [35]

During the first decade of the magazine, Du Bois published established authors, such as W. S. Braithwaite, Benjamin Brawley, Charles Chesnutt, James Corrothers, and Paul Laurence Dunbar, as well as new writers. He was particularly interested in the *Crisis* record with "unknown names." As illustrators, there were Richard Brown, William Farrow, William Scott, Albert Smith, and Lorenzo Wheeler; as poets, Otto Bohanan, Fenton Johnson, Georgia Johnson, Roscoe Jamison, and Lucian Watkins; and as prose writers, Jessie Fauset and Mary Effie Lee, along with countless others.[36]

The literature published in *Crisis* from 1910 to 1920 stimulated the artistic patterns of the 1920s. The general emphasis was on black pride, and some of the compositions bore particular lessons. Two stories, "The Beginning of Sorrows," by Lew Wallace, and "The First Stone," by Joseph Lyndel Bowler, stressed that Afro-Americans must identify with appropriate models: black children with black dolls, stated Wallace, and Afro-American readers with heroes and heroines from their own race, wrote Bowler. The ideas in other pieces came more implicitly. There were, for example, love songs to beautiful black women, such as "Ebon Maid and Girl of Mine," by Lucian Watkins; tributes to humble, hard-working folk, as illustrated in "The Washer-Woman," by Otto Bohanan; and testimonials to a rich cultural heritage, both past and present. Evocations of earlier glories came in such poems as Virginia Jackson's "Africa" and Paul Dunbar's "Black Sampson of Brandywine." Dunbar believed that Sampson, a great Afro-American soldier, represented the material out of which black literature should be made:

> Noble and bright is the story,
> Worthy the touch of the lyre,
> Sculptor or poet should find it
> Full of the stuff to inspire.[37]

Writers in all the literary genres, including drama, found inspiration in the black involvement in World War I. They emphasized the Christ-like courage of Afro-American soldiers who risked their lives fighting for a country which had refused them full citizenship. In "Negro Soldiers," which Braithwaite considered the best poem written about black involvement in the war, Roscoe Jamison portrayed men "Shedding their blood like Him now held divine, / That those who mock might find a better way!" [38]

Du Bois did not forget the future generation. From 1910 to 1920 he published occasional book reviews of children's literature, as well as poems and stories written by and for the younger set. Once a year he issued a children's number of *Crisis*, replete with prize-winning photographs of Afro-American babies. In 1919 and 1920 he and Jessie Fauset edited in connection with *Crisis* a magazine called the *Brownie's Book*, which was designed for all children, but especially for the black. Among the purposes behind the publication were: to make black children proud of their heritage; to teach them behavior suitable in interracial situations; and to educate them for race leadership, for "definite occupations and duties with a broad spirit of sacrifice." [39]

One genre, Afro-American drama, seemed particularly lacking in those days to Du Bois. He believed that such a drama could emerge out of pageants, and thus he published in *Crisis* and staged in several large cities his pageant on black history, entitled "The People of Peoples and Their Gifts to Men." Ever the teacher, Du Bois saw pedagogical as well as aesthetic ends in pageants, as he explained in the magazine. Dramatizing significant historical episodes, he believed, could educate Afro-Americans in their past and could help whites see blacks as human beings. These ends seemed so worthwhile that Du Bois founded the Horizon Guild, with himself as president, to encourage the development of the art.[40] The guild seemingly did little, probably because drama both by and about Afro-Americans began to appear more frequently, but it was important for another reason. Dedicated to promoting one of the arts, it became a forerunner of the small groups of blacks, many of them dedicated to literature, which would appear in various urban areas in the 1920s.

As the decade ended, Jessie Fauset joined the staff as literary editor. She served in that capacity from November 1919 to May 1926, the period of *Crisis*'s most active involvement in the arts. Fauset was no stranger either to Du Bois or to readers of the magazine. In 1903, she had asked Du Bois in a letter to help her find a summer teaching position in a Southern school.[41] From 1912 she contributed book reviews, essays, poems, and short stories to *Crisis*. She continued, after becoming literary editor, to publish such pieces in the magazine.

In several respects Fauset recalls Pauline Hopkins. Both women had a similar understanding of Afro-American literature. And thus they helped create a climate conducive to the most contemporary writers. They did this even though both identified with their middle-class black origins, Fauset among old Philadelphians and Hopkins among old Bostonians. In her book reviews, Fauset encouraged New Negroes, as Hopkins had promoted the work of earlier radicals. She applauded creative writers such as Claude McKay for depicting blacks honestly and artistically. She praised black scholars, including Carter Woodson, for *The History of the Negro Church*, and Benjamin Brawley, for the *Social History of the American Negro*. The latter book seemed particularly worthwhile because "it presents American history as it must have appeared to black men." [42] Those who falsified the lives of Afro-Americans met with her displeasure, as did T. S. Stribling. *Birthright*, one of his novels, made her wonder "whether or not white people will ever be able to write evenly on this racial situation in America." She saw Afro-American life as the province of artists from her own race: "The portrayal of black people calls increasingly for black writers." [43]

In her essays, Fauset endorsed the politics of Du Bois—Pan-Africanism, among other involvements—as Hopkins had promoted his work of an earlier day. Again like Hopkins, she wrote a series of biographical studies and on some of the same persons, including Robert Brown Elliott. She felt, as had Hopkins, that black youth especially needed black images. "No part of Negro literature needs more building up than biography," she insisted. "It is urgent that Negro youth be able to read of the achievements of their race." [44]

Fauset re-created, in her many short stories published in *Crisis*, a milieu familiar to the readers of Hopkins's fiction. She pictured structured and elite black communities, modeled after old Philadelphia, and she portrayed black professionals—industrious physicians, teachers, engineers, and businessmen and women. She wrote of people who live on the borderline of two races and who flirt with the idea of passing. These were not the concerns of many younger writers, who valued Fauset nevertheless. In *A Long Way from Home*, Claude McKay paid his respects: "Miss Fauset has written many novels about the people in her circle. Some white and some black critics consider these people not interesting enough to write about. I think all people are interesting to write about." He went on to say that "all the radicals liked her, although in her social viewpoint she was away over on the other side of the fence." In his autobiography, *The Big Sea*, Langston Hughes advanced Fauset as a major mover of the literary renaissance: "Jessie Fauset at the *Crisis*, Charles Johnson at *Opportunity*, and Alain Locke in Washington, were the three people who midwifed the so-called New Negro literature into being." [45]

Working together, Du Bois and Fauset published the most prominent black writers of the 1920s in *Crisis*. Essays by E. Franklin Frazier, book reviews by Alain Locke, poems and stories by Gwendolyn Bennett, Arna Bontemps, Countee Cullen, Rudolph Fisher, James Weldon Johnson, Claude McKay, and Jean Toomer studded its pages. Many of the writers had never been published before, as was the case with Hughes when the editors accepted "The Negro Speaks of Rivers" for the June 1921 *Crisis*. Among the young authors were those, such as Sterling Brown and Frank Marshall Davis, who would emerge prominently in black periodicals of the 1930s. [46]

The 1920s bedazzled some of the writers, who were unaccustomed to the sudden attention. Not only were their pieces accepted for publication, but their work was solicited for literary and artistic competitions. Such contests became something of a rage, being offered by concerns as diverse as the Alpha Kappa Alpha Sorority, Boni publishers, and by *Crisis* and *Opportunity*, the most important black magazines of the day. The two journals publicized the competitions elsewhere but remained discreetly silent over each other's respective efforts. They both held similar contests at approximately the same time and for basically identical contestants.

Amy Spingarn paid for the first two of three annual competitions sponsored by *Crisis* in 1925, 1926, and 1927. The wife of Joel Spingarn, she provided $600 for each year, to be distributed among the first-, second-, and third-place winners in five categories: stories, plays, poems, essays, and illustrations. In 1927 she contributed $350 in prize money, while women's clubs and business organizations gave additional funds for further categories of competition. Black businesses, including eight banks and five insurance companies, were generous in support, offering $725. But they were exceedingly pragmatic, wanting stories, essays, and cartoons which would, in their words, "stimulate general knowledge of banking and insurance in modern life and specific knowledge of what American Negroes are doing in these fields." [47] In 1928 *Crisis* discontinued the annual contests and provided small monthly prizes for the best contributions published in each issue of the magazine. The awards, funded by Amy Spingarn and the black businesses, were designated as Charles Waddell Chesnutt Honoraria and the Economic Prizes.

The most successful among the *Crisis* competitions were the first two annual contests. Du Bois involved some influential judges, white as well as black, for each category of competition. Among others, there were Charles Chesnutt, Sinclair Lewis, and H. G. Wells for fiction; Babette Deutsch, Robert Morss Lovett, and James Weldon Johnson for poetry; Eugene O'Neill for drama; Winold Reiss for illustrations; and Du Bois himself for the essays. Winners included the most exciting Afro-American writers and artists of the day, such as Arna Bontemps, Countee Cullen, Aaron Douglas, Rudolph Fisher, and Langston Hughes. After identifying the winners in the magazine, Du Bois published comments from the judges regarding the most successful entries.

The Economic Prizes represented the only failure among *Crisis* competitions. Winners were never announced, because a sufficient number of contestants could not be found. The first time around, the Economic Prizes attracted only 13 out of 375 contestants, "to our great surprise," announced Du Bois. [48] The draw, which never really improved, suggested that many New Negroes were not interested in directing their art toward practical ends.

In the 1920s, art and propaganda became an issue within Afro-American literary circles, and Du Bois found himself in the middle of heated polemic. He was not always ready for the debate, since his ideas on aesthetics were undergoing considerable transformation during the first half of the decade. Explication of his aesthetics becomes difficult, because Du Bois modified his position mid-decade and because he never sufficiently defined "art" and "propaganda" for his readers. His position becomes understandable only by piecing together the many comments in *Crisis* he directed to the issue.

In the first part of the decade, Du Bois advanced art over propaganda. He did not interpret art, however, as meaning any position approaching art-for-art's sake. To Du Bois, a literature which did not exist for a moral purpose was a decadent, socially dangerous activity. He equated art with truth in those years. Afro-American writers should, he believed, depict black life honestly, the bad along with the good. They should not, he claimed, limit their horizons to propaganda, which he saw as the exclusive presentation of only the most favorable images.

The truth about Afro-American life in fiction by whites and blacks was slow in coming, Du Bois explained in the first half of the 1920s. White writers in the past had given portraits of a humbled, corrupt people. Contemporary black writers were trying, in response, to right the wrong by depicting irreproachable and, to Du Bois, totally unbelieveable heroes and heroines. "We have criminals and prostitutes, ignorant and debased elements just as all folk have," he reminded his contemporaries in a 1921 editorial. "We want everything that is said about us to tell of the best and highest and noblest in us," he continued. He then summarized his position: "We insist that our Art and Propaganda be one. This is wrong and in the end it is harmful." The emphasis continued into 1925, when Du Bois said he would try, in *Crisis*, to present more portraits "frankly critical of the Negro group." [49]

With the new year, and after reading *The New Negro*, edited by Alain Locke, Du Bois changed his tune. In the January 1926 number, he praised the format but criticized the premise behind the book. "Mr. Locke," he wrote, "has newly been seized with the idea that Beauty rather than Propaganda should be the object of Negro literature and art." By using the passive voice, "has newly been seized," Du Bois suggested that Locke had not developed an aesthetic theory with care but that he had succumbed to a whim. Moreover the text itself, a collection of pieces by New Negroes, disproved the premise, "filled and bursting" as it was with propaganda. Du Bois had come to believe that black art should be propaganda, according to his earlier definition of the term. He decided that Afro-American literature could shape public opinion in a constructive way only if it dealt primarily with the black middle class, which he considered essentially decent and industrious. Thus he emphasized the danger he saw in Locke's approach: "If Mr. Locke's thesis is insisted on too much it is going to turn the Negro renaissance into decadence." [50]

Du Bois underscored his change of mind in the January editorial, which is an interesting blend of frank assertion and somewhat tentative commentary. He began boldly: "We want especially to stress the fact that while we believe in Negro art we do not believe in any art simply for art's sake." He concluded with understatement: "In *The Crisis* at least, you do not have to confine your writings to the portrayal of beggars, scoundrels and prostitutes; you can write about ordinary decent colored people if you want." He added, in an offhand way, "use propaganda if you want." [51] Presumably, the tentative quality emerged from Du Bois's embarrassment over his sudden about-face and from his unfamiliarity with ideas not yet fully explored.

Du Bois quickly became sure of his position. With the passing of another month, the hesitancy disappeared. The February issue of *Crisis* contained a questionnaire Du Bois had developed for circulation among his contemporaries. In seven rhetorical questions, he asked them essentially to agree that Afro-American writers ought to concentrate on the lives of educated blacks. Typical among the queries was number four: "What are Negroes to do when they are continually painted at their worst and judged by the public as they are painted." [52]

Du Bois supplied his own answers in the October 1926 *Crisis*. The publication was timely, coming after the summer issuance of Carl Van Vechten's *Nigger Heaven*, after the months in which Wallace Thurman had been making radical statements in *Messenger*, and just before the November appearance of Thurman's *Fire*, an outspoken and highly controversial little magazine. Feeling challenged on all sides, Du Bois made the emphatic statement which literary scholars have since remembered as his only response to art and propaganda: "All Art is propaganda and ever must be, despite the wailing of the purists. I stand in utter shamelessness and say that whatever art I have for writing has been used always for propaganda for gaining the right of black folk to love and enjoy. I do not care a damn for any art that is not used for propaganda." [53]

Du Bois did not "care a damn" for *Nigger Heaven*, or for any other creative work outside the pale of art as constructive propaganda. He concluded the year with a hostile review of *Nigger Heaven*, a book he considered "a blow in the face," a handful of "surface mud" and refuse. The novel revelled in pimps and prostitutes, "gin and sadism," and "one damned orgy after another." It totally ignored the majority of Harlemites, who were, said Du Bois, "as conservative and as conventional as ordinary working folk everywhere." He directed the same commentary, two years later, to Claude McKay's *Home to Harlem*. McKay had sold out his own race, best represented by the respectable folk of Harlem and other black communities, in order to satisfy "prurient" interests on the part of white consumers. The book "nauseates me," confessed Du Bois, "and after the dirtier parts of its filth I feel distinctly like taking a bath." Du Bois liked to deal in extremes. In the same review he hailed Nella Larsen's *Quicksand* as "the best piece of fiction that Negro America has produced since the heyday of Chesnutt." The book explored the lives of middle-class blacks and thereby reminded him of Jessie Fauset's *There Is Confusion*, another novel Du Bois considered exemplary within black fiction.[54]

By his insistence on art as propaganda, Du Bois consolidated his supporters, who included Benjamin Brawley and Allison Davis, among others. At the same time, he alienated some of the most influential among the New Negro writers and their friends. In answering the questionnaire, many indicated their disagreement with Du Bois. Langston Hughes, for example, wrote one comment to cover all seven queries: "What's the use of saying anything—the true literary artist is going to write about what he chooses anyway regardless of outside opinions." Van Vechten, who secured white publishers for some of the black authors, replied that "the squalor of Negro life, the vice of Negro life, offer a wealth of novel, exotic, picturesque material to the artist." [55]

McKay broke with Du Bois after reading the review of *Home to Harlem*. In an angry letter dated June 18, 1928, he satirized the tone of *Crisis*, "so holy-clean and righteous-pure," and charged Du Bois with incompetency in matters of art. "Nowhere in your writings do you reveal any comprehension of esthetics," he asserted, "and therefore you are not competent nor qualified to pass judgment upon any work of art." Du Bois had confused politics for aesthetics, he believed: "Therefore I should not be surprised when you mistake the art of life for nonsense and try to pass off propaganda as life in art!" [56]

Crisis declined as a literary power in the latter part of the 1920s. Never again would it be so influential in Afro-American literature as during the second decade of the twentieth century, when it laid a solid foundation for the black renaissance, and during the renaissance itself, when the magazine did much to encourage young writers. As a promoter of literature, Du Bois had no rivals among black editors from 1910 to 1920. During the 1920s, though, he experienced intense competition from Charles S. Johnson, editor of *Opportunity* from 1923 to 1928.

Opportunity was the journal of the National Urban League, which was founded in 1911 to meet the housing and occupational needs of Southern black migrants. Johnson came to the league by way of the University of Chicago, where he had studied sociology under Robert Park. In 1917, when still a student, he assumed direction of the Department of Research and Investigation of the Chicago Urban League, presided over by Park. In 1921, he went to New York as Director of Research and Investigation for the NUL, a position he maintained for the next seven years. Park, founder of the NUL's Bureau of Investigation and Research, had urged the appointment.

As Director of Research, Johnson edited the first NUL periodical, the *Urban League Bulletin*, which appeared bimonthly during 1921 and 1922. The position gave him ample opportunity to demonstrate his considerable editorial skills. Distinctly a house organ, featuring news about the local leagues and national body, the *Bulletin* nevertheless had space for editorials, which Johnson filled with incisive comments about migration and other topics of current interest. Successful as the *Bulletin* was, it did not satisfy John T. Clark, then president of the Pittsburgh League. "At every annual conference held by the National Urban League," recalled Eugene Kinckle Jones, executive of the NUL, "John T. Clark made his appeal for an official organ." He wanted a journal complete with advertisements and second-class mailing privileges, which the *Bulletin* did not have.[57] Finally in October 1922, an NUL conference in Pittsburgh agreed to such a magazine.

Opportunity: Journal of Negro Life appeared immediately thereafter, on January 19, 1923, with Johnson as editor. The name was taken from the NUL slogan, "Not Alms, but Opportunity," and expressed the optimism felt by many New Negroes. Readers came readily, 4,000 to the first issue, but the statistics did not mushroom as they had with *Crisis*. By 1927 *Opportunity* reached a circulation of 11,000, which was sizeable but still considerably below the audience attracted to *Crisis* at that time.[58] *Opportunity* never did become self-sufficient, and thus it always depended, during Johnson's editorship, on an $8,000 annual grant which the Carnegie Foundation first made available to the NUL in 1921. It never could pay contributors, which initially caused some friction between Locke and Johnson. Locke had once accused Johnson, in a letter, of using contemporary authors to advance the journal. The comment troubled Johnson, who responded on August 8, 1924: "I wish we were a well endowed literary magazine. . . . It hurts me to the quick and I cannot shake off the suggestion that the young writers are being exploited by us." [59]

Locke provided much information on *Opportunity*, both in his letters and publications. In an essay which appeared in 1945, he emphasized the ready transformation of *Opportunity* from an organizational to a cultural journal. He stressed the "unexpected" quality of the change, saying that literature and art had never been the primary focus of the NUL. "All the more credit," he then concluded, "that this chance for constructive service was promptly and effectively seized when it arrived on scene." Praising both Jones and Johnson, Locke noted the harmony existing between the national leadership and the editor: "*Opportunity*, the official magazine of the League, could and perhaps should have been exclusively a 'house organ.' But under the able editing of Charles S. Johnson and the wise sponsorship of Eugene Kinckle Jones, it was not." [60]

The January 1923 issue began quietly, with Johnson assuming a low profile. A lead editorial came from Jones, who stressed understanding rather than confrontation, science rather than art. "We shall try," he explained, "to set down interestingly but without sugarcoating or generalization the findings of careful scientific surveys and the facts gathered from research, undertaken not to prove preconceived notions but to lay bare Negro life as it is." The contents of the issue followed suit. There were no poems or stories, but there were articles on such topics as black labor, housing, and child placement. The very next issue, in February, suggested a slight modification of the policy asserted by Jones. In an editorial, Johnson repeated Jones's emphasis and added: "There are aspects of the cultural side of Negro life that have long been neglected." [61] The clarification, which Johnson did not then provide, came in following issues.

In April he published poetry for the first time: "The Dance of Love," by Countee Cullen, and "Voyaging," by Leslie Pinckney Hill. He called for more creative work in August, with an announcement which would be reprinted on the table of contents page for each number until October 1925, when the quantity of manuscripts submitted made it clear that such encouragement was no longer needed: " 'Opportunity' desires the following contributions: drawings, paintings and photographs for covers; fiction, poetry, local news of interest, with photographs; and authentic articles." The statement produced immediate results, and Johnson was able to publish a short story, Eric Walrond's "The Stone Rebounds," for the first time in September. The December issue included poems by Georgia Johnson, Gwendolyn Bennett, and Countee Cullen; a translation of an African folk tale, by Monroe Work; and a tribute to Roland Hayes, by Alain Locke. From then on creative work appeared increasingly in each issue, along with sociological essays by writers both black and white, such as E. Franklin Frazier, Adam Clayton Powell, Sr., Horace Mann Bond, Victor Calverton, and Melville J. Herskovitz. The most literary numbers came once a year from 1925 to 1927, when Johnson gave an entire issue to the publication of winners in the literature and art contests sponsored by *Opportunity*. Johnson published more creative work in those numbers than Du Bois or his successors ever did in a single issue of *Crisis*.

As editors, Johnson and Du Bois represent a study in contrasts. They differed in personal relationships: Johnson was relaxed and at ease with peer and subordinate, Du Bois impatient with and often intolerant of his associates. They had different approaches to their reading audiences. While Du Bois met them in a direct often dramatic way, Johnson kept discreetly out of sight, concentrating attention instead on the facts of Afro-American life. His editorial style was an example of deliberate and rational analysis, usually objective, often subtle, generally complex and balanced in judgment. Many of his editorials involved statistical analyses of census information, social surveys, and industrial and employment studies. As such, his statements were persuasive but not necessarily memorable; they were scientific, not poetic; well phrased, but not worthy of extensive quotation or analysis.

Johnson consciously rejected the personal journalism practised by Du Bois. In an editorial for 1925, he suggested a significant contrast between the two magazines. Speaking of *Opportunity*, he concluded that "its policy has been one of intelligent discussion rather than fireworks; of calm analysis rather than tears." He was pleased that the journal had "capitulated to no wrong, or vanity, or arrogance. Its shibboleth has been facts—facts useful, incisive, stimulating." [62] In 1928 he specified further his distaste for Du Bois's approach. He declared, in a discussion of black magazines, that *Crisis* always had "more than a tinge of personal journalism," that "the race was defended rather than explained," and "agitation was justified editorially." Years later he remembered that Du Bois was unquestionably "brilliant, highly cultured, and racially sensitive," but that he was also bitter and even destructive. "He got attention but scant acceptance," Johnson summarized.[63] Du Bois, for his part, uncharacteristically held his tongue about *Opportunity* and its editor. In *Crisis* he routinely announced the beginning of *Opportunity*, commented occasionally about an *Opportunity* contest, and briefly noted the "uneven quality" of *Ebony and Topaz*, edited by Johnson.[64] Beyond that he would not go, presumably because he respected Johnson and the work of the NUL.

The differences between Johnson and Du Bois emerge clearly in a comparison of their respective approaches to similar issues. Locke contrasted the two in their responses to art as propaganda. Du Bois, he felt, erred both as a creative writer and editor. *Dark Princess*, for example, "falls an artistic victim to its own propagandist ambushes," he wrote in *Opportunity* during 1929. In 1945 he claimed that *Crisis* had done pioneering work in black literature and art but that it lost its influence in the 1920s because Du Bois insisted on "an old-fashioned and soon to be outmoded formula." *Opportunity* assumed the predominate role during the black renaissance because it offered a new way, "substituting self-expression and interpretation for racial rhetoric and overt propaganda." [65]

It is important that Locke qualified "propaganda" with "overt." Johnson understood the social function of literature, but he expressed his ideas in a more diplomatic way than did Du Bois. He avoided the expression art-as-propaganda, and he suggested repeatedly that writers and artists had a responsibility to themselves as well as to the community. When Du Bois became most emphatic about propaganda, in 1926, Johnson spoke increasingly of freedom and self-expression for the creative writer. All along Johnson realized that authors and artists present images which shape responses to interracial relations. In "Public Opinion and the Negro," an article published in the July 1923 issue of *Opportunity*, Johnson explored social myths: "Jokes about Negroes, news stories, anecdotes, gossip, the stage, the motion pictures, the Octavus Roy Cohen, Hugh Wiley and Irvin S. Cobb type of humorous fiction repeated with unvarying outline, have helped to build up and crystallize a fictitious being unlike any Negro." If the beliefs could be questioned, and the images dissolved, "many of our inhibitions to normal, rational and ethical conduct" would be "removed." [66]

Johnson became more explicit by mid-1925, when Du Bois was still distinguishing between art and propaganda. "Art should be—and undoubtedly will be—the powerful and compelling liaison officer between nations and races," he wrote in an editorial for May. During the summer of 1926, Johnson made two statements which clearly distinguished his approach from that of Du Bois, who was by then a firm believer in art-as-propaganda. In June, he stated that *Opportunity* needed artistic as well as scientific expression. "This journal," he explained, "is designed to inform and interpret, both through sociological discussions, and through what it may offer of the cultural experiences of Negroes." Significantly, he never specified the type or quality of interpretation needed. Instead, in an editorial comment published in August, he stressed aesthetic freedom: "What is most important is that these black artists should be free, not merely to express anything they feel, but to feel the pulsations and rhythms of their own life, philosophy be hanged." [67]

In the months immediately following, *Opportunity* and *Crisis* differed dramatically in their approaches to the most controversial novels of the day. The discussion surrounding *Nigger Heaven* is a case in point. With a few comments in September, or three months before the appearance of Du Bois's review, Johnson introduced the book to *Opportunity* readers. He began as a gentleman: "Comes *Nigger Heaven*, Carl Van Vechten's amazing novel of Negro Harlem, with the already evident promise of warm debates within the 'belt' on proper racial nomenclature." He continued as a scholar, coolly and objectively discussing the varying connotations of "nigger" and "Negro." [68] He acted the diplomat in allowing others to review the book itself. Interestingly, the reviews came from those who had contributed repeatedly to *Crisis* but who would not have pleased Du Bois with their favorable estimates of Van Vechten's book.

In the October 1925 *Opportunity*, James Weldon Johnson called *Nigger Heaven* "the most revealing, significant and powerful novel based exclusively on Negro life yet written." He liked the characters, considering them believable, and the milieu, in which "the scenes of gay life, of night life, the glimpses of the underworld . . . set off in sharper relief the decent, cultured, intellectual life of Negro Harlem." [69] Gwendolyn Bennett defended *Nigger Heaven* from September 1926 to April 1928 in her *Opportunity* column, "Ebony Flute." She began by describing the book as "splendid . . . a perfect piece of research," continued with a defense of Van Vechten, saying "his has been a rather intimate knowledge" of blacks, and concluded by reaffirming her loyalty. "We've always liked *Nigger Heaven*," she testified in 1928, "regardless of what many of our friends have said or thought about it." [70]

Van Vechten reciprocated in kind. He sent a note to *Opportunity*, which was published in the issue for December 1926, the same month in which Du Bois aired his response to *Nigger Heaven*. "It seems to me," he declared, "that this magazine has made such strides, that it is no longer fair to merely say that it is better than any other Negro periodical." He demonstrated his gratitude by giving Johnson $200 for a literary contest to be sponsored by *Opportunity*.[71]

Johnson made his greatest contributions to black literature of the 1920s through the *Opportunity* contests and dinners. He was so successful—more successful than was Du Bois with the *Crisis* contests—because he could better interest a variety of influential persons and an important segment of the press. Locke praised Johnson for the "stage-managed publicity . . . which paid distinct dividends in regular publication and publicity for many young Negro artists." [72] The publicity came with the dinners, the first of which was held at the Civic Club in New York on March 21, 1924. Johnson essentially arranged the dinner, as revealed in a letter he sent to Locke on March 4, 1924. He wanted an occasion to honor the young writers meeting regularly at NUL offices to discuss literature. He mentioned names—Regina Anderson, Gwendolyn Bennett, Countee Cullen, Jessie Fauset, Langston Hughes, Harold Jackman, Eloise Bibb Thompson, Eric Walrond—but he had no label beyond the "little group" or "the 'movement.' " Locke, he hoped, would act as master of ceremonies.[73]

In May, Johnson publicized the event with an article he had written for *Opportunity*, called "The Debut of the Younger School of Negro Writers." He identified the group as the Writers' Guild and the purpose of the dinner as a tribute to Jessie Fauset, upon publication of *There Is Confusion*. The program went smoothly. Johnson spoke about "the object of the Guild" and then introduced Locke, who served as master of ceremonies and talked about "the new currents manifest in the literature of this younger school." "With soft seriousness," as Johnson wrote, Locke introduced Du Bois as a "representative of the 'older school.' " So categorized, Du Bois graciously complied with remarks about the pioneering nature of earlier black literature. There were several other speakers, including Horace Liveright, the publisher, and Carl Van Doren, editor of *Century*. After his description of the occasion, Johnson printed "To Usward," the poem Gwendolyn Bennett had dedicated to the affair. The poem had a second publication during the same month, for Du Bois reproduced it in the May issue of *Crisis*.

The guest list merits brief consideration, for it shows the formula Johnson used for the promotion of Afro-American literature. Along with many prominent blacks, he invited influential white publishers and editors: Frederick L. Allen of Harper Brothers; Paul Kellogg, editor of *Survey Graphic*; Devere Allen, editor of *World Tomorrow*; Freda Kirchwey and Evans Clark of *Nation*; Louis Weitzenkorn of

New York *World;* Oswald Garrison Villard, editor of *Nation;* Herbert Bayard Swope, editor of New York *World;* and George W. Oakes, editor of *Current History.*[74] All but the last three attended the event. Locke thought the interracial contacts most valuable and stated that the Civic Club dinner and the others which followed did much to destroy "the artistic ghetto."

He praised the *Opportunity* contests, too, seeing them as the result of a "shrewd editorship." [75] The contests were meritorious but not, at first glance, appreciably different from the *Crisis* competitions, so often neglected in literary history. The *Opportunity* contests appeared in 1925, 1926, and 1927, the same years as those at *Crisis*. Prize money came not from the magazine but from friends—in 1925 from Mrs. Henry Goddard Leach, an NUL board member; in 1926 from Casper Holstein, a black businessman in New York; and in 1927 from George Buckner, a black businessman in St. Louis. The judges were an impressive lot, including William Rose Benet, Van Wyck Brooks, Robert Frost, Vachel Lindsay, Jean Toomer; but then, so were the judges for the *Crisis* contests. Some, in fact, served in both competitions, such as Benjamin Brawley and Montgomery Gregory. The winners in the categories—originally listed as short story, poetry, essays, plays, and personal experience sketches—represented the best writers of the day. For the 1925 contest, first- and second-place winners included, in respective order: John Matheus and Zora Neale Hurston for the short story; Langston Hughes and Countee Cullen for poetry; and E. Franklin Frazier and Sterling Brown for essays.

Where the contests differed between the rival magazines was in mood. Du Bois did a workmanlike job with his competitions. Johnson created an electric excitement. He attracted 732 competitors to the 1925 contest and 1,276 to the 1926 event.[76] Johnson, to put it simply, offered greater rewards than did Du Bois: there was the possibility of inclusion in the prestigious contest numbers of May 1925, June 1926, and July 1927; of praise at the dinners following each competition; and of publication by an established firm or within another journal. It became common knowledge that contacts made at the dinners led to book publication for both Hughes, with *The Weary Blues,* and Cullen, with *Color.* One such occasion also inspired Paul Kellogg with plans for a special Afro-American issue of *Survey Graphic* and Albert Boni with ideas about a novel contest for black writers. The possibilities seemed endless when Johnson wrote in *Opportunity* about the "magnificient assemblages" of 300 or 400 people, of guest lists including Albert Boni, Jessie Fauset, Fannie Hurst, Alain Locke, Emmett Scott, Stuart Sherman, Arthur Spingarn, Carl Van Vechten, Clement

Wood and, as Johnson noted, "many other white and Negro persons interested in letters." [77]

The third *Opportunity* contest, which lacked the excitement of its predecessors, signalled the end of an era. The judges were again influential, including Benjamin Brawley, Theodore Dreiser, Robert Kerlin, Paul Robeson, Ridgely Torrence, and Eric Walrond, but they were not as numerous as in the past. Although many of the winners were prominent authors, such as Arna Bontemps, Sterling Brown, Eugene Gordon, Georgia Douglas Johnson, and Helene Johnson, some of the familiar names were missing. A new spirit was abroad, as Johnson suggested in his description of the third *Opportunity* dinner in his June editorial. He could no longer see the renaissance as the special province of Harlem, for many of the successful entrants lived "beyond the limits of the recognized cultural centers." Johnson had done good work; he had seen a boom period in Afro-American literature to its logical conclusion. He could afford, then, to take a new tack, to become more the critic and less the promoter. In the same editorial, he stressed the need for craftsmanship, saying that too many of the contestants had submitted "hasty work." He emphasized the same in his September editorial, when he ended the contests, although at that time he thought he was merely suspending them for one year. "More time for the deliberate working of manuscripts will yield vastly more valuable results," he explained.[78]

The Van Vechten Awards came as a denouement, with $200 given to the single best contribution published in *Opportunity* during 1927 and then again during 1928. The judges for the first competition—Charles S. Johnson, James Weldon Johnson, and Robert Morse Lovett—tagged Dante Bellegard as the winner for his essay, "Haiti Under the United States." The judges for 1928—Charles Johnson, and Henry Leach, editor of *Forum*—awarded the prize to E. Franklin Frazier for his article on "The Mind of Negro America." Johnson obviously found satisfaction in awarding essayists, for he had noted in the past that while black writers excelled in poetry and short stories, they had hardly made a beginning with plays and essays, which "offered the most formidable difficulties." [79]

The year 1928 also saw the end of two regular *Opportunity* columns: Gwendolyn Bennett's "Ebony Flute," which appeared from August 1926 to May 1928, and Countee Cullen's "Dark Tower," published from December 1926 to September 1928. Johnson had originated the columns in response to the times. He had noticed, mid-decade, the emergence of black literary groups throughout the country. Involved in the activities of Harlem writers, he had considered these other groups isolated, in need of the "informal literary intelligence" Gwendolyn Bennett could provide through the "Ebony Flute." He praised Bennett as "versatile and accomplished" and the title of her column as "exceptionally engaging." As Bennett explained later, the title came from William Rose Benet's "Harlem": "I want to sing Harlem on an ebony flute." [80] The line captured Bennett's intention, to bring information from the metropolis to the outlying areas. The intention for the "Dark Tower" is not so clear, since neither Johnson nor Cullen discussed it. Johnson did, though, explain that he had appointed Cullen as poetry editor for *Opportunity* because such a "step [was] virtually decreed by the demands of that awakening generation to which this magazine, in many of its interests, has consistently addressed itself." [81]

The two columns developed in basically similar ways. Bennett and Cullen reviewed theatrical presentations, books, and some of the new little magazines, such as *Fire* and *Harlem*. Both commented on black literary groups, although Bennett demonstrated more knowledge about the doings of the Quill Club of Boston, the Saturday Nighters and the Literary Lovers of Washington, D.C., and the Ink Slingers of Los Angeles, to name a few of these societies. They included revealing and often amusing anecdotes about prominent writers and artists. "Dr. Rudolph Fisher has very endearingly nick-named his new baby 'the new Negro,' " Bennett told her readers coast-to-coast. They engaged, too, in personal journalism. Cullen, for example, wrote movingly of his first journey into the deep South. "Strange incredible stories stirred to remembrance within us," he recalled of his train trip through Georgia and Alabama. "We shuddered at the sight of a charred bit of stick stretched like a slumbering snake along the road; we knew not of what insane rites it might have been part, what human torches it once might have served to light." [82]

The last publication of "Dark Tower" appeared in the September 1928 issue, which was the last number which Johnson edited. The October editorial announced that Johnson had resigned from the magazine in order to become chairman of the Department of Social Sciences at Fisk University. Johnson had long wanted to head such a department and had also been an admirer of Thomas Elsa Jones, the young and energetic president of Fisk. The move seemed timely, particularly because the future of *Opportunity* appeared cloudy. The Carnegie Foundation had discontinued its $8,000 grant to the NUL in 1927 and another satisfactory benefactor had not been found. A disgruntled Eugene Kinkle Jones was scrutinizing the budget and wondering aloud whether the magazine was "an effective instrument for carrying out the League's purposes." [83]

When Johnson resigned, two men assumed his former positions, Ira Reid as director of the Department of Research and Investigations and Elmer A. Carter as editor of *Opportunity*. Carter came to the editorship as a former teacher and organizational worker. A Harvard graduate, he had taught at Prairie View State Normal, in Texas, and had served as executive secretary of the urban leagues in Louisville, St. Paul, and Columbus, Ohio. In his opening editorial published in October, he listed his seven commitments, the first three to "the idea of interracial cooperation," to the secretaries of local leagues, and to members of the NUL. Not until the fourth statement did he mention cultural priorities: "I have a charge to keep," he wrote, "to the younger Negro artists who have freed themselves from a slave psychology and are striving to depict their race and its environment in fine drawings and paintings and in enduring sculpture and with beautiful words." [84] In the following years, Carter tried to keep that charge and did publish poetry and fiction in *Opportunity*. In comparison with his predecessor, however, Carter was not so involved in the arts, and during his editorship *Opportunity* became more the vehicle for sociological and economic studies than it had been during the high mark of the black renaissance.

In *The Big Sea*, Langston Hughes described *Crisis* and *Opportunity* as "house organs of inter-racial organizations" and *Messenger* as "God knows what." He explained about the latter, saying: "It began by being very radical, racial, and socialistic, just after the war. . . . Then it later became a kind of Negro society magazine and a plugger for Negro business, with photographs of prominent colored ladies and their nice homes in it." [85] Hughes's comment provides some insight into *Messenger*, but it does not do justice to the function performed by the magazine in its later years. While *Messenger* did not develop into a society magazine, it did originate as Hughes suggested. A. Philip Randolph and Chandler Owen founded the publication one year before the armistice, in November 1917. Under their leadership, the magazine went from socialism to union politics. From 1925 to its demise in 1928, *Messenger* served as the official organ of the Brotherhood of Sleeping Car Porters, which Randolph organized and headed. Politics were always the main focus, but the journal did engage itself in the cultural renaissance of the 1920s.

In response to the arts, *Messenger* moved through four discernible stages. Randolph and Owen, in an editorial statement for the first issue, established a tone for the initial period, which stretched roughly from 1917 to 1922. They defined their journal as one "written in fine style; its matter . . . logically presented; its interpretations . . . made calmly and dispassionately." "Our aim is to appeal to reason," they announced, "to lift our pens above the cringing demagogy of the times and above the cheap, peanut politics of the old, reactionary Negro leaders." [86]

In subsequent issues, Randolph and Owen took steady aim at the existing black leadership, especially at Du Bois. The most explicit attack appeared in a "Who's Who" column of 1918, penned by " 'Who's Who,' Editor." The anonymous author identified Du Bois as a radical for the last two decades and also as "the leading literateur [sic]." The "also" introduced a sweeping criticism of Du Bois's work, from the *Souls of Black Folk*, which he regarded as "more literature than information," to *Quest of the Silver Fleece*, "a third rate piece of fiction," to *Crisis*. The organization of *Crisis* seemed skewed, as shown in one section of the magazine: first came "Music and Art"; then " 'Meetings,' which signify the gathering of literateurs"; next " 'The War,' which inspires pictures and scenes for literary description and word painting"; and last, "Industry" and "Politics." The pattern was significant, said the writer, for it illustrated "a logical product of Du Bois's celebration." *Messenger*, on the other hand, followed the editorials with "Economics and Politics." "This is natural for us," wrote the Editor, "because with us economics and politics take precedure [sic] to 'Music and Art.' " [87]

A bias against the arts continued in issues immediately following. In a review of *Darkwater*, published in 1920, William Colson described Du Bois "as a *poet* rather than a thinker." The work showed Du Bois as a "romanticist of a high order" even in his "more serious essays," which "are never mere prose." Colson stated that he had seen the impressive personality of Du Bois emerge in the pages of *Darkwater*. He did not believe, though, that personality and literature could adequately meet the major questions of the day. In a paraphrase of Du Bois's famous statement on the centrality of the color line, he declared that the "distribution of wealth and knowledge is the problem of the twentieth century." [88]

In those early years, Randolph and Owen published creative work, primarily verse, only if it served the social and economic ends of the magazine. They favored poets who were political radicals, such as Frederick W. Falkenburg, Betuccio Dantino, Miriam S. de Ford, and Claude McKay. In "Labor's Day," published in the September 1919 issue, McKay reevaluated traditional poetry in light of recent economic developments and found it

> Hollow . . . and cold,
> Like imitated music, false and strange,
> Or half truths of a day that could not hold
> Its own against the eternal tide of change.

He believed "modern songs of hope and vision" would come from the working classes and would transform this "poor blind" society into "a new world under labor's law!" [89]

Messenger went through another phase from 1923 to 1925. As Randolph and Owen became increasingly involved with union politics, they shifted editorial control of the magazine to George Schuyler and Theophilis Lewis, who had become contributing editors in 1923 along with Abram Harris and William Pickens, among others. From 1923 to 1928, Schuyler and Lewis served essentially as de facto editors, although the masthead never gave them full credit for their work. They were listed as contributing editors until January 1927, when George Schuyler gained the title of assistant editor. In April, and until the end of the magazine, the masthead designated Schuyler as managing editor and Lewis as dramatic editor.

With the involvement of Schuyler and Lewis, *Messenger* immediately showed a new receptivity toward the arts. Socialistic verses basically disappeared, to be replaced by creative work from such poets as Countee Cullen, Langston Hughes, and Georgia Douglas Johnson; and such short story writers as Josephine Cogdell, Thomas M. Henry, Eric Walrond, and Lewis himself. Lewis and Schuyler came before the public with two monthly columns, which were continued until the end of the journal and which reviewed artistic and cultural happenings of the day. In September 1923, Schuyler originated "Shafts & Darts," which he shared with Lewis in 1924 and 1925, and then authored by himself from September 1925 to 1928. Throughout the column, and especially in his famous series of "Aframerican Fables," Schuyler used a sharp and often bitter prose to advance his militant, integrationist views on race and culture. Hughes enjoyed "Shafts & Darts," calling it "verbal brickbats" and the best feature of the magazine.[90]

Lewis's most significant involvement in the magazine was with his monthly column of drama criticism which appeared from September 1923 to July 1927. Throughout the series, he evaluated the black theater, including little theater groups, and white companies that attempted Afro-American themes. In so doing he tried to develop an ideology for a national black theater. He urged cultural independence, saying that Afro-American playwrights should concentrate on race materials. By commenting with thoroughness, depth, and frequency, Lewis provided a criticism of black drama which was more sustained and influential than that found anywhere else in the 1920s.

He called the column "Theatre: Souls of Black Folk." The subtitle echoed Du Bois, but the series showed no fondness for his approach to drama. Lewis satirized the name of the Krigwa Players Little Negro Theatre, founded by Du Bois: "It sounds like somebody with a sore throat trying to gargle." He satirized the man himself as an impractical dreamer, as "the well known astrologer who erstwhile dwelt apart from the world in an ivory tower out of a lofty window of which he would occasionally poke his head and announce mysteriously, 'The answer is in the stars.' " [91]

Dominated by Lewis and by Schuyler, who was assuming the role of managing editor, *Messenger* remained critical of Du Bois. The magazine identified good literature with propaganda at the very time Du Bois was calling for a separation between the two. The April 1924 issue of *Messenger* included "Art and Propaganda" by William Pickens, a contributing editor to the journal. Pickens never mentioned Du Bois, but he did express opinions considerably different from those printed in *Crisis* until 1926. "Propaganda," he asserted, "is the *raison d'etre* of the greatest arts. As a physic is concealed under the sugar-coating, so is propaganda best concealed under art." [92]

For a few months in 1926, Wallace Thurman held sway at *Messenger* and brought the magazine into the third phase of its artistic involvement. He came into the magazine through the encouragement of his friend Theophilis Lewis, who had earlier secured his initial editorial position in New York with the *Looking Glass*, a short-lived newspaper. Thurman first appeared in *Messenger* with "Christmas: Its Origins and Significance," a conventional essay published in the December 1925 issue. With the new year, he exerted increasing influence in the magazine. The table of contents for the April and May numbers bore an announcement presumably of Thurman's doing. "Writers Attention!" it read. "The editors of The Messenger desire short stories of Negro life and will pay liberally for those found available for publication." The statement got results, and for the next several issues *Messenger* included contributions from black writers with emerging reputations: stories from Anita Scott Coleman, Zora Neale Hurston, Dorothy West, and Thurman himself; and poems from Arna Bontemps, Langston Hughes, Georgia Douglas Johnson,

Helene Johnson, Bruce Nugent, Edward Silvera, and again from Thurman.

For the May issue, Thurman reviewed *Flight*, by Walter White. In developing his assessment, he enunciated an aesthetic which had not been heard before in *Messenger* but which represented the opinions of many New Negroes. His ideas countered, at the same time, the aesthetic views Du Bois stressed in *Crisis* from January 1926. Thurman drew an emphatic line separating art from propaganda. He claimed that White was not a good creative writer because he went to "the propagandist school." Thurman was weary of "the ballyhooing" of that approach and ready "for the genuine performance to begin." His summary comments approximated the statements Charles Johnson was making in *Opportunity*: "All art no doubt is propaganda, but all propaganda is most certainly not art. And a novel must, to earn the name, be more than a mere social service report, more than a thinly disguised dissertation on racial relationships and racial maladjustments." [93]

Thurman served as managing editor of *Messenger* in July and August, when Schuyler took a leave of absence from the magazine. Thurman wrote an editorial for August which is significant in its apparent attempt to redirect the magazine, to make it "an agent provocateur [*sic*] for new energies and new aspirations." He re-emphasized the centrality of economic analysis, but added that henceforth the readers would "find ample evidence of the contemporary cultural renaissance." [94] Evidently, Thurman wanted to involve more of the Harlem literati in the pages of *Messenger*. The management presumably did not see the magazine as an "agent provocateur," at least according to Thurman's definition of the word.

When the September issue came, Schuyler was back in his old post and Thurman was making a final appearance in *Messenger* with a review of *Nigger Heaven*. On his way out, Thurman was in a mood to shock former associates and overstated his enthusiasm for the novel. "I would not be surprised," he ventured, "should some of our uplift organizations and neighborhood clubs plan to erect a latter-day abolitionist statue to Carl Van Vechten on the corner of 135th Street and Seventh Avenue, for the author has been most fair, and most sympathetic in his treatment of a long mistreated group of subjects." He showed himself to be a habitué of Harlem nightspots by saying he would like to attend a black mass like the one described by Van Vechten. "Where, oh where," he cried," is this Black Mass in Harlem." Thurman even used the word "ofays," a term which had not been appearing in *Messenger* or the NAACP and NUL magazines.[95]

The partnership between Thurman and *Messenger* had not been easy, since other editors and contributors could not endorse many of Thurman's ideas. *Nigger Heaven* and Van Vechten moved Schuyler, for example, to satiric laughter. In the October issue of "Shafts & Darts," he announced the coming of "a great public debate" in Harlem between Van Vechten and David Belasco: "They are to debate on which one is most entitled to be known as the Santa Claus of Black Harlem." [96] Thurman, for his part, was dissatisfied with *Messenger*. He wanted a radical little magazine dedicated to literature and art, not a journal committed first to union politics. And thus during the summer of 1926, he and friends like Hughes and Gwendolyn Bennett made plans for the November appearance of *Fire*.

With the departure of Thurman, the magazine entered its final stage. Schuyler and Lewis reasserted their influence and attracted a new list of contributing editors, including Eugene Gordon, James Ivy, and Alice Dunbar-Nelson. They continued to publish creative writing: poems from Lewis Alexander, Langston Hughes, and Ann Lawrence, and stories from Elmer Carter, Hughes, Schuyler, and Josephine Cogsdell, along with others. The April 1927 issue carried the first short story Hughes ever published, "Bodies in the Moonlight." Two of his other stories appeared in the same year, "The Young Glory of Him" in June and "The Little Virgin" in August. Hughes said the pieces came into *Messenger* by way of Thurman, who thought they were "very bad stories, but better than any others they could find." Unlike the other larger magazines, *Messenger* paid its writers, as Hughes clearly recalled: "They paid me ten dollars a story." [97] The money for contributors did not last, however, and by early 1928 Randolph concluded that the journal was too great a drain on the financial resources of the Brotherhood of Sleeping Car Porters. The May–June issue was the last.

In comparison with *Crisis* and *Opportunity*, *Messenger* occupied a valuable but secondary position in the black cultural renaissance. The journal matched the others in the quantity of literature published between 1923 and 1928. Quality was another matter, though, and many black writers turned to *Messenger* only after their work had been rejected elsewhere.[98] They were not as interested in *Messenger* because the magazine, in comparison with the others, was not as involved in the arts. The journal had Schuyler and Lewis, but it did not have a literary editor. It published considerable amounts of creative work, but it did not have literary contests, promotional dinners, or a sizeable audience. Schuyler recalled that *Messenger* never sold more than 5,000 copies a month.[99] Most of those copies went to members of a black union, not to an interracial audience ready and willing to encourage promising young writers.

The year 1928 was pivotal as the larger magazines met reversals and the little magazines began to proliferate. *Messenger* folded; the literature and art contests ended at both *Crisis* and *Opportunity;* Charles S. Johnson resigned from his editorship; and Du Bois faced new difficulties in maintaining his editorial position. Significant as these occurrences were, they did not revive the old graveyard metaphors. Locke indicated the sense of the times in a retrospective review published in the January 1929 issue of *Opportunity.* He never commented on the discouragements among larger journals because he was so enthusiastic over the black little magazines.

Locke saw "the spread of beauty to the provinces," [100] with the appearance of *Harlem* in New York, the *Saturday Evening Quill* in Boston, and *Black Opals* in Philadelphia. *Stylus* continued from Howard University, and the *Carolina Magazine*, at the University of North Carolina, came out with a number devoted exclusively to black poetry. In addition, Afro-American art and dramatic groups were appearing in such places as Chicago, Cleveland, Dallas, and Indianapolis. In publicizing the cultural renaissance to cities across the land, the larger journals had encouraged the development of smaller journals and artistic groups. As the organizational periodicals faltered, black little magazines appeared ready to carry on the standard and to suggest new approaches to Afro-American literature.

3. Black Renaissance

Little Magazines and Special Issues,

1916–1930

The first black little magazines of the twentieth century came immediately after *Crisis* had achieved financial independence from the NAACP. In November 1915, Du Bois announced that *Crisis* was solvent. In January 1916, the journal paid his entire salary, and all other operational expenses, for the first time. Two small black journals appeared shortly thereafter, as if the success of Du Bois had bolstered the confidence of others who wanted to start periodicals. *New Era* of Boston emerged in February and *Stylus* of Washington, D.C., in June of that year. Other black little magazines followed, as did Afro-American issues of essentially white periodicals, but they arrived after the war had ended and the postwar depression had eased. *Survey Graphic,* a journal published in New York and concerned broadly with social questions, featured in 1925 a special number on Harlem, its literature and its people. Established in Guadalajara, Mexico, a little poetry magazine called *Palms* published an issue devoted to Afro-American literature in 1926. The next year saw the first Afro-American number of the *Carolina Magazine,* a student publication at the University of North Carolina. Inspired by the quality and influence of that number, the students followed with a special issue of black literature in 1928 and also in 1929. The black little magazines began in Harlem with two radical and short-lived publications, *Fire* in 1926 and *Harlem* in 1928. More conservative Afro-American journals appeared elsewhere on the East Coast, as did *Black Opals* in Philadelphia during 1927 and 1928, and the *Saturday Evening Quill* in Boston during 1928 to 1930.

Pauline Hopkins came to the fore again with *New Era.* She established the journal because she sensed the beginning of "a really new era in America," and wanted to be part of that beginning. She did not succeed in addressing the contemporary scene, however, and the magazine collapsed after its first two issues of February and March. In the opening number, she introduced her compeers, saying "the roll of the staff presents a few familiar names, but for the most part we are as young in public life as is the new year." [1] The controlling voices came out of the past, though, for Hopkins was listed as editor and Walter Wallace, her colleague on the staff at *Colored American Magazine*, as managing editor. The contributors even included Sarah Allen, or Hopkins writing under the maiden name of her mother, her previous practice when she lowered her profile.

In both issues Hopkins elaborated on the functions of *New Era*. Her commentary indicates that she envisioned the journal in three roles: as an agitator for race rights, as an historian of race progress, and as a promoter of black literature and arts. Her accents rang as of old when she placed the journal firmly within the protest tradition: "We know that there are able publications already in the field, but the pang that has set our active world a-borning is the knowledge that the colored man has lost the rights already won because he was persuaded and then bullied into lying down and ceasing his fight for civil liberty." [2] Hopkins understood the importance of journals as preservers of tradition. As editor of *New Era* she voiced sentiments reminiscent of those expressed much earlier by Max Barber. "We are," she claimed, "sparing neither time nor money to make this Magazine the most authentic historian of the race's progress." She recognized the importance of black journals in providing an outlet for Afro-American writers. She promised, then, that *New Era* would "do its utmost to assist in developing the literature, science, music, art, religion, facts, fiction and tradition of the race throughout the world." In this connection, she hoped to establish a "Race Publishing House" in Boston which would "stand as a permanent and lasting monument of race progress." [3] Undoubtedly she envisioned the publishing house along the lines of the Colored Co-operative Publishing Company which had issued the *Colored American Magazine*, as well as books by and about blacks.

In many respects, the contents of *New Era* paralleled the contents of the *Colored American Magazine* when edited by Hopkins. *New Era* emphasized biography, with each issue featuring several sketches of prominent persons. Hopkins probably wrote all the sketches, those left unsigned as well as those carrying her name, because the pieces bore her stylistic idiosyncracies, with didactic introductions and conclusions stressing the value of individual effort. She envisioned the biographical essays as a continuation of her earlier effort, as indicated in the February issue: "The series of sketches prepared by Miss Hopkins some years since on 'Famous Men of the Negro Race,' will have a worthy sequel in this series entitled 'Men of Vision.' " [4] She likewise planned a series on "sacrificing women" of the race, including Frances Harper, Sojourner Truth, and Harriet Tubman. As in the past, her favorite subjects were New Englanders, men like John Trowbridge whom she identified as the "Last of the Famous Group of New England Authors." [5]

She continued to feature fiction and verse. The table of contents for each issue noted two short stories and one poem, and then Hopkins went ahead and included several other creative pieces which were not announced. Foremost among the poets was William Stanley Braithwaite, whose "picture adorn[ed] our cover" for the February issue, and whose lyrics appeared in prominent positions in the March issue. [6] The most significant fiction came from Pauline Hopkins, who was engaged once again with a serialized novel, this time called "Topsy Templeton." She planned her effort to "run through several issues," and consequently readers never did learn what finally happened to Topsy. The first two installments were sufficient, however, to show that Hopkins had not changed as a creative writer. Once again she concentrated on interracial relations, in this story between the white Newbury sisters and Topsy, the little black girl they adopted. She ended the first episode with much suspense and an apparently dead Topsy. In the second issue, she revived a scene which had figured significantly in *Of One Blood*, serialized in *Colored American Magazine*. A physician having psychic powers recognizes Topsy's condition as "suspended animation" and "reanimates" her before some wondering colleagues and two very grateful Newbury sisters. [7]

Not all of the journal was a look backward. Hopkins had the foresight to include a regular column, headed "Helps for Young Artists," by the sculptor, Meta Warrick-Fuller, who was art editor for the journal. In her column, Fuller urged black artists to form groups in order to experiment with suggestions advanced in the column. By so doing, she became one of the first writers in a black journal to stress the need for such organization. Only Du Bois had preceded her, with his call one year earlier for Horizon clubs dedicated to Afro-American pageantry. Hopkins recognized the merit in Fuller's comments and encouraged involvement by announcing a prize to be awarded "to the individual or group of persons . . . who will have tried out any one or more of the instructions offered in this series." [8] The journal collapsed before the plans matured, but Hopkins nevertheless anticipated Du Bois and Charles S. Johnson who later realized the value of artistic competitions and prizes.

New Era went quietly. Du Bois never alluded to its demise in *Crisis*, but then he had never announced its initial appearance. He kept a fine eye on the press, so he probably knew about *New Era*. Most likely he did not welcome the magazine because he saw it as a potential rival to *Crisis*. He would not have criticized Hopkins because she had battled long and hard in the past for a free black press and for other concerns he himself endorsed. It would have been ungracious to express satisfaction over the failure of her later attempt with a magazine rivalling his own. And so Du Bois said nothing. No one else said much about the magazine either. As a result, it slipped out of memory, forgotten by editors and literary historians.[9]

Whereas much of *New Era* echoed the past, *Stylus* looked to the future. The support for the journal came in the winter of 1915–16, when Professors Alain Locke and Montgomery Gregory organized a literary society at Howard University. Called Stylus, the group included students, to be selected from biannual competitions, and several faculty and honorary members. From the beginning, members wanted to stimulate writing based on Afro-American culture and to encourage artistic expression in the black community, especially among youth. Gregory remembered that the society had "a vision, a vision which embodied in the not too distant future a Negro literature that should secure recognition along with that of other peoples." [10] The *Howard University Record* recalled in later years that the efforts of Stylus were not limited to Howard University, but that they extended "to the Negro race and to civilization." Benjamin Brawley noted that the organization "hoped to make a genuine contribution to racial advance." [11] To further their ends, Locke and associates issued a journal which bore the same name as the organization and which was the first purely literary magazine published at any black college. Appearing in June 1916, *Stylus* featured student efforts and special contributions by honorary members, such as Braithwaite, Brawley, and James Weldon Johnson.

World War I interrupted the work, sending Stylus members and supporters to distant parts. Efforts did not resume until peace returned and a handful of the former participants came back to campus. With that nucleus Professors Locke and Gregory attracted new student members, including Zora Neale Hurston, and additional honorary members, notably Charles W. Chesnutt, W. E. B. Du Bois, Alice

Moore Dunbar, and Arthur A. Schomburg. The second number of *Stylus* appeared in May 1921.

In his "Foreword" to that issue, Montgomery Gregory voiced sentiments which would be echoed by New Negroes emerging in the latter half of the decade. "It becomes clearer daily," he stated, "that it must be through the things of the Spirit that we shall ultimately restore Ethiopia to her seat of honor among the races of the world. The Germans have amply demonstrated the futility of force to secure a place in the sun. Any individual or people must depend upon the universal appeal of art, literature, painting, and music—to secure the real respect and recognition of mankind." Gregory urged his colleagues onward with promise of better days ahead: "*The Stylus* is on the right track although like all bearers of Truth they are in a minority for a day. Theirs are the future years, rich with the promise of a fulfilment of the visions of those whose love for their race embraces humanity." [12] *Stylus* reserved further statements for future years. The third number, to be discussed later, did not appear until 1929.

Du Bois lent his name to *Stylus*, but he was not much impressed with the journal. He mentioned it only once in *Crisis*, and then with faint praise. "The poems of Otto Bohanan seem to be the only notable contributions," he asserted about the publication in 1916. Du Bois did not say so, but *Stylus* launched the careers of writers much more influential than Bohanan. Probably the most outstanding student published in the journal during its early years was Zora Hurston. In her autobiography, *Dust Tracks on a Road*, she traced her literary career from her involvement in the Howard group. She explained how Charles Johnson, who was then planning the first issue of *Opportunity*, read a short story of hers included in *Stylus* and asked her to contribute to his magazine. Hurston sent him "Drenched in Light," which he published. Later he published a second story, "Spunk," and counselled her to move to Harlem, which he considered the hub of literary activity. Hurston responded enthusiastically to his promptings: "So, beginning to feel the urge to write, I wanted to be in New York." [13] *Stylus* also served as the testing ground for Locke. From his editorial experience at Howard, he went on to involve himself in the more significant black journals of the 1920s. He related well to numerous, often conflicting groups and became the most ubiquitous Afro-American literary presence in that period.

The Harlem number of *Survey Graphic* appeared in March 1925, edited by Locke. Contemporaries applauded Locke for his role but then dickered over who gave Paul Kellogg, editor of the magazine, the idea for the issue. Du Bois claimed the credit for his own staff. At the Civic Club Dinner of March 21, 1924, he explained, Kellogg had sat next to Augustus Dill, business manager of *Crisis*, who acquainted him with those in attendance. Then "it occurred to the editor of *The Survey*," wrote Du Bois, "that here was material for a *Survey Graphic*." Despite his own cautions, "still he hesitated and feared the 'social uplifters' of the United States with a mighty fear," he acted on the inspiration encouraged by Dill and went ahead with plans for the special issue.[14]

Charles S. Johnson saw it differently, as indicated in a speech made in 1955 at Howard University. He explained that Locke had written a series of important essays for *Opportunity*, variously entitled "The Black Watch on the Rhine" (1921), "Apropos of Africa" (1924), and "Back Stage on European Imperialism" (1925). Johnson found the essays so insightful that he offered to share publication with *Survey Graphic* in order to find them a larger audience. Kellogg gladly published the articles at hand and requested further essays from Locke. "Thus began," declared Johnson, "an important relationship with the editor of the *Survey* and *Survey Graphic*." At the Civic Club affair, which Johnson carefully distinguished as an *Opportunity* dinner, Kellogg asked Locke to edit an issue of *Graphic* which would "carry the entire evening's readings." [15] Johnson does deserve a large share of the credit, since ideas for the number originated during the occasion he had staged, and since the editor was the essayist he had introduced to Kellogg.

The catchword in the issue became "Harlem," with essays, stories, poems, and drawings considering life in that urban center. The cover of the number bore the designation, "Harlem: Mecca of the New Negro." In the lead editorial, entitled "Harlem," and in another article, Locke ascended the scale to near religious ecstacy, labeling the area "a race capital," "the sign and center of the renaissance of a people," and finally, "the home of the Negro's 'Zionism.' " In Harlem, he believed, "the masses" would lead black writers toward the making of a vital folk literature. "In a real sense," he noted, "it is the rank and file who are leading, and the leaders who are following. A transformed and transforming psychology permeates the masses." [16] With such an emphasis, Locke enunciated ideas which would become increasingly prevalent throughout the decade and which would emerge, recast, as dominant in the 1930s with the pronouncements of Richard Wright and others.

Locke reinforced his ideas with an essay by James Weldon Johnson,

"The Making of Harlem"; an essay by Konrad Bercovici, "The Rhythm of Harlem"; with portraits by the German artist, Winold Reiss, on "Harlem Types"; with seven well-wrought poems by Countee Cullen on "Harlem Life"; and with "The South Lingers On," sketches of life in Harlem by Rudolph Fisher. The south lingered in the new migrants, in Jake Crinshaw who came from "Jennin's Landin'," Virginia, in unsuccessful pursuit of work in Harlem, in Reverend Ezekiel Taylor who followed his congregation north—"But where were they?"—in a grandmother who thinks her Jutie has lost her soul in Harlem, "this city of Satan." [17]

Another slogan in the issue was "the New Negro." After "Harlem," the Table of Contents listed Locke's essay, "Enter the New Negro." Revised, the piece became the lead article in Locke's edition of *The New Negro*. "Enter the New Negro" illustrates the balanced prose and memorable phrases Locke used to capture the attention of his contemporaries. Gone, he declared, is the "Old Negro," who was more fiction than actuality: "The day of 'aunties,' 'uncles' and 'mammies' is equally gone. Uncle Tom and Sambo have passed on, and even the 'Colonel' and 'George' play barnstorm roles from which they escape with relief when the public spotlight is off. The popular melodrama has about played itself out, and it is time to scrap the fictions, garret the bogeys and settle down to a realistic facing of facts." The facts included a "younger generation . . . vibrant with a new psychology," a black population "awake" in a "new spirit." The awakened generation was conscious, he explained, of being "the advance-guard of the African peoples in their contact with Twentieth Century civilization." [18]

He wrote again about the New Negro in "Youth Speaks," an essay printed midway in the issue. In expanding upon his ideas, he entered headlong into the controversy over art and propaganda. He talked about literary pioneers—Du Bois, along with Chesnutt, Dunbar, James Weldon Johnson, Lucian Watkins, and others—and said they had spoken "for the Negro," meaning they had tried to interpret the race to others. The new generation wrote instead "as Negroes" and attempted to express the quality of Afro-American life to Afro-Americans. Thus had come "the happy release from self-consciousness, rhetoric, bombast, and the hampering habit of setting artistic values with primary regard for moral effect." Among the New Negroes were Rudolph Fisher, Willis Richardson, Eric Walrond, and the young poets published on the very next pages, including Countee Cullen, Langston Hughes, Claude McKay, and Jean Toomer.[19]

The issue featured a heady sampling of those influential in interracial circles. There were essays from Melville Herskovitz, the cultural anthropologist; Arthur Schomburg, who was establishing his collection of books on black history and culture; Walter White, who was assistant secretary of the NAACP. The number also included an essay by Charles S. Johnson, on "Black Workers and the City," and a piece by Du Bois, called "The Black Man Brings His Gifts." Du Bois used an ironic style, by then familiar to *Crisis* readers. He developed a story to illustrate the pretensions of some white midwesterners who believe they have the best of everything. "We've got a pretty fine town out here in middle Indiana," the white persona declares at the beginning of the story. When told of the contributions blacks had made to American life, she and her friends become huffy and shun the speakers, who include a white professor and an educated black woman. The persona confides to the reader that the ideas of the black speaker especially "made me sick and I turned and glared right at her." [20]

The Harlem number of *Survey Graphic* was important for several reasons. The issue sold over 40,000 copies, thereby establishing a circulation record which the magazine did not match until the 1940s. The number led immediately to Locke's *The New Negro,* which was published by Boni in the fall of 1925 as an expanded form of the issue. The book was also significant, considered by Charles S. Johnson to be the "standard volume of the period," "the portal to a new world of adventure." [21] The editors of *Messenger* praised the Harlem number of the magazine for something far less tangible, for "the spirit which gave it birth." They saw in it the sign of a new day, as expressed in an editorial for April 1925: "It marks an interesting turn in the attitude of intellectual white America toward the Negroes. It was planned by black and white intellectuals. This is as it should be." Writing much later, in his study of Paul Kellogg, Clarke Chambers emphasized the uniqueness of the magazine: "In focusing on the contributions rather than the problems of the American Negro, in stressing the constructive cultural advances emerging in Harlem, in using Negro authors and critics to set forth the truths of the Negro renaissance, the *Survey Graphic* was far ahead of its time. Other journals might publish sympathetic articles now and again, but the *Graphic's* adventure stands alone as a classic account." [22]

The Harlem number was unique, but it did not stand alone in the 1920s. By its example, it encouraged other magazines to feature issues on black literature and life. In October 1926, Idella Purnell and her associate editor, Witter Bynner, published a special number of *Palms,* a poetry journal issued six times a year from Guadalajara. [23]

The October table of contents carried this statement: "Countee Cullen is the editor of this issue of *Palms* which is entirely the work of Negro poets." The comment was apt in that the emphasis was on black poets rather than on black poetry. The writers included the best of the day: Lewis Alexander, Gwendolyn Bennett, Arna Bontemps, William Braithwaite, Countee Cullen, W. E. B. Du Bois, Jessie Fauset, Langston Hughes, Helene Johnson, and Bruce Nugent. Most of them wrote about love and nature, not about topics specifically pertinent to Afro-American readers. The first stanza of Du Bois's "Poem" did not, for example, run true to his customary ejaculations:

> O Star-kissed drifting from above,
> On misty moonbeams, sunshine shod,
> Dim daughter of the lips of God,
> To me and angels—Thou art Love!

Two other verses followed, one addressed to Life and the other to Truth.

There were exceptions in the issue, such as the other poem by Du Bois. In "The Song of America," Du Bois sounded a familiar theme, as a few lines from the persona, the U.S.A., indicate: "I writhe, I rave, / To chain the slave / I do the deed, I kill!" The most notable exception was "Black Madonna," by Albert Rice. The particular emphasis emerged clearly in the first two stanzas:

> Not as the white nations
> know thee
> O Mother!
>
> But swarthy of cheek
> and full-lipped as the
> child races are.[24]

Du Bois liked the composition so much that he published it, along with an announcement of the *Palms* issue, in the November 1926 *Crisis*. In the next number, he reprinted Braithwaite's "Age and Autumn," one of the best-crafted poems in the October *Palms*.

The special issue of *Palms* figures in the cultural renaissance of the 1920s. It publicized contemporary work with two timely essays: a discussion of "The Negro Renaissance" by Walter White, and a favorable review of Hughes's *The Weary Blues*, by Alain Locke.[25] It encouraged the best from young writers with two poetry contests open to anyone who cared to apply. As announced in *Palms*, Langston Hughes won the Witter Bynner Undergraduate Poetry Prize Award for 1926, as well as the John Keats Prize one year later. In her

Opportunity column, "Ebony Flute," Gwendolyn Bennett acknowledged Hughes's award and reminded readers that they could still enter the Witter Bynner competition for 1927. In retrospect she declared that "of no small importance was the Negro issue of *Palms*." [26] The number not only provided further support for black writers, but it also indicated the widespread interest in Afro-American literature.

With their literary journal, *Carolina Magazine*, the students at the University of North Carolina gave further testimony to that interest. They published a "Negro Number" in May 1927, a "Negro Poetry Number" in May 1928, and a "Negro Play Number" in April 1929. The editors, who changed with each new year, received materials for each special issue from Lewis Alexander, a poet, an actor, and a member of both the Washington Saturday Nighters and the Quill Club of Boston. Alexander managed to include most writers who had been published in other black magazines and issues, save for Du Bois, who did not appear in any of the numbers. He clearly favored the efforts of Charles S. Johnson, whom he identified as the founder of *Opportunity*, "the ablest Negro journal in America." Johnson wrote the lead article, "The Negro Enters Literature," for the 1927 issue and one of the featured essays, "Jazz Poetry and Blues," for the 1928 number.[27] The lead article for the "Negro Poetry Number" of May 1928 was Alain Locke's "The Message of the Negro Poets."

The underlying theme in the essays of both Johnson and Locke was that New Negro poets had gained immeasurably by leaving the old propaganda emphases behind. Both men echoed statements they had made elsewhere. Locke's commentary, for example, recalled opinions he had asserted in *Survey Graphic* and made basic to *The New Negro*: "Yesterday it was the rhetorical flush of partisanship, challenged and on the defensive. This was the patriotic stage through which we had to pass. Nothing is more of a spiritual gain in the life of the Negro than the quieter assumption of his group identity and heritage; and contemporary Negro poetry registers this incalculable artistic and social gain." [28]

Some of the plays, stories, and poems included characters and situations which would not have been acceptable to Du Bois or others concerned with respectability. "The Hunch," a play by Eulalie Spence, gave a lesson in the numbers game:

MRS. REED. Ah dream Ed an' me—Ed's mah fus husband—Ah dream Ed an' me was lyin' in bed—
MITCHELL. Is he dead?
MRS. REED. Bin dead five years.

MITCHELL. That's 9.

MRS. REED. The door opened an' in walks Joe, mah secon' husban'—Lookin' mad tuh kill.

MITCHELL. Is he dead, too?

MRS. REED. Yeah. Died las' year.

MITCHELL. That's 2. Your number's 295. Play the combination an' yuh can't lose.[29]

Hughes, represented by several poems, wrote about a "Boy" who preferred to be "a sinner . . . and go to hell," about a "Boy on Beale Street" who lost his dream in "dice and women / And jazz and booze," and about an "African Dancer in Paris" who traded her native lover "for coins of gold." Waring Cuney sang the blues about "Once Bad Gal":

> Ah'd go straight if
> Ah thought Ah could,
> Say Ah'd go straight
> If Ah thought Ah could,
> But a once bad gal
> Can't never be good.[30]

Alexander put together the special issues by relying extensively on prizewinning literature from the *Crisis* and especially the *Opportunity* literary contests. The May 1927 number carried such pieces from *Opportunity* in each of the major genres: Arthur Huff Fauset's "Symphonesque" had placed first in the short story section for 1926; Helene Johnson's "Fulfillment" was first honorable mention in the poetry division for the same year; and Spence's "The Hunch" took second place in the 1927 drama competition. The editorial for the April 1929 issue identified the playwrights—Eulalie Spence, Willis Richardson, John F. Matheus, and May Miller—by their previous success: "All won prizes in *The Crisis* and *Opportunity* contests." In the same number, Alexander reflected on the meaning of those competitions, since they had by then ceased. "The contests and prizes offered reassured the race writers that it was worth while," he explained; "for some of them . . . had been writing a decade or more with little or no attention at all. The new spirit of the contests reincarnated the old writers and moved aspiring young dreamers to take up their pens and write." [31]

Crisis never acknowledged the compliment. In the November 1929 issue, Du Bois simply mentioned the drama number and then added that it included a drawing by Aaron Douglas "done for *The Crisis* and reprinted without credit." *Opportunity* responded graciously, with several laudatory reviews of the special issues. In June and July of 1927, Countee Cullen and Gwendolyn Bennett wrote in a similar vein about North Carolina University and the black number for that year. Cullen, in June, called the school and its journal "oases in that barren land," while Bennett praised the institution for its "fine liberality of thought." By July, both had recognized the number as a pioneering effort. Cullen spoke at greater length than Bennett, saying the May *Carolina Magazine* was "a number of historical importance in race relations in this country. For the first time, as it were, in the time of man, a Southern university magazine has given over one of its numbers to the work of Negro writers." [32]

Cullen was particularly impressed because he recalled an ugly episode he had written about in the December 1926 installment of "Dark Tower." He had noted that Julian Starr and R. K. Fowler, "erstwhile" editors of *Carolina Magazine*, had been "deposed" in 1926 for publishing a story having a white girl and a mulatto as principal characters. The incident had seemed, to Cullen, an immense step backward: "And this just after we had been turning double somersaults and triple handsprings because that same issue carried a sketch by Eric Walrond, along with a pronunciamento asking for contributions from people of all races, colors, creeds, and political leanings!" [33]

For some time, there had been students and teachers at North Carolina University interested in black literature and folklore. The special numbers of *Carolina Magazine* stressed this interest, describing it as part of a rich cultural legacy. The dedication to the May 1928 number called it "fitting" that the journal should feature black poetry. One of the earliest Afro-American poets, George Horton, had been a familiar figure on campus, and one of the New Negroes represented in the issue, Donald Hayes, was a native of Raleigh, North Carolina. In the April 1929 number, Lewis Alexander stated that "it is quite fitting" for the magazine to emphasize black drama, "for the University of North Carolina, thru [sic] its organization The Carolina Playmakers has done more for the development of the folk play in America than any other University." He urged students at North Carolina to remain true to the example set by Paul Green, a native North Carolinian who wrote *In Abraham's Bosom;* Professor Howard Odum, who edited the *Journal of Social Forces*, which was published at the University and which included several timely articles on black culture; and, among others, Newman I. White and Walter C. Jackson, editors of the *Anthology of Verse by American Negroes* published by Trinity College Press of Durham, North Carolina.[34]

Much of the excitement of the period appears in the black little magazines, which came in the second half of the 1920s, as did the special issues from journals with white management. The little magazines represented a new stage in the evolution of Afro-American culture. In the past, political and organizational concerns had dominated purely literary interests. After World War I the emerging generation sensed opportunities never seriously considered by earlier generations, partly because of the groundwork done by the NAACP and the NUL. To many New Negroes it seemed no very difficult matter to launch an entirely new type of black periodical, one concerned primarily with the arts. In November 1926, Wallace Thurman broke with tradition and issued *Fire*. As the first black magazine that was both independent and essentially literary, *Fire* deserves a place in surveys of American cultural history. It has been excluded from most studies of the 1920s, however, and mentioned only briefly in the others. Nathan Huggins, for example, took just two paragraphs to label *Fire* as a "short-lived" journal, one of "Harlem's attempts" at a little magazine.[35] One of the few to comment at length and with insight about the journal is Langston Hughes, who discussed it in *Big Sea* and in an article published later.

In his recollections he paused fondly over memories of Sugar Hill, in Harlem. At 409 Edgecombe, the address of the "tallest apartment house" on the hill, lived Walter and Gladys White, who gave frequent parties for their friends; Aaron and Alta Douglas, who "always had a bottle of ginger ale in the ice box for those who brought along refreshments"; Elmer Anderson Carter, who succeeded Charles S. Johnson as editor of *Opportunity;* and actor Ivan Sharpe and his wife Evie. Just below the hill, in the Dunbar Apartments, lived W. E. B. Du Bois as well as E. Simms Campbell, the cartoonist. Nearby was Dan Burley, a black journalist and a boogie-woogie piano player. Hughes recalled the excitement of those days: "Artists and writers were always running into each other on Sugar Hill and talking over their problems" and the ways to fellowships and grants from benevolent organizations. One evening, Hughes and six friends gathered in the Aaron Douglas apartment and made plans for a literary magazine. Hughes remembered their motives, saying generally that they wanted "to express" themselves "freely and independently—without interference from old heads, white or Negro," and specifically that they hoped "to provide . . . an outlet for publishing not existing in the hospitable but limited pages of *The Crisis* or *Opportunity*." They readily divided responsibilities for the new magazine, establishing Wallace Thurman as editor, Aaron Douglas as artist and designer, John P. Davis as business manager, and Gwendolyn Bennett, Zora Hurston, Bruce Nugent, and Hughes as the other board members.

They selected *Fire* as a title because, in Hughes's words, they desired to "*épater le bourgeois*, to burn up a lot of the old stereotyped Uncle Tom ideas of the past...." [36] Hughes did not expand further on the meaning of the name, which merits brief examination. It represented a significant contrast with the quieter labels, such as "Colored American Magazine" and "Voice of the Negro," appearing in earlier generations. It broke as well with the import of "Crisis," which suggested that a crucial moment must be met, and "Opportunity," which implied that possibilities were at hand for the observant black. *Fire!!* with two exclamation marks in the full title, sounded an alarm that the old way would be destroyed in preparation for a new world.

The group was confident, even though members had little money of their own and no benefactors in sight. They planned to share expenses, with each of the seven contributing an initial fifty dollars. The bills mounted quickly as the board selected an expensive format. Hughes noted that "only the best cream-white paper would do on which to print our poems and stories. And only a rich crimson jacket on de luxe stock would show off well the Aaron Douglas cover design." As it turned out, Thurman became responsible for the expenses since he, with a job at *World Tomorrow*, was the only one who had steady although hardly profitable employment. Thurman wrote to Hughes that "*Fire is* certainly burning me," [37] and Hughes wondered how the number ever left the printer's office, "how Thurman was able to persuade the printer to release the entire issue to us on so small an advance payment." The available funds went to the printer, thereby leaving no money for advertising or distributing the journal. The board hoped that the magazine would quickly attract a loyal constituency who would assure solvency and a second number. They quietly asked for help on the first page of the issue: "Being a non-commercial product interested only in the arts, it is necessary that we make some appeal for aid from interested friends. For the second issue of FIRE we would appreciate having fifty people subscribe ten dollars each, and fifty more to subscribe five dollars each. We make no eloquent or rhetorical plea. FIRE speaks for itself." [38]

After November 1926, *Fire* never reappeared. "When the editorial board of *Fire* met again, we did not plan a new issue," Hughes narrated, "but emptied our pockets to help poor Thurman whose wages were being garnished weekly because he had signed for the printer's bills." Thurman's wages continued to be "garnished" for three or four more years, even after "the bulk of the whole issue" burned to ashes in the basement of the apartment in which it was stored.[39]

The end was ironic, particularly because fire had been the unifying metaphor in the periodical. Thurman autographed special copies with "Flamingly, Wallace Thurman." The "Foreword," with its provocative challenge, established the dominant motif:

FIRE . . . flaming, burning, searing, and penetrating far beneath the superficial items of the flesh to boil the sluggish blood.

FIRE . . . a cry of conquest in the night, warning those who sleep and revitalizing those who linger in the quiet places dozing.

FIRE . . . melting steel and iron bars, poking livid tongues between stone apertures and burning wooden opposition with a cackling chuckle of contempt.

FIRE . . . weaving vivid, hot designs upon an ebon bordered loom and satisfying pagan thirst for beauty unadorned . . . the flesh is sweet and real . . . the soul an inward flush of fire. . . . Beauty? . . . flesh on fire—on fire in the furnace of life blazing. . . .

> Fy-ah,
> Fy-ah, Lawd,
> Fy-ah gonna burn ma soul! [40]

The poetry section announced itself with the title from Countee Cullen's poem and appeared as "Flame From The Dark Tower." The issue concluded with "A Department of Comment" by Thurman, called "Fire Burns."

Thurman indicated the literary aesthetic behind the magazine in his comments. He began by recalling his controversial review of *Nigger Heaven*, published two months earlier in *Messenger*. Instead of being honored with a statue on 135th Street and Seventh Avenue, he explained, Van Vechten had become a likely candidate for a lynching. The wheel would revolve in a few years and Van Vechten, he predicted, would then be "spoken of as a kindly gent rather than as a moral leper." For the time being, Thurman ridiculed the detractors of

Nigger Heaven and cried freedom for black writers: "Any author preparing to write about Negroes in Harlem or anywhere else . . . should take whatever phases of their life that seem the most interesting to him, and develop them as he please." [41]

As author and editor, Thurman was primarily interested in aspects of black life generally considered disreputable by the more proper Afro-Americans, as his inclusions in *Fire* indicate. The three short stories featured characters falling far short of standards dear to the bourgeoisie, both black and white. "Cordelia the Crude: A Harlem Sketch," by Thurman, followed directly after the table of contents and Bruce Nugent's drawing of a naked African woman. The story traces the development of "a fus' class chippie," from the italicized first word of the opening sentence: "*Physically*, if not mentally, Cordelia was a potential prostitute, meaning that although she had not yet realized the moral import of her wanton promiscuity nor become mercenary, she had, nevertheless, become quite blasé and bountiful in the matter of bestowing sexual favors upon persuasive and likely young men." Later in the issue came Gwendolyn Bennett's "Wedding Day," which portrays the unsuccessful relationship between a black boxer and a white prostitute; and Zora Hurston's "Sweat," which tells the tragic end of Sykes, a loafer who loses everything, including his life, because of an obsession with fat black women: "Gawd! how Ah hates skinny wimmen!" [42]

The number also included the first part of a novel, "Smoke, Lilies and Jade," by Bruce Nugent writing under the pseudonym of Richard Bruce. In his narration, Nugent detailed the amours of bisexual black artist Alex, known to his male lover Adrian (alias Beauty) as Duce. One scene, involving an interracial relationship, particularly violated the sensibilities of the middle class on both sides of the color line: "Alex ran his hand through Beauty's hair . . . Beauty's lips pressed hard against his teeth . . . Alex trembled . . . could feel Beauty's body . . . close against his . . . hot . . . tense . . . white . . . and soft . . . soft . . . soft. . . ." [43] No other black literary magazine had previously included an explicit portrayal of a homosexual affair.

The poetry section, headed by Cullen's "From the Dark Tower," included "Elevator Boy," a controversial poem by Langston Hughes. The selection bothered many, because the protagonist showed no evidence of the American work ethic: "I been runnin' this / Elevator too long. / Guess I'll quit now." "Flame From the Dark Tower" featured other poets worthy of comment, such as Lewis Alexander, Arna Bontemps, Waring Cuney, Helene Johnson, and Edward Silvera. Alexander contributed two poems, one of them about a prostitute ironically called "Little Cinderella," a girl who did not wait for her prince:

> Look me over, kid!
> I knows I'm neat,—
> Little Cinderella from head to feet.
> Drinks all night at Club Alabam,—
> What comes next I don't give a damn!...[44]

Reaction to *Fire* were mixed. As Hughes noted, the white-owned press largely ignored the journal. An exception was *Bookman*, which reviewed the periodical in November 1926. In *Big Sea*, Hughes called that appraisal "excellent," an adjective he wisely removed from his subsequent discussion of the same material. The *Bookman* review shifted in tone, telling blacks first to lift themselves into the middle class by their own bootstraps and then suggesting that Afro-American writing should be separate and distinct from "American literature." The anonymous author, perhaps editor John Farrar, initially commended *Fire* for appearing "at a time when the Negro shows ominous signs of settling down to become a good American." He continued: "As the Negro begins more and more to measure up to the white yardstick of achievement, he will gain a merited position in American society." By his conclusion, the reviewer was complimenting *Fire* for encouraging "separate but equal" in the arts: "It is to be hoped that he [the black writer] will find in this new Negro quarterly the thing he needs to keep his artistic individuality." [45]

Fire brought a greater response from black magazines and reviewers. *Opportunity* endorsed the journal enthusiastically, as it did the other black little magazines of the period. Cullen, in the January 1927 issue of "Dark Tower," suggested that the journal would offend only the unsophisticated: "There seems to have been a wish to shock in this first issue, and, though shock-proof ourselves, we imagine that the wish will be well realized among the readers of *Fire*." He called the journal "the outstanding birth of the month" and looked to the future with anticipation: "This sort of success," particularly the contributions of Hurston and Aaron Douglas, "augurs good for the development of Negro artists." Gwendolyn Bennett wrote in the same month, with the same opinion as Cullen's, but with more temperate phrasing. She undoubtedly felt constrained in using her position at *Opportunity* to trumpet her concerns elsewhere. Thus, she simply defined *Fire* as "the new literary venture of the newer Negroes," and as a quarterly which had been "hailed with enthusiasm." She kept silent about her own involvement in the journal. "To Wallace Thurman goes the praise for the editorship of this first number," she declared.[46]

Crisis did not have so much to say about *Fire*. Hughes claimed that "Dr. Du Bois in the *Crisis* roasted it," although he provided no supporting quotation. Hughes remembered inexactly, probably because he and others had wanted and expected Du Bois to respond with indignation. "As we had hoped—even though it contained no four-letter words as do today's little magazines—the Negro bourgeoisie were shocked by *Fire*," Hughes recalled. In his January 1927 review of the magazine, Du Bois showed that he was still capable of surprising contemporaries who tried to push him to the periphery of artistic circles. He graciously accepted the magazine: "We acknowledge the receipt of the first number of *Fire* 'devoted to Younger Negro Artists.'" He praised the format and the contributions by Douglas: "It is strikingly illustrated by Aaron Douglas and is a beautiful piece of printing." And he even endorsed the publication: "We bespeak for it wide support." [47]

Some unexpected criticism came later in the year from Alain Locke, who reviewed the magazine in *Survey*, August 15–September 15, 1927. Ever the diplomat, Locke commended before he corrected. He began with a statement which would please Thurman and the others, saying that with *Fire*, "the youth section of the New Negro movement has marched off in a gay and self-confident manoeuver of artistic secession." "Obvious artistic cousins" of the journal were, he observed, the *Little Review*, edited by Margaret Anderson, and the *Quill*, a magazine of Greenwich Village. Then he came to the sore point. True, *Fire* was "a charging brigade of literary revolt, especially against the bulwarks of Puritanism," but it raised the wrong standard. Simply put, *Fire* exceeded Locke's limits: "If Negro life is to provide a healthy antidote to Puritanism, and to become one of the effective instruments of sound artistic progress, its flesh values must more and more be expressed in the clean, original, primitive but fundamental terms of the senses and not, as too often in this particular issue of Fire, in hectic imitation of the 'naughty nineties' and effete echoes of contemporary decadence." [48]

The commentary appeared eight months after Hughes had sent his own bemused reactions to bourgeois readers in a note to Locke, dated December 28, 1926. He chortled over the review in the *Afro-American*, especially the part saying that at least Locke had been left out of the magazine. Under the heading, "Writer Brands Fire as Effeminate Tommyrot," Rean Graves of the Baltimore *Afro-American* had declared: "I have just tossed the first issue of Fire—into the fire, and watched the cackling flames leap and snarl as though they were trying to swallow some repulsive dose." [49]

Benjamin Brawley provided the most hostile review in "The Negro Literary Renaissance," published in the April 1927 issue of the *Southern Workman*. He did not believe black writers and artists were undergoing any especial awakening, even though promise was shown in the efforts of Claude McKay, Jean Toomer, Eric Walrond, and Walter White. The sign of the times appeared in jazz, "a perverted form of music," and in *Fire*, a magazine he considered the work of decadent loafers, not artists at all. By way of example, he quoted a passage from "Smoke, Lilies and Jade." "I certainly hope the compositor will set it up exactly as we give it to him," he added:

> he wondered why he couldn't find work . . . a job . . . when he had first come to New York he had . . . and he had only been fourteen then was it because he was nineteen now that he felt so idle . . . and contented . . . or because he was an artist . . . but was he an artist . . . was one an artist until one became known . . . of course he was an artist . . . and strangely enough so were all his friends . . . he should be ashamed that he didn't work . . . but . . . was it five years in New York . . . or the fact that he was an artist . . .

About "Cordelia the Crude," he claimed it "ought not to have been written, to say nothing of being published"; about Hughes's "Elevator Boy," he "submit[ted] simply that the running of an elevator is perfectly honorable employment and that no one with such a job should leave it until he is reasonably sure of getting something better." The last paragraph expended on *Fire* gave his summary comment: "About this unique periodical the only thing to say is that if Uncle Sam ever finds out about it, it will be debarred from the mails." [50]

Thurman commented on the outrage over *Fire* in "Negro Artists and the Negro," an essay published in the August 1927 number of *New Republic*. He explained, essentially, that the more conservative readers had been shocked once too often, first by *Nigger Heaven* and then by *Fine Clothes to the Jew*, "a hard, realistic" volume of poems by Hughes. The latter book appeared when "Negroes were still rankling" from *Nigger Heaven* and thereby uncovered "a store of suppressed invective that not only lashed Mr. Van·Vechten and Mr. Hughes, but also the editors and contributors to Fire." The magazine was "experimental," noted Thurman, who went on to define the term for those confused about the magazine: "It was not interested in sociological problems or propaganda. It was purely artistic in intent and conception. Its contributors went to the proletariat rather than to the bourgeoisie for characters and material." Unlike Jessie Fauset and Walter White, those contributors were interested in black Americans, not Negroes who were "totally white American in every respect save color of skin." [51]

As the ashes settled, some of the younger writers began to think of a new journal. And thus Zora Hurston turned to Alain Locke, whose reputation survived intact from the *Fire* controversy. In a letter to him, dated October 11, 1927, she touched on the past lightly, saying *Fire* had been a good idea which failed for lack of "better management." In surveying the present, she reiterated complaints heard previously about *Crisis* and *Opportunity*, that they were "house organ[s]" of political groups and were consequently "in literature" only "on the side." Before soliciting his aid, she asked him a rhetorical question: "Dont you think . . . that it is not good that there should be only two outlets for Negro fire?" She followed with another question, posing an intriguing triumvirate: "Why cant our triangle—Locke—Hughes—Hurston do something with you at the apex?" She concluded with a statement which flattered but which also gave testimony to Locke's influence among diverse literary circles: "I am certain that you can bind groups with more ease than any other man in America." "Will you think it over?" she added.[52]

The "triangle" never did get together. Locke had too many responsibilities with his writing and his work at Howard, which included sponsorship of *Stylus*, a magazine needing some attention. Hughes was no longer interested, for the demise of *Fire* had educated him in the ways of literary periodicals: "That taught me a lesson about little magazines. But since white folks had them, we Negroes thought we could have one, too. But we didn't have the money." And then a member outside the threesome was already setting the basis for another journal.

After the collapse of *Fire*, Thurman "laughed a long bitter laugh," Hughes remembered, and set to work again.[53] Determined to avoid problems that had ended *Fire*, he planned for a journal that both looked professional and lasted. He secured an office on Seventh Avenue and peopled it with young writers who wanted to handle the business affairs of the journal. He kept the managing board small, with himself as editor of the magazine, Aaron Douglas as art editor, and S. Pace Alexander as managing editor. He tried to repair communication with influential persons disturbed by *Fire*. In a letter of October 3, 1928, sent on *Harlem* letterhead stationery, he asked Locke to support the venture with a short article "of some kind" for the first number. He assured Locke that *Harlem* would be no *Fire*. He described the effort as a "general magazine," with all types of literature, creative and critical, and for all kinds of people: "We are not confining ourselves to any group either of age or race." The journal would, though, fill a gap left by the larger race journals: "The Crisis and The Messenger are dead. Opportunity is dying. Voila here comes Harlem, independent, fearless and general, trying to appeal to all." Thurman had not fully considered his plans, as his unlikely conjunction of "fearless" with "general" indicated. Of one matter, however, he was sure: "I am mighty glad of the chance to be able to edit a magazine and let someone else worry about the financial end, in fact, after Fire, that is the only way I would ever venture forth again."

Locke responded with a letter dated October 8. He was "committed" to the new magazine, he said, because "dear friends," whom he did not specify, were promoting it. Then, too, he agreed with Thurman over the need for an "independent journal—especially a journal that will recognize that there is more than one side to most issues." He would contribute to the first issue with an article called "Art or Propaganda,—Which?" [54]

Thurman carefully organized the one and only issue of *Harlem*, published in November 1928. He alternated the essays, which explicitly indicated the focus of the magazine, with poems, stories, and illustrations. As if to emphasize the contrast between *Harlem* and his previous little magazine, he started the issue with a political discussion he had solicited from Walter White. At the onset of his essay, "For Whom Shall the Negro Vote?" White quoted from Thurman's letter to him, which had asked for an examination of "the dilemma of Negro voters today—surveying the attitude of the old guard toward loyalty to the Republican party and the attitude of another group which is openly advocating a bolt from the traditional party of our fathers." In his analysis, White adopted a moderate, well-balanced tone, seemingly in keeping with Thurman's approach to his new journal. He acknowledged great inadequacies in Al Smith and Herbert Hoover, candidates for the United States presidency, but he did not call for new political parties. Seeing that black voters held a balance of power in about ten states, he urged them to "trade ballots for justice," to make white candidates listen to the needs of black people. [55]

After the political discussion came artistic considerations, including a story by Hughes, a poem by Helene Johnson, and the essay from Locke. With diplomacy, Locke considered the most debatable aesthetic matter of the times, and from the opening sentence: "Artistically it is the one fundamental question for us today,—Art or Propaganda.

Which?" The query was rhetorical to anyone who had read Locke's earlier pronouncements. He asserted that "After Beauty, let Truth come into the Renaissance picture,—a later cue, but a welcome one." He distinguished between truth and propaganda, saying that the latter is monotonous and that it encourages feelings of "group inferiority even in crying out against it." Metaphors followed theory, with Locke comparing Afro-American propagandists with "too many Jeremiahs" occupying too much "drab wilderness." He likened the larger black journals to Jeremiahs and the black little magazines to David, confronting the Philistines with confidence and with "five smooth pebbles." He thought *Harlem* could be a most valuable magazine if it developed as "a sustained vehicle of free and purely artistic expression." [56]

The editorial came midway in the issue, after Locke had calmly discussed the matter of art and propaganda. Thurman considered the same issue in a basically similar way, echoing some of Locke's imagery and much of his approach. He sketched the history of black magazines, beginning with "the old propagandistic journals," such as *Crisis*, *Opportunity*, and *Messenger*, which had served their day but were "emotionally unprepared to serve a new day and a new generation." They had been "Jeremiahs," either "alarmed and angry," or "weeping and moaning." All they could offer the aspiring young writer was an occasional page, "but the artist was not satisfied to be squeezed between jeremiads or have his work thrown haphazardly upon a page where there was no effort to make it look beautiful as well as sound beautiful." The only recourse, until the latter 1920s, was the white press. Few blacks, though, would continually buy "white magazines" in order to read an occasional poem or story by an Afro-American writer.[57]

In 1926, *Fire* seemed to herald a new era. As Thurman remembered, it "was the pioneer of the movement. It flamed for one issue and caused a sensation the like of which had never been known in Negro journalism before." Wisely, he did not elaborate on the "sensation" but went on to credit more moderate magazines which had since developed—*Black Opals* in Philadelphia, "a more conservative yet extremely worthwhile venture," and the *Saturday Evening Quill* in Boston, published by and for members of a literary group. These little magazines had problems, however, as Thurman so well recalled: "The art magazines, unsoundly financed as they were, could not last."

With *Harlem*, Thurman thought he had the formula for success. He would lower his own profile, become relaxed, genial, tolerant.

The magazine "enters the field without any preconceived editorial prejudices, without intolerance, without a reformer's cudgel," he told readers. He stated his goal with modesty, saying the journal "wants merely to be a forum in which all people's opinions may be presented intelligently and from which the Negro can gain some universal idea of what is going on in the world of thought and art." [58] He subtitled the magazine, "A Forum of Negro Life."

Thurman was not so balanced in his other contributions which appeared later in the number, after poems by Georgia Douglas Johnson, Alice Dunbar Nelson, and Effie Lee Newsome, a story by George Little, and essays by Theophilus Lewis and Bruce Nugent. When tucked into the back of the issue, Thurman felt free to be outspoken and controversial. He attacked the aesthetics of Du Bois in a review ostensibly directed towards *The Walls of Jericho*, by Rudolph Fisher, and *Quicksand*, by Nella Larsen. In the opening paragraph, he recalled that Du Bois had criticized Fisher in *Crisis* for not portraying the people he knew best, the "better class Negroes." Thurman had "chanced" upon the review, which "set my teeth on edge and sent me back to my typewriter hopping mad." He thought Du Bois ought to have known better, to have realized that "the entire universe is the writer's province." Du Bois had served his race "so well," asserted Thurman, "that the artist in him has been stifled in order that the propagandist may thrive." Thurman also came to the next novelist through a consideration first of Du Bois: "The author of *Quicksand* no doubt pleases Dr. Du Bois for she stays in her own sphere and writes about the sort of people one can invite to one's home without losing one's social prestige." [59]

Thurman was unrestrained in the "Harlem Directory: Where To Go And What To Do When in Harlem," included among the advertisements in the last pages. The initial line, with its neat parallelism, surely offended the same persons shocked by *Fire*. "There are four main attractions in Harlem," he announced with some glee: "the churches, the gin mills, the restaurants, and the night clubs," which he considered in order. He went for the exotic in churches, listing first the "largest congregations" and mentioning then "a great number of Holy Roller refuges, the most interesting of which is at 1 West 137th Street." Prohibition had made the "gin mills" more appealing, if anything: "As a clue to those of our readers who might be interested we will tell them to notice what stands on every corner on 7th, Lenox, and 8th Avenues. There are also many such comfort stations in the middle of the blocks." The most attractive night clubs, he said, were best seen in company "with some member on the staff of *Harlem*." "Only the elect and the pure in heart are admitted to these places," he explained.[60]

Perceptive readers would have detected the old Thurman not only in the last part of *Harlem* but also in the stories and poems included throughout the issue. Hughes contributed three poems dealing with drunkenness, boredom, and jazz, and a short story called "Luani of the Jungles," which portrays the fatal attraction between a white European man and a black African woman. The other short stories offered pictures no more appealing to the black bourgeoisie. Roy de Coverly's "Holes" and George W. Little's "Two Dollars" both consider prostitution and murder. Only George Schuyler offered a respectable character in "Woof," a story about the courageous and commanding First Sergeant William Glass of Company H, Twenty-fifth U.S. Infantry.

Thurman had planned succeeding issues of *Harlem*. With this in mind, he challenged readers to support his effort. In the last page of his editorial he wrote: "It now remains to be seen whether the Negro public is as ready for such a publication as the editors and publishers of *Harlem* believe it to be."[61] He gave further evidence of his plans at the end of the journal, when he listed prominent writers who had been asked to contribute to future issues, such as Heywood Broun, a columnist for the New York *Telegram* and the *Nation*; Clarence Darrow, "noted liberal and attorney"; Eugene Gordon, editor of the *Saturday Evening Quill*; Charles Johnson, former editor of *Opportunity*; Claude McKay, author of *Home to Harlem*; H. L. Mencken, editor of the *American Mercury*; and Frank Alvah Parsons, President of the New York Schools of Fine and Applied Arts.

As a literary editor, Thurman failed once again. In part he himself was responsible, since he had not been able to develop a magazine sufficiently different from *Fire*. Thurman had a bad name with many readers, who merely shook their heads knowingly when they saw his book review, his tips on the town, and his friends sandwiched in among more respectable contributors. It was not in Thurman to edit a truly "general magazine." He had an uncontrollable urge toward controversy, of a type which readers were not buying, especially in the face of the Great Depression. In 1932, upon the appearance of Thurman's *Infants of the Spring*, Theophilus Lewis wrote that *Fire* and *Harlem* came to their end for financial reasons. "It was a lack of money," he explained, "not a dearth of merit which caused the ... magazines to disappear."[62] Lewis did not elaborate. Thurman lacked funds because times were hard, especially for Afro-Americans, but also because he was too outspoken to attract the type of support he needed.

Lewis was one of the few to note the demise of *Harlem*. Contemporary responses were negligible, with neither *Crisis* nor *Opportunity* venturing a comment. So many enterprises were collapsing in those days that another unsuccessful attempt by Thurman raised few eyebrows. Lewis covered essentially new ground in 1932, when he reviewed Thurman's editorial career for the New York *Journal and Guide*. The title of the piece reflects the reputation Thurman had acquired: "Wallace Thurman Adores Brown Women Who Have Beauty Mark On Shoulder; Prefers Sherry To Gin." As an editor, Thurman went from the *Outlet* in Los Angeles, to five periodicals in New York—*Looking Glass, Messenger, World Tomorrow, Fire,* and *Harlem*. The first magazine had been his most successful, wrote Lewis, because it lasted for six months. Editorial longevity remained his dream, as Lewis added: "His ambition, he says, is to be the editor of a financially secure magazine." [63]

The ambition went unmet. Disillusioned by the loss of *Harlem*, Thurman never again attempted a literary journal, and he became more and more convinced that the black renaissance had failed. In *Infants of the Spring*, he compared the 1920s to a scene at a drunken party. Raymond, who represents Thurman in this novel, describes the situation: "Whites and blacks clung passionately together as if trying to effect a permanent merger. Liquor, jazz music, and close physical contact had achieved what decades of propaganda had advocated with little success." Raymond concludes that "this . . . is the Negro renaissance, and this is about all the whole damn thing is going to amount to." Through his protagonist, Thurman also reevaluated some of the main figures of the period. He reserved gentle satire for Alain Locke, who "played mother hen to a brood of chicks, he having appointed himself guardian angel to the current set of younger Negro artists." [64] Parke appears several times in the novel, always "clucking" after a brood of scattering chicks.

The other little magazines of the period showed several "guardians" and many coteries of young writers. Arthur Huff Fauset, the brother of Jessie, and other of the "older New Negroes," developed *Black Opals* as an outlet for young Philadelphians. Arthur Fauset edited the first issue, which appeared in the spring of 1927. Two other issues followed: the Christmas 1927 number under the leadership of guest editor Gwendolyn Bennett and an editorial staff composed of Fauset,

Nellie Bright, Allan Freelon, and James Young; and the June 1928 number under the control of the same editorial board, with the exception of Bennett.

The first number stated motivations clearly, indicating that *Black Opals* "is the result of the desire of older New Negroes to encourage younger members of the group who demonstrate talent and ambition." The process was more important than the product, since the editors expected to feature "embryonic outpourings of aspiring young Negroes," along with a few contributions by recognized writers. Young aspirants, who primarily wrote poetry, were students in the Philadelphia public schools and at the Philadelphia Normal Schools, Temple University, and the University of Pennsylvania. With the possible exception of Mae Cowdery, then a senior at the Philadelphia High School for Girls, most of these students did not emerge later as established poets. Identification of "older New Negroes" came on the contributors' page of issue one and included persons knowledgeable about little magazines: Lewis Alexander and Langston Hughes, "well known New Negro poet[s]," and Alain Locke, "the father of the New Negro movement." [65]

From a historical perspective, the most significant material in all three issues is "Hail Philadelphia," a short essay written by Locke and included in the initial number. The piece reinforces the picture of Locke as politician, steering cleverly between the old ways and the new, endorsing the new without a flat rejection of the old. To introduce his thesis, he criticized the elders of Philadelphia, but with humor: "Philadelphia is the shrine of the Old Negro. More even than in Charleston or New Orleans, Baltimore or Boston, what there is of the tradition of breeding and respectability in the race lingers in the old Negro families of the city that was Tory before it was Quaker. Its faded daguerotypes [*sic*] stare stiffly down at all newcomers, including the New Negro (who we admit, is an upstart)—and ask, 'who was your grandfather?' and failing a ready answer—'who freed you?' "

In his next paragraph, Locke made a gesture toward the "Old Negro" of Philadelphia and elsewhere, saying that "I was taught to sing 'Hail Philadelphia' (to the tune of the Russian anthem), to reverence my elders and fear God in my own village." After a few more conciliatory lines, he turned to the youth and remained in that direction to the end of his comments. He warned young readers about the past—"I hope Philadelphia youth will realize that the past can enslave more than the oppressor"—and came to his conclusion with a metaphor. By his references to barnyard fowl, Locke developed the very imagery Thurman would associate with him in *Infants of the Spring*: "If the birth of the New Negro among us halts in the shell of conservatism, threatens to suffocate in the close air of self complacency and snugness, then the egg shell must be smashed to pieces and the living thing freed. And more of them I hope will be ugly ducklings, children too strange for the bondage of the barnyard provincialism, who shall some day fly in the face of the sun and seek the open seas." Quieting his essay, Locke ended with a direct address to young black writers willing to experiment: "Greetings to those of you who are daring new things. I want to sing a 'Hail Philadelphia' that is less a chant for the dead and more a song for the living. For especially for the Negro, I believe in the 'life to come.' " [66]

Locke established a tone for the journal, but he did not control the publication. Arthur Fauset, the moving force behind the magazine, was more conservative than Locke, even though he could make a gesture in the philosopher's direction. Fauset was not, to use Locke's image, in a mood to smash the "egg shell . . . to pieces." Neither was he in a position to do so, publishing mostly the "embryonic outpourings" of interested students. The last number of *Opals* concluded with Fauset's review of *Quicksand*. Fauset introduced his appraisal with sentiments acceptable to Locke, among others. He praised Larsen's novel as "a step forward" in Afro-American literature. "For the first time, perhaps, a Negro author has succeeded in writing a novel about colored characters in which the propaganda motive is decidedly absent." In qualifying his comment, Fauset showed that the older New Negroes were not in complete harmony on the way to instruct youth. The propaganda novel, like the "pure" literature advanced by many contemporary black writers, had its place, Fauset asserted: "If the 'pure' artist desires to create pure art, then of course let him create pure art; but whoever set up any group of Negroes to demand that all art by Negroes must conform to such a standard?" [67] Clearly, the focus of *Opals* was to guide the young, not shock their elders. In this, it bore similarities to *Stylus* at Howard University.

The editors of *Opals* kept open the lines of communication with the larger black magazines. The Christmas 1927 number, edited by Gwendolyn Bennett, praised young Philadelphians who had distinguished themselves in the *Crisis* and *Opportunity* contests. "Pardon Us For Bragging," the older New Negroes said, as they went on to commend Nellie Bright, Mae Cowdery, Allan Freelon, James Young, and Idabelle Yeiser.[68] Du Bois was happier about *Opals* than he had been with other of the small black magazines. He liked the "little brochure," even saying that the poems were of a "high order." [69] *Opportunity* editors were just as pleased but more expansive, as they had traditionally been. Again Cullen and Bennett echoed each other in their respective columns. After applauding the journal, both looked to the larger picture. Cullen hoped the *"Black Opals* venture" would "sweep the country as the Little Theatre movement has done." Bennett, more chatty than Cullen, noted that the Philadelphia group was going to visit the Quill Club of Boston. "Mayhap some year," she dreamed, "both of these groups with one or two of New York's younger, newer Negroes will get together and go to visit the *Ink Slingers* in California." [70]

The Boston Quill Club issued the first number of the *Saturday Evening Quill* in June 1928, the very month when the Philadelphia group brought forth the last number of *Opals*. For the next two years, the *Quill* appeared annually, the second number in April 1929 and the third and final number in June 1930. The magazine included a majority of locals, but there was a scattering of writers developing national reputations. The editor was Eugene Gordon, who was on the editorial staff of the Boston *Post* and who contributed regularly to *Opportunity* and *Messenger*. Among the contributors were Waring Cuney, Helene Johnson, and Dorothy West, all prizewinners in the *Crisis* and *Opportunity* literary competitions.[71] In *Infants of the Spring,* Thurman singled West and Johnson out from among their peers for commendation. Both had "freshness and naïveté," rare among contemporary black authors, Thurman asserted, and both had skill as writers: "Surprisingly enough for Negro prodigies, they actually gave promise of possessing literary talent." [72]

With "A Statement to the Reader," printed in the first issue of the *Quill,* club members expressed their reasons for publishing a journal. As the comment indicated, they did not want to start a revolution; they did not want to make money, never offering the *Quill* for sale until the third number; and they did not want to exhibit their literary wares before a wide audience. On behalf of his colleagues, Gordon wrote: "They have not published it [the *Quill*] because they think any of it 'wonderful,' or 'remarkable,' or 'extraordinary,' or 'unusual,' or even 'promising.' They have published it because, being human, they are possessed of the very human traits of vanity and egotism." In other words, they wanted to try their work out, preferably on a close circle of friends. As explained further, they paid for the periodical out of their own pockets.[73] Evidently their pockets were more full than those of Thurman and his associates, since they were able to sustain their effort for three years.

Unlike *Opals*, which specialized in verse, the *Quill* printed fiction, drama, poetry, essays, and illustrations. Some of the selections had a decidedly conservative message, such as the poem by George Margetson, which lauded Abraham Lincoln as the black savior: "To every dark-skinned child a hope he gave, / And made four million hearts beat happily." [74] Most of the contributions, though, considered themes conventional in black magazines of the 1920s—the problems between white employer and black employee, between social worker and welfare recipient, between husband and wife, between dark-skinned blacks and "high-yaller," or those who passed as white. The same considerations had appeared in *Fire* and *Harlem*, but with different treatment. Thurman's writers employed various dialects, rural and southern, urban and northern, and a variety of terms widely considered offensive, such as "coon" and "cracker." Eugene Gordon and his colleagues depended on standard educated English, the type of language they used in their everyday professions.

In the *Quill* as elsewhere, Gordon carefully separated himself and his involvements from radical positions in literature and politics. He de-emphasized the relationship between Afro-Americans and Africa, thereby disagreeing with such contemporaries as Locke, who had no discernible role in *Quill*. In his editorial for the first issue, he urged associates to look to the ground on which they stood, not to hanker after some distant jungle. Basically, he considered the Afro-American to be as American as apple pie: "The colored artist is trained in the same schools that train the white artist, and at the hands of the same instructors. He gets the same stereotyped formulas of technique and style. He stands to the rendering of the Star Spangled Banner, and even, at times, tries to sing it. He salutes the flag throughout the farthest reaches of the land; eats baked beans and brown bread on Saturday night, in Boston; sneers, in New York, at 'the provinces'; falls in line to shake the President's hand at New Year's, in the District of Columbia; laughs at the comic strip; and he worships wealth and caste in true American fashion." Gordon realized that black writers had some rich sources unavailable to whites, but he asserted that they must use the "same method" and "the same medium," or language, available to white authors.[75]

To further his views, Gordon included an essay by William Edward Harrison, Harvard-trained journalist, in the third number of the *Quill*. Like Gordon, Harrison declared that American blacks could hardly look for inspiration to Africa, which was surely a "terra incognita" after some three hundred years. Summarizing Gordon's ideas, he claimed that black writers should use materials from their own environment in an effort to reach out to all people, black and white: "This literature must be at once profoundly racial and still universal in its appeal." He then stated opinions which were held by other club members but had not been explicitly asserted in the *Quill*. Looking to the success of the Boston and Philadelphia literary organizations, Harrison asserted that Harlem could no longer be the moving force in the black renaissance. He believed that the "Harlem theme" had grown "stale," as had writers like Thurman and George Schuyler: "Through the efforts of these and their satellites Harlem, the Negro quarter of New York, has been relegated to the place of a satrapy of Babylon or Sodom; it is the epitome of the bizarre and the unregenerate asylum of Vice in capitals, if we may trust these literati; it means somehow knowing nods and winks, and suggests forbidden *diableries*." [76]

By the turn of the decade, many reviewers agreed that the Harlem theme was indeed "stale." Writers for the New York *Amsterdam News* and the *Commonweal*, among others, called *Quill* the best of the black little magazines. A reporter for the *Amsterdam News* urged "Harlem writers" to follow the "example" of the Boston group, while the reviewer for *Commonweal* praised the journal for its "admirable absence of jazz and Harlem posturings." W. E. B. Du Bois liked the fresh beginning he saw in *Quill* and commended the journal in *Crisis*: "Of the booklets issued by young Negro writers in New York, Philadelphia and elsewhere, this collection from Boston is by far the most interesting and the best. . . . It is well presented and readable and maintains a high mark of literary excellence." Charles Johnson, in an unsolicited letter, went so far as to call the journal one of the few solid artistic achievements of the decade: "Here we have what seems to me the best evidence of a substantial deposit after the feverish activity of the last few years." [77]

As the Depression began, *Quill* came to an end, as had its predecessors. By 1930 *Stylus*, which had led the way for the others, was the only black little magazine alive. During the 1920s, *Stylus* remained dormant as Locke preoccupied himself with literary activities especially in Harlem, which he saw as the center for a great cultural awakening. The second number of *Stylus* appeared in 1921 and the third was delayed until June 1929. Then in the middle of the Depression, the magazine emerged on a more regular annual basis.[78] The journal continued, while others fell, largely because of university support.

From his perspective on the Howard campus, Locke evaluated the 1920s and presented his conclusions in "Beauty and the Provinces," an essay published in the 1929 *Stylus*. He began his remarks with definitions, calling a capital a center for creative work and a province a place empty of poets, a place "where living beauty . . . is not." Using these distinctions, Locke pointed to New York as the capital of the United States and to Harlem—"the mecca of the New Negro"—as the vitality of that capital. Washington, D.C., on the other hand, was a province, in touch only with the "nation's body." It was not, wrote Locke, "the capital of its mind or soul." Locke had endorsed the situation in the mid-1920s, but he felt some regret by the end of the decade, when Harlem seemed less promising than it once had. He suggested that Washington, D.C., could have become a true capital if "Negro Washington" had dropped its "borrowed illusions" and encouraged its wealth of "intellectual and cultural talent." Had this occurred, the metropolis could have "out-distanced Harlem" and led the way in the cultural renaissance. As it was, the District "merely yielded a small exodus of genius that went out of the smug city with passports of persecution and returned with visas of metropolitan acclaim." [79]

Criticizing "Negro Washington" in general, Locke neither accepted nor apportioned any blame. He liked to issue praise and he wanted to feel comfortable about his own role in the 1920s. Thus he turned to "certain exceptions" in Washington, pointing with "collective pride" to the "pioneer work" done by *Stylus*. As Locke remembered, the Howard group was among the first to advocate an Afro-American literature rooted in racial consciousness, or on "the foundation of the folk-roots and the race tradition." Locke also remembered the many groups which had followed elsewhere, such as the Writers' Guild of New York, Krigwa of New York and other cities, the Dixwell Group of New Haven, the Scribblers of Baltimore, the Ethiopian Guild of Indianapolis, the Gilpin of Cleveland, the Ethiopian Folk Theater of Chicago, the Cube Theater of Chicago and, among others, the Dallas Players of Texas. The very enumeration of these societies irresistibly recalled the expression Locke had used in his retrospective review of 1928, published in the January 1929 issue of *Opportunity*. "The provinces are waking up," he concluded, "and a new cult of beauty stirs throughout the land." [80]

Locke's essays, particularly the two noted from 1929, give valuable insight to the 1920s. More than any other contemporary, Locke was involved in nearly every Afro-American magazine and special number of black literature issued during that period. By his publications, his correspondence, and his personal contacts, he saw better than anyone else the cultural renaissance taking place up and down the

4. Renaissance to Reformation

House Organs,

Annual Reviews, and Little Magazines,

1930–1940

Black literature became more diversified in the 1930s than it had been in the 1920s, but the market for that literature was limited in comparison with the outlets provided in the preceding decade. The diversity has not been fully recognized, with scholars concentrating primarily on proletarian emphases of the day. Neither has the literary market been discussed sufficiently. In *Blacks in the City,* for example, Guichard Parris and Lester Brooks restated the opinion held by many that black writers had a broader opportunity in the 1930s than they had experienced in the past ten years. They claimed that "the thrust of the Negro Renaissance dispersed under the impact of the Great Depression and the opening of other journals, the previously closed 'white' magazines, to black authors and artists." [1]

Fuller insight into the 1930s came from Alain Locke writing at the onset and Langston Hughes commenting at the end of the decade. In his retrospective review published in 1929, Locke used the image of a graph to describe much of the contemporary interest in black literature and culture. He traced "the typical curve of a major American fad," with the high point being reached in 1928: "The year . . . represents probably the floodtide of the present Negrophile movement. More books have been published about Negro life by both white and Negro authors than was the normal output of more than a decade in the past." He predicted that the curve would swing downward, as indeed it did in the 1930s.[2]

Hughes summarized the situation in a speech made in 1939 to the third Congress of the League of American Writers in New York City.

He explained that the market for black writers was "definitely limited" because publishers classified black literature as exotica, in a category with Chinese, Bali, or East Indian writing. "Magazine editors will tell you," he asserted, that " 'we can use but so many Negro stories a year.' (That 'so many' meaning very few.) Publishers will say, 'We already have one Negro novel on our list this fall.' " Publishers also told writers that they wanted formula representations of black literature or no representations at all: "Those novels about Negroes that sell best, by Negroes or whites, those novels that make the best-seller lists and receive the leading prizes, are almost always books that touch very lightly upon the facts of Negro life, books that make our black ghettos in the big cities seem very happy places indeed, and our plantations in the deep South idyllic in their pastoral loveliness." [3]

In the 1930s, the larger magazines controlled by whites—*Atlantic Monthly, Saturday Review,* and *Scribners,* among others—did not appreciably alter the policies they had pursued in the 1920s. They accepted occasional pieces from established black writers, who in the early 1930s included Countee Cullen, Langston Hughes, and Claude McKay. Only the leftist periodicals, such as *Partisan Review, New Masses, Midland Left, Anvil,* and *Left Front* of the John Reed Clubs, welcomed contributions from newer Negroes. Many of those writers, however, thought the more radical publications were not sufficiently concerned with creative literature and with Afro-American culture and interests.

While the black little magazines offered an alternative, they were not so abundant in the 1930s as they had been in the past decade. The newer writers had outlets only in *Challenge,* edited by Dorothy West from 1934 to 1937, and *New Challenge,* edited by West, Marion Minus, and Richard Wright in 1937. Claude McKay was the only contemporary Afro-American to attempt a small journal for more conservative literary emphases. His efforts did not coalesce until the end of the decade, though, and then they were abortive.

The larger black periodicals provided another, albeit limited, outlet. The popular magazines reached maturity in the 1930s with *Abbott's Monthly* and published poems and stories from writers who could attract a wide readership. Many of the serious authors did not fit into that category, except perhaps in the early stages of their career. *Opportunity* and *Crisis* tried to encourage a black literati as they had in the past. Both magazines had difficulties merely surviving, however, and had to cater more to the interests of their audience than was formerly the case. In "Our Literary Audience," an essay published in the February 1930 issue of *Opportunity*, Sterling Brown listed attitudes he found predominating among black readers:

> We look upon Negro books regardless of the author's intention, as representative of all Negroes, i.e. as sociological documents.
> We insist that Negro books must be idealistic, optimistic tracts for race advertisement.
> We are afraid of truth telling, of satire.
> We criticize from the point of view of bourgeois America, of racial apologists.

Brown suggested that black literature could not flourish in such a climate. He reminded readers of Whitman's words: "Without great audiences we cannot have great poets." [4]

The editorial board had difficulty determining the role of *Opportunity* in the 1930s. Some board members, such as Hollingsworth Wood and William Baldwin, worried about circulation and thought *Opportunity* should be a popular journal. Editor Elmer Carter answered them by referring to considerably different types of periodicals: "How much money do you think the *Economic Review* makes?" he asked, or "How much money from circulation and advertising does the *Harvard Monthly* make?" Others on the board thought that *Opportunity* should be a house organ of the National Urban League or that the journal should function more as a literary magazine, as it had in the 1920s.[5] The board never settled on one of these options, and thus *Opportunity* served the 1930s in a variety of ways not necessarily consistent with each other. Along with organizational news, the journal included a variety of articles having popular appeal, as a sampling of titles indicates: "A Survey of Occupations for Negroes," "Are Negro Banks Safe?" "The Negro Athlete and Race Prejudice," and "What I Have Learned About Tuberculosis."

In its literary capacity, *Opportunity* published a considerable amount of creative work, usually one or two short stories and three or four poems an issue. It printed many obscure contributors as well as writers of note, such as Robert Hayden, Chester Himes, Langston Hughes, Margaret Walker, and Dorothy West. Carter and the editorial board tried to encourage young authors by reviving the contests which had been so successful under the direction of Charles S. Johnson. "The *Opportunity* awards of a few years ago attracted the attention of America's literati to the efforts of Negro writers," Carter reminded readers of the magazine in an editorial for October 1931.

In the same statement, he announced that an anonymous donor had offered an annual prize of $100 for the best short story or essay of 5,000 words on "Negro life" by a black writer. The donor believed in the social function of literature, as did Carter, who wrote: "Through distinctive literary achievement the Negro artist might conceivably bring about a change in the attitude of his oppressors." [6] Short story writers took the top awards during the three-year duration of the contest: Charles Cranford won in 1931 with "A Plantation Episode," Arna Bontemps in 1932 with "A Summer Tragedy," and Marita Bonner Occomy in 1933 for "Tin Can."

The competition took new form in 1935 and quickly failed. Carter announced, in January, that ten dollars would be given each month to the college student, "whatever his race," who wrote the best essay on some subject considered in a recent issue of *Opportunity*.[7] The approach would encourage young authors both to read the journal and to write essays, which had been neglected in the previous contests. The competitions failed because they did not meet the needs of the audience. The contests were open to all races, but *Opportunity* was primarily interested in promoting black writers and culture. Then, too, they were limited to college students. In the Depression, many of the most talented young writers were not part of that privileged class. In all, the competitions seemed out-of-date, the expression of an earlier generation.

Opportunity made its most significant contribution to black literature of the 1930s through publishing essays by Alain Locke in particular and by Sterling Brown, a poet and a professor of English at Howard University. Brown's column, "The Literary Scene: Chronicle and Comment," appeared monthly with some exceptions from December 1930 to December 1935.[8] Brown believed that the task of the "chronicler," as he called himself, was to examine issues and texts pertinent to black readers. In some months he considered particular subjects, such as Afro-American drama, or the qualities universal in minority literatures. At other times he devoted entire columns to discussions of writers he liked, including Charles Chesnutt, Claude McKay, and Richard Wright, and of those he found harmful, such as Fannie Hurst.

The column was both informative and entertaining. In March 1935, Brown railed against the ridiculous in Hurst's *Imitation of Life*, a book which dealt in cultural stereotypes and which brought to his mind "something unmistakably like a wild horse laugh." An indignant Hurst wrote to Carter, in a letter reprinted in Brown's installment for April, that the reviewer had used "carping, petty angles of criticism" and had revealed an attitude both "ungrateful" and "unintelligent." Brown, in a letter of response reprinted in the same column, reaffirmed his original estimate of the book and concluded with a smile: "Concerning my ungratefulness, let me cheerfully acknowledge this degree of unintelligence: that I cannot imagine what in the world I have to be grateful for, either to Universal Pictures or to Miss Hurst." Several issues of the column ended memorably, as did the one for August 1931: "For the chronicler remembers his persistence in the face of an old gentleman's studied avoidance of pointed questions about cruelty. Finally, the old man said, 'Was dey evah cruel? Certainly dey was cruel. But I don't want to talk about dat.' And he closed his eyes. . . ." [9]

In some of his concerns, Brown paralleled Locke. He refused, for example, to accept formula approaches to black literature and stereotyped responses to black people. Living in Washington, D.C., he believed that the cultural renaissance had not been limited to Harlem but that it had "spatial roots elsewhere in America." [10] He encouraged McKay, along with others, to look beyond "those strait purlieus that he and others staked off in the rush, and worked exhaustively. There is other gold in other hills, thereabouts." He satirized white writers, such as Roark Bradford and Richard Coleman, and publishers who used cultural stereotypes and talked knowingly about "the Negro" or "the Southern Negro." He quoted publicity from Macmillan Company which drew "the true Southern Negro" as a composite of "superstition . . . primitive fanaticism . . . sensuality, lightheartedness, easy humor and violence." Harper, which he also cited, had rhapsodized about "the mercurial moods of the careless, happy, colored people of the South." The quotations spoke for themselves, but Brown could not resist ironic commentary and added that "these literary masters are white folks, they ought to know." [11]

As essayists, Brown and Locke differed significantly in their prose styles. Brown wrote with more fluidity, using imagery, dialect, and irony to excellent advantage. He brought to his column techniques adapted from his poetry. Locke was more philosopher than poet, more analytic than moving or witty. He excelled as a cultural critic, as one interested in literary trends rather than in isolated examples. He used imagery well, but he tended to repeat and sometimes to belabor his metaphors. When he discussed his own work, as he frequently did in *Opportunity*, he adapted the military imagery which had appeared in previous of his essays, as well as in the work of other writers: "A critic's business is not solely with the single file reviewing-stand view of endless squads of books in momentary dress parade but with the route and leadership of cultural advance, in short, with the march of ideas." [12] The metaphors were familiar, but the particular sense of purpose, almost of mission, singled Locke out from other black critics of the day. When he reviewed the work of the year past, he not only looked backward, but he tried to predict future developments, which was a risky venture and not duplicated with comparable frequency by his colleagues. In his first retrospective review, Locke announced that such an essay "ought to give us some clue as to what to expect and how to interpret it. Criticism should at least forewarn us of what is likely to happen." [13]

During the Depression, Locke had enviable access to varying literary groups, the more radical as well as the more conservative. He was not, however, quite so important in that period as he had been in the 1920s. He had been around long enough to alienate certain of his contemporaries, most especially Claude McKay. As a voice from the previous decade, he seemed an elder statesman to some of the younger writers, who were eager to rally around Richard Wright rather than Locke. He was, nevertheless, an influential figure, largely because of his *Opportunity* essays. He understood the value of keeping a historical record and had the means to provide full documentation through his contacts with Carter. He also had the will and energy to make a painstaking analysis of the literary events year by year in the 1930s. No one else and no other Afro-American journal attempted a like venture, and Locke's retrospective reviews thus provide valuable insight into the decade, as well as into the evolving concerns of one of the most significant black literary figures of the period.

Locke's *Opportunity* reviews appeared annually from 1929 to 1942, with the exception of 1930. He issued them in two parts, the first being published in January as a survey of creative work and the second in February as an analysis of scholarly studies. He examined an impressive variety of materials, including the following categories as he listed them: Fiction, Poetry and Belles Lettres, Biography, Drama, Sociology and Race Relations, Anthropology, and Africana. The essays were lengthy, with each year's edition covering usually eleven printed pages, although the 1940 installment comprised fifteen pages. Locke had an eye for catchy titles. He based them on favorite metaphors, as in "Deep River; Deeper Sea," on familiar biblical phrases, as in "This Year of Grace," and on timely references. The captions alluded to contemporary views of blacks—"The Negro: 'New' or 'Newer' "—and to contemporary literature—"Dry Fields and Green Pastures" and "Of Native Sons: Real and Otherwise."

Throughout the decade, Locke examined and re-examined the relationship between the 1920s and the 1930s. To newer Negroes scornful of the earlier period, he readily admitted the weaknesses of the 1920s, saying that some of the literature of that day had been adolescent, guilty of excess, exhibitionism, and overt propaganda. At the beginning of the 1930s, he suggested that outside pressures had prohibited a complete flourishing of creative work: "To win a hearing, much exploitation has had to be tolerated. There is as much spiritual bondage in these things as there ever was material bondage in slavery." [14]

By mid-decade, Locke had modified his original estimate and asserted that black writers had to assume responsibility for their own failure. "Using the nautical figure to drive home the metaphor," he noted, "we may say that there was at first too little ballast in the boat for the heavy head of sail that was set. Moreover, the talents of that period (and some of them still) were far from skillful mariners; artistically and sociologically they sailed many a crooked course, mistaking their directions for the lack of steadying common-sense and true group loyalty as a compass." Locke believed in a biblical sense of justice, that past wrongs must be expiated in the present. And thus he claimed that writers in the 1930s had to "pay artistic penance for our social sins," that they had to experience a reformation after the renaissance.[15] Locke was willing to accept collective but not any personal responsibility for the failings of the 1920s. To *Opportunity* readers, he cast himself in a prophetic mold. As he talked about the reformation of the Depression years, he reminded them of his commentary in "Our Little Renaissance," an essay published in *Ebony and Topaz*, the volume edited by Charles S. Johnson: "In self-extenuation, may I say that as early as 1927 I said . . . 'Remember, the Renaissance was followed by the Reformation.' " [16]

Locke saw the literary reformation as a continuing, not a countering, of the renaissance. In one essay, he conveyed the sense of a developing tradition with water imagery, extended through three long paragraphs and introduced with a discreet apology to the audience: "If the reader has patience, let us try a simile." Locke compared black literature and art to an ever-deepening river leading inevitably to the sea of universal expression. He considered the literature of the 1920s and 1930s as stages in an evolutionary process, not as periods complete in and of themselves. Writers of the Depression had got further down the river than had their predecessors, but they had not yet reached the sea: "Here we are at the end of 1935, I think, on the wide brackish waters of the delta, waiting not too comfortably or patiently in the uninviting vestibule of the ocean of great, universalized art." [17]

At the end of the decade, he wrote more explicitly, probably to quiet the increasingly outspoken newer generation of writers. He started his essay of 1939 with a rhetorical question, asking "whether today's Negro represents a matured phase of the movement of the 20's or is, as many of the youngest Negroes think and contend, a counter-movement, for which incidentally they have a feeling but no name." He suggested a response by quoting extensively from "The New Negro," his essay in his volume of the same name. One statement in particular carried an emphasis Locke saw as dominant in the 1930s: "A transformed and transforming psychology permeates the masses. . . . In a real sense it is the rank and file who are leading, and the leaders who are following." Answering his initial query specifically, he asserted that the 1920s had provided a "spiritual surge and aesthetic inspiration" and the 1930s had given "social analysts in deployed formation." He held onto the metaphor a moment longer: "And so, we have only to march forward instead of to counter-march; only to broaden the phalanx and flatten out the opposition salients that threaten divided ranks." [18]

To Locke, as well as to others of his generation, it was "important" to show "today's literature and art, an art of searching social documentation and criticism," as "a consistent development and matured expression of the trends that were seen and analyzed in 1925." [19] Years later, others stressed the same understanding Locke championed in *Opportunity* in the 1930s. John Hope Franklin, for example, stated that the 1920s were only the first stage of a renaissance continuing in the decades following: "It takes little perspective to realize that the Harlem Renaissance that began shortly after the close of World War I continued into the sixties. The interruptions of the Depression and World War II were slight, and, in some respects, these two disturbances served as stimuli for the greater articulation of the Negro American." [20]

In his retrospective reviews, Locke showed the ways in which writers of the 1930s recast the major aesthetic topic of the 1920s, involving art and propaganda. He tried both to interpret the ideas of newer Negroes for the reading public and to influence those authors in the literary styles he thought best. By so doing, he indicated how far a reasonably enlightened member of an older generation could go in meeting the radical pronouncements of the next generation.

He greeted the 1930s with unqualified enthusiasm and a rush of metaphors. He concentrated in one review on imagery of passage, on what had gone out the door and on what should be retained. "Greater objectivity and a soberer viewpoint are good gift-horses to stable," he cautioned, "and lest they flee overnight, let us lock the stable-doors." Adopting biblical language, he applauded "a wholesale expulsion of the money-changers from the temple of art" and urged his readers to "rejoice and be exceedingly glad." At the birth of a new day, he believed he saw the retreat of propagandistic literature: "One of the symptoms of progress in the field of fiction is the complete eclipse of the propaganda novel." [21]

Locke soon discovered the inaccuracies in his original estimate, as proletarian literature came to the fore, much of it advancing the needs of the lower socioeconomic classes, especially the black. Rather than reject the new approach outright, he modified the position he had held throughout the 1920s, when he had stressed time and again: "After Beauty, let Truth come into the Renaissance picture,—a later cue, but a welcome one." In the Depression years, Locke transposed the order of the nouns, saying that truth must come first, that beauty could not emerge until writers had an understanding of "Who and What Is Negro." [22] When writers had struggled with definitions, they could then develop work in which "Black Truth and Black Beauty" were one and the same. After reevaluating his position, Locke concluded that the new emphases would not be pleasant but that they were necessary and would bring health to black literature.

He could intellectually accept contemporary approaches, but he had trouble with his emotions, as his imagery indicated. The new literature was "merciless," characterized by hot "grill[s]" and "a dozen steely mirrors." The reformation may have been a "tonic," but it had a "bitter tang" which made him nostalgic for the "sweetness and light of a Renaissance." Contemporary writing seemed "bitter," an adjective which appeared often in Locke's reviews, partly because it so frequently involved propaganda. Locke complained: "Half of the literature of the year isn't literature but a strange bitter bracken of commingled propaganda and art." He refused, however, to revive the old dialectic over art and propaganda, a phrase he essentially discarded from his vocabulary in the 1930s, and emphasized the positive: "Our art is again turning prosaic, partisan and propagandist, but this time not in behalf of striving, strident racialism, but rather in a protestant and belligerent universalism of social analysis and protest." He put it simply: "In a word, our art is going proletarian." [23]

Locke discerned both a new mecca and leader for the younger writers. Chicago, he noted, had usurped the place Harlem had occupied as the capital of the Afro-American arts, and Richard Wright had become the man who would write the influential essays for his generation as Locke had done previously. Locke had much praise for

Wright's creative work, saying that even his early poems were an artistic blend of beauty and truth. He wrote extensively about *Native Son*, calling it a masterpiece in the tradition of Zola. In his evident admiration for the work, he endorsed proletarian literature more enthusiastically than he had in the past. He thereby approximated the type of critical statements Wright was making elsewhere. In "the present crisis," Locke declared in 1941, *Native Son* was more significant as a social statement than an artistic achievement. He came close to a near reversal of the claim he had made in "Art and Propaganda," published in Thurman's *Harlem* of 1928: "More than ever we want either the truth and nothing but the truth, or what we feel is the writer's humanly best effort to get at it," he stated. His nostalgia had evaporated before the power of *Native Son*: "Yesterday's charm and irresponsibility we now think reprehensible." [24]

Wright's essays on aesthetics were another matter. Locke could not simply hand the critical standard to Wright, and he rounded off the 1930s by stating the limitations he saw in much of the new literature. He quoted extensively from Wright's foreword to *12 Million Black Voices*, citing paragraphs which included the type of imagery Locke himself used in other contexts: "This text assumes that those few Negroes who have lifted themselves, through personal strength, talent or luck, above the lives of their fellow-blacks— like single fishes that leap and flash for a split second above the surface of the sea—are but fleeting exceptions to that vast tragic school that swims below in the depths, against the current, silently and heavily, struggling against the waves of vicissitudes that spell a common fate." In subsequent lines, Wright explained that he had chosen to write of "the humble folk," or "the broad masses," because he wanted to capture "that which is qualitatively and abiding in Negro experience." [25]

Locke's criticism followed, stated in his gentlemanly manner. He noted, first, that each artist had a right to his own theories and that Wright's views were perfectly reasonable for a proletarian writer. "But" came next. Locke's quarrel, it appeared, was with part of the philosophy Wright had enunciated and many had pursued. Locke claimed that the younger writers were repeating the errors of their elders: "The fallacy of the 'new' as of the 'older' thinking is that there is a type Negro who, either qualitatively or quantitatively, is the type symbol of the entire group." Locke emphasized, as had Sterling Brown before him, that "there is, in brief, no 'The Negro.'" Afro-Americans came in all classes, he explained, and writers must recognize the existence and importance of "the intellectual elite, the black bourgeoisie as well as the black masses." Locke, it became clear, could travel with the newer Negroes only so far. "We should no longer be victims of the still all-too-prevalent formula psychology," he lectured them.[26]

As the decade ended, Locke held one other brief for the younger writers. In a review called "Dry Fields and Green Pastures," published in 1940, he told newer Negroes that he was on their side, that he preferred the "dry fields" of contemporary writing to the "green pastures" of romantic and sentimentalized literature. Where he differed with many of the writers was in the definition of "dry." He thought the term allowed for an occasional flower, as did the desert, while they thought it gave license only to stark but accurate documentation. Speaking more explicitly, he said that too often the newer Negroes were developing studies rather than creative literature. Locke stressed that the quality of realism must not be "merciless" but that it should be poetic or artistic in presentation.[27] Throughout his retrospective reviews, he had pointed to favorable examples where he could find them, to the poetic realism of the Chicago group, especially the creative work of Richard Wright, and to the poetry of his colleague, Sterling Brown.

During the 1930s, Locke essentially stayed out of *Crisis*, largely because the magazine no longer functioned, in an important way, as a literary journal. He gave Roy Wilkins only one notable essay, "Freedom Through Art," which was published in the July 1938 issue. The article does not bear close examination, since it merely reaffirmed the ideas expanded upon in the retrospective reviews for *Opportunity*. The title bore the theme, which stressed that the arts of a minority group should not be dilettantish entertainment but a vital means to "spiritual freedom." As a tool, the arts would assume a "social significance . . . often shading them unduly with propaganda or semi-propaganda and for whole periods inflicting them also with an unusual degree of self-consciousness and self-vindication, even to the point of cultural exhibitionism and belligerency."[28] Again, Locke was saying that the literature of the 1930s would be beneficial even if not very much fun.

Crisis did not feature any regular contributor who would counter the retrospective reviews published in *Opportunity*. Indeed, the journal was so concerned with survival itself that it had little time for competition. The closest it came to a sustained literary column was with "Books by Negro Authors," compiled by Arthur B. Spingarn and published annually from 1936 to 1966. The subtitle, "Paragraph Reviews for the Guidance of Crisis Readers," indicated the nature of the effort. Spingarn made short, perfunctory statements about the many texts which he had perused but included nothing at all, not even a publisher's blurb, about materials he had not examined. "No comments are made . . . on books which the compiler has not read," he confessed in the headnote for each yearly installment. Spingarn listed books, but he did not pursue "the march of ideas," as Locke was doing. He neither compared texts nor indicated dominant literary tendencies. In general, the effort was well-intentioned but not very effective.

The literary emphasis in *Crisis* declined considerably during the 1930s. After the departure of Du Bois, the magazine included occasional stories, fewer poems, and other works by writers who were more popular than talented. Articles of general interest predominated, on such issues as employment, housing and relief projects, and with such titles as "Jim Crow in Steel," "Picking Cotton by Machinery," "New Job Frontiers for Negro Youth," and, for diversity, the "Saga of Jesse Owens." In addition, the literary competitions collapsed.

Sponsored by Louise Mathews, a white New Englander and the mother-in-law of Oliver La Farge, the *Crisis* contests were to offer $1,000 in 1932 for prose fiction, in 1933 for prose nonfiction, and in 1934 for poetry, at which time the rotation would begin anew. As it turned out, no one took honors in 1932, since none of the entries was "first rate" according to La Farge, trustee of the awards.[29] James Weldon Johnson won the laurels in 1933, with *Black Manhattan*. The 1934 contest never materialized, undoubtedly because Du Bois resigned in that year and the competitions had been associated with his name. Mathews had stipulated that the yearly award of $1,000 be known as the "Du Bois Literary Prize." "Your name," she wrote him, "will be an inspiration to the Negro youth of future generations." Du Bois had accepted the honor because, as he explained to *Crisis* readers, he thought it might advance the literary theories he had been so long promoting: "There are many reasons why this prize might be named after some one else, but there is one reason for having my name used which overcomes any feeling of modesty on my part. And that is, that I have been striving in recent years to induce the stream of Negro-American literature, especially of our younger writers, to return to a normal, human and truthful channel, rather than to be led astray by considerations of income and sensationalism. I have talked so much about this that I hope that my name in connection with this prize will emphasize my thought and feeling still more."[30] Neither the name, nor the *Crisis* dinners

Du Bois tried to establish in 1932, were enough to assure that the award would be continued.

Du Bois left his successor with a weighty assignment. As Roy Wilkins later recalled, "the gloomy future of the magazine fell into my hands. The big job was keeping alive." The editorial board was not exactly sure how to achieve survival, and thus, as Wilkins explained, it made *Crisis* do the duty of two very different types of magazines: "It was the official organ of the NAACP and it was carrying on the tradition of being a magazine of general discussion." It was no longer, however, trying to function as a literary journal. Wilkins noted that the NAACP, which was paying the bills for *Crisis*, insisted that there be more popular and far less literary materials in the magazine. "In fact," he remembered, "to recover lost circulation, we had to carry more popularly written material, for the devotees of fine writing have never been able, alone, to keep a 'cause' magazine going." [31] The new policy helped *Crisis* through the Depression, but it essentially removed a literary outlet which serious writers had depended upon in the 1920s.

The Depression years afforded another alternative, though, in the black popular magazines. Such journals tried to entertain rather than to instruct or lead the larger Afro-American reading public. One editor, for example, declared that his periodical "has no ax to grind; no fish to fry; it has no politics and no policy. Its sole aim and purpose is to amuse, to interest and to entertain." [32] In pursuit of this aim, black popular magazines featured light fiction, including true confession stories, success stories, gossip columns, and discussions of fashion, homemaking, and sports. Early versions of the type had appeared in Boston, with *Negro American* (1897–1901) and *Alexander's Magazine* (1905–1909); in Philadelphia, with *McGirt's Magazine* (1903–1907); and in Pittsburgh, with *Competitor* (1920–1921). The black popular journal reached maturity in Chicago, as a steady succession of periodicals came to the fore, including *Half-Century* (1916–1925), *Reflexus* (1925), *American Life Magazine* (1926–1928), *Bronzeman* (1929–1933), and *Abbott's Monthly* (1930–1933). The most successful among these publications were *Bronzeman*, with its sampling of "Bronze Beauties," and most especially *Abbott's Monthly*.

Robert S. Abbott, founder of the *Chicago Defender*, began *Abbott's Monthly* at the worst of times, one year after the crash on Wall Street. Elmer Carter, struggling to keep *Opportunity* afloat, admired Abbott's daring. "Only a courageous man would undertake the establishment of a magazine in these perilous and uncertain times," he noted in *Opportunity*. He also admired the man's skill: "Robert S. Abbott knows the Negro reading public, and his experience as a successful editor and publisher will undoubtedly serve him in good stead in this venture." [33] Carter's confidence in Abbott proved well-founded. Abbott secured Lucius C. Harper, an imaginative black journalist, as his editor. Abbott and Harper then put together in their magazine an almost irresistible mix, approximately 100 well-illustrated pages of, among other items, tantalizing feature articles—"He Left the Jungle to Become an Artist's Model"—and fiction—"His Hula Hula Wife." The first number sold an unprecedented 50,000 copies. Shortly thereafter, the statistics soared to 100,000, as the journal broke all circulation records for a black popular magazine. Onlookers were impressed. "It is really different," declared the Detroit *Independent*. "There have been many literary ventures of this sort, and magazines upon magazines but not of the caliber of *Abbott's Monthly*. It has outstripped the imagination of all and upon perusal proves to surpass any other endeavors." [34]

Ultimately, both *Abbott's Monthly* and *Bronzeman* fell victim to the deepening Depression, each ceasing publication in 1933. Only a few popular magazines appeared during the remainder of the decade and into the 1940s. Those that did, such as *Dawn* (1935), *Metropolitan* (1935), *Mirror* (1936), and *Brown American* (1936–1945), reached primarily local or, at best, regional audiences. Not until *Ebony* emerged in 1945 would a black popular magazine match the audience attracted to *Abbott's Monthly*.

As a medium for serious writing, the black popular magazines had significant limitations. They specialized in stock literature, the type that could be penned to formula by the inexperienced or the hack writer. The more talented and dedicated authors would have scorned these journals if the period had afforded more variety in publishing outlets. Since options were not plentiful in the 1930s, the popular magazines attracted contributions from established as well as new names. Edited by Bertha Meeks Riley, *Metropolitan* pursued a wide audience with work from eminent authors, including Jessie Fauset, Rudolph Fisher, and Countee Cullen.[35] *Abbott's Monthly* stood out among the others because it published, along with sensationalist writers, a sizeable sampling of older and newer talent, an article by J. Max Barber, occasional poems by Langston Hughes, and fiction by Richard Wright and Chester Himes. *Abbott's Monthly* was, in fact, the first magazine to publish a short story by either Wright or Himes.

The popular magazines were important in creating a market for serious Afro-American writers, as Elmer Carter recognized in 1930. He saw in the present the historic problems experienced by black authors: "It is no secret that this reading public, which is largely white, has certain ideas and concepts about Negro life which publishers hesitate to derange for obvious reasons." Popular magazines, he hoped, would "enlarge the Negro reading public" as they wooed the general reader. An increase in the number of black readers would provide a strong and sympathetic base for Afro-American magazines and writers. As the founder of such a journal, Robert Abbott was, then, a worthy colleague, one rendering "to American literature a unique and not insignificant service." [36] To a lesser extent, the same could be said for the other editors of black popular magazines. As they chased the general reader and the increasingly elusive dollar, they figured with some significance into the evolution of black literature.

The serious and independent black writers became restive, however, because of the limitations apparent in the popular and organizational journals. They wanted black little magazines, in the tradition of the independent journals of the 1920s but adapted to the needs of the 1930s. With a straitened economy, they could manage only a few such publications, which served a variety of purposes. The political and social magazines did their part, albeit in a small way, for creative writers. One of these journals, *Race,* was published by the Conference on Social and Economic Aspects of the Race Problem and appeared just twice, in the winter of 1935–36 and the summer of 1936. In a study of literary periodicals, it merits attention for two pieces, both from established writers trying to adapt to contemporary styles. The authors disagreed on aesthetic matters and thereby showed a fragmentation among the older writers as they confronted newer approaches. With "Elderly Race Leaders," [37] Hughes rejected "the old, the cautious, the over-wise," in politics as well as in literature. As the last stanza indicates, he had left lyricism and the blues behind:

> Elderly,
> Famous,
> Very well-paid,
> They clutch at the egg
> Their master's
> Goose laid:
> $ $ $ $ $ $ $ $ $
> $ $ $ $ $ $ $
> $ $ $ $ $

$ $ $

$

In his essay, characteristically dubbed "Propaganda—or Poetry?" Locke criticized extremes, as he was doing in his retrospective reviews for *Opportunity*. He repeated advice by then familiar and urged black writers to create a proletarian literature which was poetic: "The fire of social protest should flame, not smoulder," he cautioned; "and any expression on behalf of the Negro masses should exhibit the characteristic Negro folk artistry." He pointed to both the good and the bad, to the poems of Sterling Brown and Frank Marshall Davis on the one hand and, on the other, to the most recent compositions of Hughes: "turgid, smouldering rhetoric, rimed propaganda, and the tone of the ranting orator and the strident prosecutor." [38]

Aesthetic questions were discussed in more sustained fashion in the small literary magazines, in *Challenge*, edited by Dorothy West, and in *New Challenge*, edited by Dorothy West, Marion Minus, and Richard Wright. Literary historians have said no more about the little magazines of the 1930s than they did of those in the previous decade. They have recognized *Challenge* and *New Challenge*, but just in passing. Robert Bone was one of the few to see the importance of the publications. In the *Negro Novel in America*, he noted that "the dominant tendencies of a literary period often crystallize in its little magazines," and that *New Challenge* especially showed the involvement of black writers in "proletarian art." Harold Cruse was not so charitable, calling the *Challenge* magazines "very undistinguished." He thought the editors and contributors confused and unproductive— "off in a quiet, contemplative cultural eddy watching the fireworks elsewhere." They had new names—Ralph Ellison, Margaret Walker, Frank Marshall Davis—but they represented the old ways: "*New Challenge* was a belated effort to rally the tattered and defeated forces of the Harlem Renaissance. . . ." The attempt accomplished little, he claimed. The journal expired, as had so many before it, and it left nothing for those who would follow: "Yet another Negro publication had failed to sustain itself . . . and its only bequest to the next young generation, its ideological poverty." [39]

Cruse to the contrary, the little magazines of the period provide a rich story, indicating the relationships between generations and among the more radical and conservative Afro-American writers. They put theory to practice, giving working examples of the aesthetic notions and styles discussed by Locke in *Opportunity*. Dorothy West, who would write *Living is Easy* in 1948, was the first to attempt such a publication in the Depression. In formulating her plans, she chose a different confidant from the one traditionally selected by her predecessors. She obviously knew Locke's work, but she considered James Weldon Johnson "the dean of Negro letters." She found it easy to relate to Johnson and thus wrote to him, on October 23, 1933, about her nostalgia—"there is behind me much lost loveliness"—and guilt— "It occurred to me that I could make up for much I have wasted by some way finding space for young dark throats to sing heard songs." She wanted a publication for New Negroes, "that they may know a rebirth," but especially for "the newer voices, that we may light their literary way a little." Johnson, she thought, could write the best introductory editorial, since he could attract the attention of both the younger and older black writers.[40]

In a letter of October 30, she suggested ideas for the editorial, which Johnson had agreed to author. She thought he should scold the older writers, "I and my contemporaries who did not live up to our fine promise." Young writers should be cautioned, told that "the majority of us, their literary elders, degenerated through our vices." All needed inspiration, an essential West thought Johnson could well supply.[41]

The editorial, drafted by Johnson on the bottom of West's letter, was more instructional than inspirational. He claimed that younger writers could be a "tremendous force" in destroying stereotypes about the race if they avoided the excesses of the past decade and if they dedicated themselves to hard work. "Writing is not only an art," he explained, "it is also a trade, a trade that demands long, arduous and dogged effort for mastery." [42] West found the advice timely and thanked Johnson for the piece on November 11. "It is precisely what I want," she stated. "It is mellow." Johnson returned the compliments after reading the first issue of the magazine, dated March 1934: "I heartily congratulate you on *Challenge*. It is away and beyond superior to any Little Magazine that we have yet launched. I hope it is going to be a success. It deserves to be. It is certainly a necessity." [43]

West began her magazine in high hopes but soon became frustrated, partly because she could not, in the first several issues, formulate a clear and consistent editorial policy. Her difficulty emerged because of her own personal evolution, from one who could endorse the relatively conservative positions of Johnson to one attracted to the more militant stands of Richard Wright. As she became surer of herself and of the period, she wrote more exact editorials, calling explicitly for a literature of social realism. At the same time, she became increasingly critical of her contributors and delayed publication of several numbers. Originally announced as a literary monthly, *Challenge* was designated a quarterly with the second issue, even though it never appeared more than twice a year.

The editorial page of the first number announced the journal as "an organ for the new voice." That issue and number two, published in September 1934, depended primarily, however, on well-recognized writers, including Arna Bontemps, Countee Cullen, Langston Hughes, Zora Neale Hurston, Helene Johnson, and Claude McKay. The best contributions probably came from Bontemps, who dramatized the lower socioeconomic classes in an article, "Saturday Night: Alabama Town," and a short story, "Barrel Staves." In the story, though, he depended on caricatures and thus deflected attention away from the urgent concerns of city folk. The action, set in the upper Bronx of New York City, centers on the abortive love affair between "old good-lookin'," "big-eyed" Adina, who likes "tropical fruits, green vegetables and pork meat," and "bad-luck Skeeter Gordon," who "ain't one o' dem jack rabbit mens"—"I's a true-love boy." [44]

Langston Hughes, who had been on the editorial board of *Fire*, enjoyed seeing the old names again in a little magazine. He urged West to solicit pieces from other members of the *Fire* staff: "Get something from Gwendolyn Bennett, Zora (Hurston), Wallie (Thurman), a cover from Doug (Aaron Douglas). All the oldtimers aren't dead. If they're dozing, you ought to wake 'em up." Wanting to be in the front of a new age, West was not so pleased, as she indicated in the editorial for issue two: "We had to fall back on the tried and true voices. And we are that embarrassed." She criticized younger writers with a general statement, not specific advice: "We were disappointed in the contributions that came in from the new voices. There was little that we wanted to print." [45]

West felt much better about the third number, published in May 1935. In the editorial, she announced that "we are rather pleased with this issue," because most of the contributors were new and young. She ticked off ages: Frank Yerby at seventeen years, Myron Mahler at twenty-one, Morton Freedgood at twenty-two. She cited backgrounds on the authors' page, including that of Russell Garner, convict 13386, who sent his experimental story from Leesburg Farms, New Jersey. The promise of these young writers swelled her "matriarchal bosom," making her feel both proud and old.[46]

The young and older writers contributed more frequently the kind of literature West desired, dealing with both race and class. With his short story, "Alabama Welcomes You," Myron Mahler dramatized the tragic absurdities of an Alabama town, which carried two signs on the main road: "Opedeika, Alabama Welcomes You," and "Nigger Don't Let The Setting Sun Find You In This Town." Waring Cuney, who had been published in the 1920s, wrote a poem about a "desperate folk," the "working class." [47] If West had only commended such contributions as well as their authors, she might have encouraged better work for future issues.

As it was, the fourth and fifth issues, of January and June 1936, did not fulfill the promise West had glimpsed in number three. Most of the pieces were conventional in both style and substance. The numbers are memorable mostly because they indicate West's evolution toward the political left. She published, for example, Louis Martin's article endorsing the spirit of the National Negro Congress, held in February 1936. At the Congress, Martin noted the absence of the "old guard"— Du Bois, James Weldon Johnson, and Charles S. Johnson—and the search for a new leadership: "Certainly we must say that for once at least 'God's dark chillun'' were 'red' in spirit if nothing more." In an editorial, West clearly indicated her enthusiasm for proletarian literature, if it were well written. "Somebody asked us," she recalled, "why *Challenge* was for the most part so pale pink. We said because the few red articles we did receive were not literature. We care a lot about style." She concluded with statements which would bring her to the attention of Richard Wright, among others: "We would like to print more articles and stories of protest. We have daily contact with the underprivileged. We know their suffering and soul weariness. They have only the meagre bread and meat of the dole, and that will not feed their failing spirits. Yet the bourgeois youth on the southern campus, who should be conscious of these things, is joining a fraternity instead of the brotherhood of serious minds." [48]

Issued in the spring of 1937, the last number of *Challenge* was transitional, signifying the end of West's venture and the beginning of a cooperative, much more radical publication. Generally well written, the inclusions lacked the note of protest West had called for in the previous issues. There were two exceptions, however, both of which suggested West's developing relationship with more progressive writers. "Big Men," by Everett Lewis, was a poem more revolutionary than those formerly included in *Challenge*. The "Big Men" were those building America on "Jim-Crow and misery," "the KKK and the DAR," and on "company unions." There would be revenge, as the last lines of the piece suggested: "For this is your fitful end. . . . / Big Men. . . . / Your final hour." In a statement on contributors, West endorsed the piece: "We like this poem, which is the sort of present-day

things [*sic*] *Challenge* wishes in its pages." She also introduced Marian
Minus, represented in the issue by an article entitled "Present Trends
of Negro Literature." A graduate of Fisk and then an anthropology
student in Chicago, Minus was "in the vanguard of the young
Chicagoans." [49]

With her final editorial, West introduced the young Chicagoans
to her readers. She said the group met regularly for discussion, of
each other's work and of publications elsewhere. "*Challenge* has
come in for considerable dispraise," she revealed, "but we have never
resented honest opinions." She responded by offering the young
writers space, "a special section in a forthcoming issue that they may
show us what we have not done by showing us what they can do." [50]

The one issue of *New Challenge* emerged in the fall of 1937,
heralded by left-wing magazines and announced in the report of the
Second American Writers Congress of June 1937, which was dominated by communists.[51] Dorothy West and Marian Minus were listed
as editors, although Richard Wright, as associate editor, did the bulk
of the work. In compiling the number, Wright drew on experience he
had gained earlier. He had been on the editorial board of *Left Front*
from January to May 1934, when the journal folded. In April 1936,
he had organized the South Side Writers' Group, which West termed
the young Chicagoans. The literary club numbered twenty members,
among whom were Frank Marshall Davis, Robert Davis, Marian
Minus, and Margaret Walker.[52] As the predominant voice in the organization, Wright interested members in *New Challenge*, establishing
Margaret Walker and Russell Marshall as contributing editors. The
other contributing editors also numbered among Wright's associates and included some influential persons—Sterling Brown, Collins
George, Robert Hayden, Eugene Holmes, Langston Hughes, Loren
Miller, and Arthur Randall.

In the opening statement, dominated by Wright's ideas, the editors
recalled comments made in *Challenge* but went further. They asserted
that the renaissance of the 1920s "grew unsteadily and upon false
foundations" and made plans for a true flourishing of black literature.
They announced *New Challenge* as a medium for writers dissatisfied
with journals like *Opportunity* and *Crisis*, "those Negro magazines
which are sponsored by organizations and which, therefore, cannot
be purely literary." Through their publication, they wanted to encourage a literature of social realism, based upon "the life of the
Negro masses" and the "great fertility of folk material." Perhaps
thinking of *Left Front*, by 1933 the official journal of the midwestern
John Reed Clubs, the editors mentioned hopes for a national organiza-

tion: "We want to see *New Challenge* as the organ of regional groups composed of writers opposed to fascism, war and general reactionary policies." Loren Miller and Langston Hughes were to introduce the magazine to writers on the West Coast, while Sterling Brown, Arthur Randall, and Alain Locke would publicize the journal in Washington, D.C., and elsewhere. Such ambitions captured the imaginations of many, who directed congratulatory letters to the editors. One of the most intriguing notes came from Donald Ogden Stewart, president of the League of American Writers. Suggesting Communist interest in the publication, Stewart sent a donation "as a token of my desire to help *New Challenge* in every way possible." [53]

Richard Wright's essay, "Blueprint for Negro Writing," was the focal point for *New Challenge*, as "Art or Propaganda" had been for *Harlem*. Wright centered his argument around a rhetorical question, as Locke had done in his essay. "Shall Negro writing be for the Negro masses, moulding the lives and consciousness of those masses toward new goals," Wright queried, "or shall it continue begging the question of the Negroes' humanity?" He then articulated the ideas he would stress later in *12 Million Black Voices*, among other places. He said black writers must develop perspective, not one out of several but the only one possible in present conditions. They "must," he insisted, "learn to view the life of a Negro living in New York's Harlem or Chicago's South Side with the consciousness that one-sixth of the earth surface belongs to the working class." Stating ideas voiced less coherently by others, both in *New Challenge* and elsewhere, he urged his colleagues to develop a nationalistic literature based on folklore and an understanding of contemporary social realities. Such a literature, rich in itself, would not be the final goal. By adopting a Marxist perspective, black writers should ultimately transcend nationalism and realize the "interdependence of people in modern society." Modern rhetoric pervaded, with Wright emphasizing the problems of workers, particularly of a minority people, and the concomitant responsibility of Afro-American artists and intellectuals, who should "stand shoulder to shoulder with Negro workers in mood and outlook." [54]

In the spirit of Wright's article, a letter from a Louisiana sharecropper appeared in the issue, along with essays, short stories, poems, and book reviews by other writers. The letter, an "authentic word-picture . . . of share-cropper life," was one of a series sent during a year to the headquarters of an unidentified union. In broken English, with a grammar fashioned from years of hard living, the worker described the attempts of white men to destroy the union on Gradnigo

Island: "Now the country is quieted down and steady and the government doing with us just like a man would do with a old poor dog." The short stories included pieces by George B. Linn, identified as a former member of the Timber Workers' Union, and Benjamin Appel, described as an established "left-wing writer." [55] Appel and Linn respectively satirized bourgeois blacks and whites, those too complacent for involvement and those reactionary in temper.

The poets were angry, speaking along both class and racial lines. In "Snapshots of the Cotton South," Frank Marshall Davis offered portraits of a land of violence, a place outlawing the socialist, the communist, and the Southern Tenant Farmers Union, a region nursing "white croppers and tenant farmers" on "banquets of race hate for the soul." In a much shorter poem, entitled "South Chicago, May 30, 1937," Robert Davis wondered where God was on the day of the riot, when "the prairie flowed red / With workers' blood." Sterling Brown contributed "Old Lem," a piece now well anthologized, and Margaret Walker sent in four protest poems best characterized by the conclusion of "Hounds":

> Beware. In black kennels all over the world
> there are hounds starving and tired of despair.
> Growing mad and terrible. When they run amuck,
> Beware.[56]

Ralph Ellison wrote a review of *These Low Grounds*, by Waters Edward Turpin. The review, Ellison's first foray into print, reflects the language of the editorial and Wright's "Blueprint": "It is the Negro writer's responsibility, as one identified with a repressed minority, to utilize yet transcend his immediate environment and grasp the historic process as a whole, and his, and his group's relation to it." [57] Locke penned one of the other reviews, his sole contribution to *New Challenge*. Under the heading, "Spiritual Truancy," he appraised *A Long Way From Home*, by Claude McKay. He damned the poet with a pun, saying that McKay was "still spiritually unmoored" and that his latest book showed him "a longer way from home than ever." Biblical stories came to mind. "One does not know," declared Locke, "whether to recall Peter before the triple cock-crow or Paul's dubious admonition about being 'all things to all men.' " When seen in relation to the times, to the "march of ideas," he found McKay wanting. In "a decade of social issues and conflicts," he "repudiated all possible loyalties," and that, said Locke, amounted to "self-imposed apostasy." Locke's last lines showed that he had mastered contemporary jargon and that he was not out of place in a journal dominated by the more radical Wright. Newer Negroes "must become truer sons of the people," he concluded, "more loyal providers of spiritual bread and less aesthetic wastrels and truants of the streets." [58]

The review lacked the diplomacy which had characterized much of Locke's work and marked him, in some circles, as a controversial, even a difficult person. As the protest over the review reached West, she wrote to James Weldon Johnson, who was a good friend of McKay, and asked him to redress the balance with another review of *A Long Way From Home*. She noted that McKay would like a reappraisal and that he would be especially pleased if it came from Johnson. McKay, in a letter, asked Johnson to avoid conflict with Locke, whom he believed contentious. Explaining further, he said that Johnson was in a unique position among black leaders. Unlike Du Bois or Locke, he appealed to considerably divergent groups of Afro-Americans. This very quality, McKay continued, would make him the ideal president for a society of black writers which McKay hoped to establish.[59]

For several months, West and McKay had not been speaking the same language, as she was becoming more politically radical and he more conservative. West became alarmed over McKay's evolution, particularly as it took shape in a rival literary organization. She tried, in conversations and letters, to win him over with compliments. "I want," she said in one note, "to ask you something about 'Challenge'. And Zora says you two are going to help me make the magazine really mean something. Oh, Claude, I am fond of you, and bless you, and go on writing your novel, and know that I believe in your talent." Later, she invited McKay to the organizational meeting of *New Challenge*. He attended the gathering, only to send West a form letter announcing the creation of his own organization. West reacted with some lines to Johnson, probably hoping that he would use his influence on McKay. "I am only sorry there will be two banners flying," she declared, "when each needs the support of the other." [60]

McKay also complained to Johnson. He summarized West's letters, even enclosing some of them in his own correspondence to Johnson. He could not trust West and her crowd. "These are the days," he confided in one note, "when the black-red hand disguised tries to pull all the strings, even your pajamas'." His concluding comment told much of the story: "So I am wary of Dorothy's sudden sweetness." [61]

The demise of *New Challenge* released Johnson from his sense of obligation to competing societies. The journal went the way of *Fire* and *Harlem*, other magazines which had not been able to meet their financial obligations. Appearing as a radical publication, *New Chal-*

lenge could not attract sufficient funds, either with subscriptions or advertisements. This left the field to McKay, who attempted both a literary society and a journal. Both efforts were unsuccessful, but both nevertheless merit examination. An abortive try at a magazine and organization can tell as much about a period as can a more successful venture. McKay, through his endeavors, showed that there was opposition to the dominant literary tendencies of the 1930s. He indicated that some of the older writers could not give control of Afro-American literary organizations and journals to blacks and whites who seemed sympathetic to communism. He engaged certain of those writers in their last gesture toward an Afro-American magazine.

In developing his plans, McKay turned for advice to James Weldon Johnson. The relationship developed for several reasons, both personal and professional. McKay felt grateful to Johnson the literary critic, for favorable reviews, and to Johnson the man, for acts of friendship. Before McKay left for Russia in 1922, Johnson gave him a farewell party. When McKay remained in Europe, Johnson urged him, in several letters, to return to the United States and to take part in the black literary movement. "You ought to be here to take full advantage of the great wave of opportunity that Negro literary and other artists are now enjoying," he counseled on January 26, 1928. "In addition—we need you to give more strength and solidity to the whole movement." To smooth his return, Johnson talked with Wilbur J. Carr, Assistant Secretary of State, and Walter White, who could probably, he told McKay, "do more at this time than anyone else to facilitate your entry into the United States." [62]

McKay confided in Johnson, moreover, because he considered his friend an astute critic of communism. McKay had not always, though, been skeptical of left-wing politics. Through most of 1920, he was a staff member of the *Workers' Dreadnought*, a small socialist weekly edited by Sylvia Pankhurst. In April of the next year, he joined the editorial board of Max Eastman's *Liberator*, then probably the leading American periodical for revolutionary politics and art. When Eastman left the journal to pursue his own literary career, McKay and Michael Gold became coeditors. McKay served in that capacity from January to June 1922, when he resigned. He had discovered ideological differences between himself and Gold and had decided that the staff, which was predominately white, was not sufficiently involved either in black America or in literature. [63] The evolution in McKay's thought proceeded apace, as recorded later in a letter. He recalled that he was somewhat disillusioned with communism when in Russia, that he became "altogether non-political" after leaving the country, and that he "lost all interest in the Soviets" when Stalin assumed leadership.[64] Long before that time he had determined that obedience to party discipline would be detrimental to his own art.

Johnson shared McKay's opinions, as recorded in his books and correspondence. In *Negro Americans, What Now?* he lectured contemporaries about their faith in revolutionary politics. "It appears to me," he declared, "that this infinite faith in Communism indicates extreme *naïveté*." He refused to join the Negro Peoples' Arts Committee, apparently a Communist organization, and the League of American Writers. In a letter dated February 4, 1938, he informed Donald Ogden Stewart of his decision: "I wish to say in reply that I am against every kind of dictatorial government, whether it be known as Fascism or Communism or under any other name. I still firmly believe that the democratic form is the best form of government. And it is to the preservation of democracy that I stand ready and willing to do all that I can." [65] McKay endorsed Johnson's action and declined membership in the same organizations, observing that the Negro People's Arts Committee "is a CP set-up." To Johnson he wrote: "What I mainly dislike about the Communists of these times is their chicanery and intrigue—so different from the forthright propaganda methods of the Communists of Lenin's time." [66]

McKay originally directed his literary organization toward two major goals. He wanted, first, to provide an outlet for writers who had been "in the thick of the Harlem Renaissance" and who felt left out of the 1930s, "more or less at loose ends." Second, he hoped to offset the appeal of the Communists, particularly among newer Negroes. "I feel very strongly about Negro writers coming closer together in cultural contact," he explained to Johnson, "and think that Negro writers who have made a reputation should do something to encourage the younger fellows and if possible keep them out of the destructive clutches of the Communists." [67]

With Johnson, McKay continued to worry over possible saboteurs, who might try to use the group for political purposes. He accordingly selected founding members carefully, choosing those who had proved trustworthy in the past, such as Gwendolyn Bennett, Jessie Fauset, Zora Neale Hurston, Henry Lee Moon and, among others, Arthur Schomburg. McKay suggested to Johnson that further steps might be taken to ensure a society "essentially democratic and non-partisan." Perhaps, he offered, the constitution should "bar from membership those who do not believe in Democracy or who pledge allegiance to any form of Dictatorship." [68]

McKay also conferred with Johnson about all documents representing the organization: the circular letter announcing the plans; the form letter calling for the first meeting, scheduled for November 1, 1937; the various drafts of the constitution, which labeled the society first as "The Negro Writers Guild" and then somewhat tentatively as "The League of Negro Writers (of America?)." [69] The latter name was possibly meant to suggest that black authors belonged with McKay and Johnson and not in the essentially white League of American Writers.

The last draft of the constitution specified that the society would be "purely cultural" and principally black: "Its aim is to foster intellectual contact among Negro Writers, help further their literary aspirations, and encourage the development of literary talent." Potential members, chosen on the basis of their artistic merit, would face close examination by the Executive Committee which recommended them and by the entire group which voted final approval. In using this procedure, the organization followed a method devised by the Stylus society at Howard University and recommended by Benjamin Brawley to McKay, in a letter dated November 12, 1937. [70]

In his excitement over the league, McKay misinterpreted the times. He moved too quickly for most of his associates, who were willing to give their name to his organization but not much of their effort. They were discouraged over the Depression, the rising tide of fascism, and the memory of other societies and journals which had failed. In letter after letter, McKay complained to Johnson that the meetings were poorly attended and that the members seemed lethargic. "Writers are so difficult to get together," he concluded. He was particularly disappointed on April 2, 1938, when reporting on the previous meeting. Only five members had come to vote on the constitution. These five did not include two of the officers: Jessie Fauset who was vice-president, and Regina Andrews who was recording secretary. The vice-president seemed particularly lax: "Jessie Fauset has not attended any meeting since we were at her house, nor has she responded to my personal notes." McKay began to wonder if his scheme were feasible after all, if it were "possible to build up an organization of writers, who are not infused with a group spirit." Johnson, who had been encouraging McKay, showed the same concern. "It begins to look doubtful that anything can be done to bring our writing group into an active organization," he admitted on April 14. "I am at a loss to know what to suggest." [71]

Then came McKay's letter of April 22. He told Johnson that everything had changed, that he had the means to "put fresh new life into our League." The publishers of the *African* had invited McKay to become editor. The journal, issued by David Talbot and Charles Cumberbatch, was faltering, or as McKay stated, "it is a good-looking thing on the outside, but bad inside." In the name of the league, and before consulting with the organization, McKay accepted the offer and made Countee Cullen his associate editor. He and Cullen had gone right to work, McKay explained, even posing "Minority" as the name for the journal. The publishers had demurred, however, since they were "a kind of remnant of Garveyism" and sentimentally attached to the word "African." McKay asked two things of Johnson: that he contribute to the July issue, the first to be edited by McKay and Cullen, and that he tell the league about the *African*, since McKay had been too busy to consult with the group.[72]

McKay and Cullen immediately devised a form letter, which went with minor changes to Johnson. Dated May 14, 1938, and written on *African* letterhead, the note identified the modified name and purpose of the magazine. The publishers had not budged on the primary designation, but they did agree to a different subtitle. Hence, *The African: A Journal of African Affairs* would become *The African: A Journal of Literary and Social Progress*. They also allowed McKay and Cullen a "free hand in policy and program," or so the new editors understood. Thus, they announced that the journal would become "an organ of group culture." They asked, in the same letter, if Johnson would serve as one of two honorary editors, the other being Du Bois.[73]

In his response dated May 17, Johnson praised the editors but said nothing about the proffered honor, probably because he wanted to study the journal first. "I look forward," he declared, "to seeing a copy of 'The African.' My judgement is that you ought to be able to do a splendid piece of work through it as a medium."[74]

McKay and Cullen next sent their form letter, with some modifications, to the distinguished black writers they wanted as contributing editors. Among others, they contacted Alain Locke. Cullen added a brief postscript, presumably to offset any hard feelings called up by McKay's signature. He claimed the venture would profit considerably by Locke's support and urged him to accept the position.[75]

The connection with the *African* was exceedingly brief. The May–June issue of 1938 heralded the change in editorship, and the July–August number cancelled the plan. A brief statement appeared next to the table of contents and underneath an advertisement for Imperial Upholstery: "Due to reasons not anticipated, the world renowned poet-novelists Claude McKay and Countee Cullen, cannot now serve in the capacities of Editor and Associate-Editor respectively as announced in the last issue of *The African*." [76] The influence of McKay and Cullen appeared in two instances in a number otherwise dominated by political articles on the third world. Gwendolyn Bennett contributed an essay, "Toward a Permanent Bureau of Fine Arts," and Cullen made a laudatory review of *Uncle Tom's Children*, by Richard Wright.

After seeing the issue, Cullen wrote two notes to McKay. He indicated his embarrassment over the review, which listed Wright's book as *Uncle Tom's Cabin*. He took the blame upon himself, explaining that he had written too hastily, and said he would send an immediate apology to Wright. In both notes, he alluded to arguments the new editors had been having with the owners of the magazine. By so doing, he revealed the primary reasons for the project's collapse. The owners, he claimed, were interested in African politics rather than in Afro-American literature, and they would not, despite earlier statements to the contrary, relinquish control of the journal to Cullen and McKay. [77] In one sense, then, McKay had come full circle. As a young man, he had left the *Liberator* because Gold desired polemics instead of art. In his maturity, he encountered a similar bias and subsequently gave over both journal and league.

Afro-American periodicals of the 1930s fit into no easy formula. As the Depression worsened, the black editor as businessman and as political radical came increasingly to the fore. The more conservative editors and writers of organizational journals experienced a difficult time gathering a following. And thus it was that the black popular magazines made money, at least for a while, the leftist little magazines established literary policy, and the house journals lost support. Through periodicals, the older generation of writers tried to shape the development of a new literature. Dorothy West looked to the left, Claude McKay to the right, and Alain Locke remained discreetly in the middle, both in politics and the arts. Newer Negroes made up their own minds, after first consulting with Richard Wright.

5. Aesthetics of Integration

Negro Quarterly, Negro Story,
Phylon, and *Harlem Quarterly,*
1940–1960

Integration became the dominant emphasis during World War II and in the postwar years, as seen in contemporary events and as dramatized by Afro-American magazines of the period. A series of developments greatly expanded the assimilation of black Americans into the broader society: the extensive Afro-American participation in the war effort both at home and overseas; the reversal of federal executive policy on racial segregation, as in the 1941 creation of a Fair Employment Practices Commission and the 1948 mandating of military desegregation; and the continued judicial undermining of the "separate but equal" doctrine. The doctrine was finally overthrown by the 1954 and 1955 Supreme Court rulings against segregated educational systems. These occurrences encouraged first in the South and then nationally a civil rights movement that eventually grew to challenge the very basis of racial caste in the nation. Determined resistance to the demand for justice largely failed to discourage those who supported increased racial integration. From the war years to the latter half of the 1950s, a majority of Afro-Americans felt optimism, guarded though it was, about race relations in the United States. With demonstrations and confident speeches black leaders, particularly Martin Luther King, fanned the hopes many had for a just society.

Magazines of the war and postwar years, as they provided further outlets for black writers, reflected the prevailing emphasis on racial cooperation. In an essay published in *Phylon* during 1944, Ira De A. Reid explained that the war had heightened interest in minority groups to a "fever." The larger periodicals—*American Mercury, Atlantic, Common Sense, Colliers, Fortune, Harper's, Life, Nation,*

New Republic, Saturday Evening Post, Survey, and *Time,* along with others—had together issued "millions of words on the Negro, all of which contained less bilge than we are usually accustomed to read on the subject." Compared to such "furious devotion and loud acclaim" the interest during the 1920s in black subjects seemed "a mere whine." In a special number of *Phylon,* published in 1950, Langston Hughes commented on the postwar market for black writers. During the past five years, he said, "the field of magazine writing has opened up considerably." He noted, as an example, that the *Saturday Evening Post* had recently included not only his own work but pieces by Zora Neale Hurston and Walter White. This development had been, he concluded, "the most striking change" in the conditions affecting Afro-American writers since the 1920s.[1] Literary scholars have subsequently made related claims. Robert Bone, for instance, declared that the majority of young black writers in the 1940s and 1950s "preferred to seek nonracial outlets for their work."[2]

Such comments need qualification, as did similar assertions about the 1930s. The war did indeed open journals which had been essentially closed to blacks, but it opened them only so far. *Negro Story,* a magazine embodying the integrationist thrust of the period, carried a note which characterized most of the new outlets for publication: "The market for stories and articles by and about Negroes is now greater than ever, and it continues to expand. Light, entertaining fiction stories and interesting feature articles (the latter dealing with outstanding Negro activities and personalities) are the new formulas wanted."[3]

The major magazines and publishing houses were issuing more work by blacks than they ever had in the past. They persisted, however, in dealing with formulas rather than reality. They wanted "light, entertaining" fiction from blacks, not stories which examined the fuller dimensions of Afro-American life.[4] For this reason, among others, Afro-American journals of the period performed a valuable service for the black literati, especially for young writers. The magazines afforded space for more serious efforts, creative work as well as essays examining the trends in black literature.

During both decades, black magazines called for integration in all areas of American life, including the arts. Proletarian literature of the 1930s had been integrationist, too, with its emphasis on collaboration between black and white workers. The theme took new form in the 1940s and 1950s, however, as many Afro-American writers concentrated on assimilation into the mainstream, and as they began to consider themselves first as American authors and then as universal writers involved in subjects common to all persons regardless of background or origin. In the journals, the reshaping of the theme began in the early 1940s. Harold Cruse, for one, noted that the war inspired the first articles on integration in *Crisis*. They were followed, he continued, by essays in *Phylon* which spoke against "the racial tag" in literature, art, and education, among other fields. Writing in *Phylon*, J. Saunders Redding stated that, as a result of Roosevelt's New Deal policies and the war, the black intellectual "could begin to explain himself and his motives and his character in terms of conditioning forces common to all humanity." [5]

Afro-American magazines of the 1940s and 1950s make most sense when viewed initially during the war and then in the postwar years. Journals extant in the early 1940s include the larger publications, *Opportunity* and *Crisis*, as well as smaller periodicals, *Negro Quarterly* and *Negro Story*. The organizational magazines survived the war, but they underwent distinct experiences, worthy of close examination.

During the war, as in past decades, *Opportunity* and *Crisis* continued to wear several hats—as house organs, as political journals, and as literary magazines. With these various efforts, *Crisis* had more success than did *Opportunity*, which suffered considerably under the restrictions imposed by the times. In the April 1942 issue of *Opportunity*, editor Elmer Carter stated the difficulties in no uncertain terms: "*Opportunity* admittedly has no mass appeal. . . . The magazine now is in desperate straits. Its continuance can only be assured if its friends, subscribers and readers come to its rescue, either by a direct contribution, or by securing additional readers." Six months later, Carter quietly and humbly resigned from his position: "And with this issue the present pilot steps down from the bridge of the ship that carried his name on the masthead. It has been a pleasant albeit at times a stormy voyage. He hopes that it has not been without benefit to the Negro and to the nation." [6] The next editor was Madeline Aldridge, who had been Carter's secretary for many years. At the onset of 1943, *Opportunity* became a quarterly, to be issued in January, April, July, and October. "Wartime restrictions" on paper and printing, along with a loss in public support, necessitated the change.[7]

Policies regarding literature did not alter. The quantity of creative work remained high, with each issue often including two poems and two stories. Newer names, such as Robert Hayden, appeared along with the old standbys, Hughes and others. For the most part, the literature did not appear as filler, entertainment, or as art-for-art's sake, but it came with a purpose—to shape and then to publicize the ways in which most blacks responded to the war. Editorials, especially some terse comments by Carter, explicitly stated the issues which creative writers presented more implicitly. Carter underlined in early editorials the commitment of Afro-Americans to the war effort: "We who comprise one-tenth of the population of the nation yield to none in our loyalty to its institutions and to its ideals." Engaged against the enemy abroad, Afro-Americans protested against the enemy at home, seen in the pervasive presence of Jim Crow. Time and again, Carter denounced the army, the navy, the Congress— "the cheap evasions . . . the vacillation, the excuses, the super-snobbery and moral cowardice. . . ." [8] At war's end, editorials written by others stressed hope for a new world, rebuilt by blacks and whites working in cooperation. White soldiers "have fought side by side with Negroes," Alphonse Heningburg reminded his readers, "and have learned that the blood of a black man is warm and red like their own." [9]

Frenise Logan called her poem "Paradox," a title which could have been the label for many poems and stories published in *Opportunity*, including "Enigma of Democracy," by Marcus B. Christian, and "Blackout," by Ruth Albert Cook. Such pieces considered the absurdity of a Jim Crow nation fighting for freedom overseas. Cook's poem, in particular, presented some good images, as "Black troops marched with empty guns / Through Southern towns / Bristling with loaded guns." With "Southern Negro Speaks," Langston Hughes addressed the same issue: "Cause I sure don't understand / What the meaning can be / When folks talk about freedom— / And Jim Crow me?" [10]

From the beginning of the war, integration captured the imagination of many literary critics and creative writers published in the magazine. The new emphasis undoubtedly inspired Frank Hercules, who re-examined the black renaissance in an article published in 1942. During the 1920s, he explained, blacks and whites worked together for "cultural purposes," a recollection that inspired him to metaphor: "That [cooperation] was as nakedly unprecedented in its incidence as a firstborn child. And when all the rubble and rococo, the sensationalism and the sham, are carted away, that monolithic achievement towers up, a splendid monument to a great social ideal." As the war went on, the new note came louder, with occasional pieces proclaiming unity between Afro-Americans and Jews, and others bespeaking the common humanity of all. In "Cosmos," published in

1945, Roger Woodbury expressed the hope of most blacks who had been reading *Opportunity*:

> On common ground we'll learn to stand
> And till the common soil
> And reap the harvest hand-in-hand
> And share the fruits of common toil.[11]

During the war, *Crisis*, which remained as a monthly, could not match the quantity of creative literature published in *Opportunity*. At best, an issue of *Crisis* included one poem or story. More commonly, a number appeared which had neither. Quality was another matter, however, as *Crisis* published some of the most outstanding black authors and some of the most influential creative work issued just before and during the war. Editor Roy Wilkins and associates drew special attention to three writers, one who recalled the historic involvement of *Crisis* in Afro-American literature, and two others who represented a continuation of that involvement.

Langston Hughes came to the fore particularly in the months preceding Pearl Harbor. In June 1941, he celebrated an anniversary, as did *Crisis*. Twenty years earlier, in June 1921, *Crisis* had published "The Negro Speaks of Rivers," which was the first of his poems ever in print. Wilkins announced the coming anniversary, in the April 1941 number, and noted that *"Crisis* will indulge in a mild celebration and a little patting of itself on the back." [12]

The June issue honored both Hughes and *Crisis*. First came accolades for the journal itself, in an editorial called, "We Take a Bow." Wilkins thought he and his colleagues could congratulate themselves, momentarily, because in Wilkins's words they had performed "no easy task." An "all-purpose magazine," *Crisis* had to manage three sometimes contradictory roles: as "a crusader for the cause of the Negro," true to the program of the NAACP; as a "general magazine of Negro life," and as a literary journal. The first and third functions posed special difficulties. As an organ of propaganda, *Crisis* chased off prospective advertisers, most of whom shy away from the controversial. In its literary capacity, the magazine generally pleased only the literati, which comprised merely a small segment of the reading audience. "The encouragement of new talent does little, if anything, to attract new readers or new revenue," Wilkins noted. After recalling such difficulties, Wilkins took "peculiar satisfaction" in ending his editorial with praise, both for Hughes and *Crisis*, and with a commitment: "We salute him. We take a small bow for ourselves, and we pledge once again that our pages will be open always to young men and women of talent." [13]

Then came a more extended tribute to Hughes. Under the title, "Twentieth Anniversary," "The Negro Speaks of Rivers" appeared once again in *Crisis*, along with a large picture of Hughes and a brief but laudatory summary of his career. The issue included two further contributions from Hughes, both of which showed his evolution from the preceding decades. Another poem, "NAACP," contrasted both in style and substance with such a piece as "Elderly Race Leaders," which had appeared in *Race* in 1936. Hughes was working more with traditional forms again, and he was actively giving his support to organizations he had earlier considered a bit stodgy: "The NAACP meets in Houston. / Folks, turn out in force! / We got to take some drastic steps / To break old Jim Crow's course." [14]

The issue also featured "The Need for Heroes," an essay by Hughes undoubtedly shocking to those who best remembered his poems of the 1920s, such as "Elevator Boy." From first sentence to last, Hughes voiced ideas similar to those enunciated in the editorials of Du Bois, when he had demanded that art be propaganda. "We have a need for heroes," he announced as his theme. "We have a need for books and plays that will encourage and inspire our youth. . . ." He declared that black writers had to counter the stereotypes developed by Hollywood, by pulp stories, and by "the Lazy Bones of the popular songs." He preached that black authors had a "social duty . . . to reveal to the people the deep reservoirs of heroism within the race." Critical of the vogue inspired by Richard Wright, Hughes generally denounced those who "write about caged animals who moan, who cry, who go mad, who are social problems, who have no guts." He did not except himself from blame: "I myself have not been sufficiently aware" of the heroism among blacks, "so I accept here and now my own criticism." [15]

Hughes practised what he preached in "One Friday Morning," a story written for *Crisis* and included in the next issue of the magazine. Strongly integrationist in orientation, the narrative portrays the talented and industrious Nancy Lee Johnson, a black student in a white high school. Refused an art prize because of her skin color, Nancy determines to win other awards and to help make more opportunities available to black students. The story ends with Nancy and her classmates pledging allegiance to the United States of America.[16]

Crisis advanced the literary career of Ann Petry as it had promoted the work of Langston Hughes and his contemporaries, especially in the 1920s. The December 1943 issue included "On Saturday the

Siren Sounds at Noon," the first of Petry's stories to appear in print. The piece details the effects of an air raid signal on a wanted man who had killed his faithless wife: "It's almost as though I can smell that sound, he told himself. It's the smell and the sound of death." [17] The story led directly to the publication of Petry's first novel, *The Street*. An editor at Houghton Mifflin liked "On Saturday" and asked if Petry were working on a novel. She sent him the first five chapters, along with a complete summary, of *The Street*. She received, in turn, the $2,400 Houghton Mifflin Literary Fellowship for 1945, which gave her the freedom to finish her novel in ten months.

Petry directed other manuscripts to *Crisis*. She submitted a story on the Harlem riot of August 1943, which was rejected because it was considered too long. The journal did, however, publish two of her short stories in 1945, "Olaf and His Girl Friend" in May, and "Like a Winding Sheet" in November. Impressed by the pieces, James Ivy interviewed Petry and published his findings, complete with revealing quotations, in the February 1946 issue of *Crisis*.

During the interview, Petry explained that she had developed some of her work around particular messages. She wrote "Olaf and his Girl Friend" as a tender love story between two West Indians because she wanted "to show that there can be true affection among Negroes," and that "Negroes can love as deeply as anyone else." She wanted to offer alternatives to the popular images of blacks, as she explained when discussing *The Street*, which she defined as a "problem novel": "I am of the opinion that most Americans regard Negroes as types—not quite human—who fit into a special category and I wanted to show them as people with the same capacity for love and hate, for tears and laughter, and the same instincts for survival possessed by all men." Lutey Johnson, the protagonist of *The Street*, does not fail because she is black or because of any personal defects. She is, as Petry said, "an intelligent, ambitious, attractive woman with a fair degree of education." She fails because she is confronted with an insurmountable obstacle, life in the black ghetto of a large Northern city. "In *The Street* my aim is to show how simply and easily the environment can change the course of a person's life," Petry told Ivy.[18]

The dedication and accomplishment of Petry made *Crisis* editors proud of having, in a sense, discovered her. The February 1946 issue included, along with the interview, an editorial reminiscent of the one published in connection with Hughes, in June 1941. It had the same title, "We Take a Bow," and the same import: "We take pardonable pride in the fact that the piece [of Petry's] which attracted the attention of the publishers appeared in this magazine." The train of thought carried Wilkins back to 1921, when *Crisis* had given first encouragement to Hughes. The tradition would carry on, Wilkins promised in the last line of his editorial as he had promised in the editorial of June 1941: "Our pages will continue to be open to aspiring and talented young writers." [19]

During the war, the pages of *Crisis* had been particularly open to Chester Himes, who published seven excellent stories in the magazine from 1942 to 1945. His stories were undoubtedly the most creative of the lot, although they did not receive special praise from the editor, presumably because Himes was contributing to other journals as well. Among the seven *Crisis* pieces, only the first, "Lunching at the Ritzmore," did not concern itself with the war. Appearing in the early months of United States' involvement in the conflict, at a time when many black readers were placing new emphasis on integration, "Lunching at the Ritzmore" focused on "the motley" "of all races" milling about Pershing Square in Los Angeles: "Drifters and hop-heads and tb's and beggars and bums and bindle-stiffs and big sisters, clipped and clippers," as they appeared immediately in the first paragraph. "It is here," the introduction goes on, that "you will find your man, for a game of pool, for a game of murder." [20] Himes had probably penned the story before the United States had entered the war. In his subsequent contributions to the magazine, which were published at the height of United States military activity, Himes addressed himself to the interests of *Crisis* readers, most of whom wanted respectable characters in their fiction and fiction dealing with the international picture.

He dramatized, in the narratives which followed, many of the situations confronting Afro-Americans during the war. "So Softly Smiling" explains, among other matters, why a young black man would willingly enter the army, how he goes from rejecting the war effort to accepting responsibility for a country he had helped build: "It got to be big in my mind—bigger than just fighting a war. It got to be more like building, well, building security and peace and freedom for everyone." "Two Soldiers" details the complex relationship between a black and a white soldier who are both caught behind enemy lines. The white soldier lets the other die, only to risk his own life transporting the body back behind Allied lines: "And even after George was dead, in his heart Private Crabtree still carried him, for days, for weeks, for years, back to home, back to Georgia." "The Song Says 'Keep On Smiling'" tells of a young woman who endures, even though her lover is at war and she herself is subject to unfair employment and other discriminatory practices at home. "Heaven Has Changed," a witty fable, predicts that the sacrifice made by black Americans in the war effort will send "Old Jim Crow . . . to hell where he belongs." [21]

Other writers of note appeared occasionally in *Crisis* during the war. Among the poets were young James Baldwin, who portrayed in "Black Girl, Shouting" the grief of a young woman whose lover had been lynched, and Frank Marshall Davis, who offered a "War Quiz for America." Davis wrote didactically, using ideas especially predominant in the 1930s:

> When white sharecropper rips the flesh of black share-
> cropper, who laughs and steals the shirts of both?
> Who gains when white laborers bolt their union doors
> in the face of their black brothers in toil?

The gist of the poem came in one passage, when he asked flatly, "Do you get it, America? / If you take my brown sons to fight abroad for democ- / racy then I have a right to expect it here." [22]

The journal also included writers who remained obscure in reputation but who contributed some moving pieces, especially about black GIs returning to the hostilities in the southern United States after the end of warfare abroad. Two such stories appeared in the June 1946 issue: " 'Hill to Climb,' " by Will Thomas, and "Look Away, Dixie Land," by Babette Stiefel. In the latter story, Josh Tatum comes back to Sterrit's Hollow, Florida, and discovers a community more polarized along racial lines than it had been before the war. Measured against his family, he has changed dramatically: "Couldn't they see he was different. He no longer had their humility. No longer wanted to walk in the gutter so the white man could have the right of way. No longer wanted to remain the servant, the obliging, easy gaited, shuffling, soft humored 'nigger.' " The great tragedy is that he finds understanding neither from his kin nor from the white community: "His valley was hemmed in with malice and hostility. He wondered what road would he find, where in all the world would there be relief from the pounding volley . . . nigger, nigger, nigger." [23]

The larger black journals, especially *Crisis*, had played an important part in World War II by articulating the responses of most Afro-Americans to the confrontation overseas, as well as to the battle remaining at home. The writers voiced protests and demands in varied ways, using editorials, essays, poems, stories, and plays. At the end of the war, and despite heroic efforts, the editors of both *Crisis* and *Opportunity* felt their journals had not moved far from Sterrit's

Hollow and that they were in danger of losing their magazines. Adjusting to the conditions of postwar America, *Crisis* and *Opportunity* entered into new phases of their long histories.

The black little magazines extant during the war did not have to make such adjustments because of their abbreviated existences. The small journals numbered but two, *Negro Quarterly* and *Negro Story*. The latter was an influential periodical, while the former was not a particularly notable venture. Even so, it did show another aspect of integration, as well as an intriguing glimpse of the young Ralph Ellison.

One of the sole commentaries on *Negro Quarterly* came from Harold Cruse, who thought no more highly of this journal than he had of previous small magazines. He had described the *Challenge* magazines of the 1930s as "very undistinguished." Using similar language, he declared that "there was nothing at all distinguished" about *Negro Quarterly* "beyond its unabashed Communist Negro-white unity editorial slant." He could not applaud the pairing of Angelo Herndon as editor with Ralph Ellison as managing editor. Neither did he favor such articles as "Anti-Negroism Among Jews" and "Anti-Semitism Among Negroes," which seemed to him to indicate "the victorious ascendancy of Jewish nationalism in Communist Party affairs." As *The Crisis of the Negro Intellectual* reveals, Cruse felt that Afro-Americans ought to have primary responsibility in all organizations purportedly black. Such an understanding seemed vindicated by the short career of *Negro Quarterly*, which expired after appearing four times between 1942 and 1944. "*The Negro Quarterly* died after four issues," Cruse concluded, "because Communist Left literary and critical values cannot sustain a 'Review of Negro Life and Culture' even when these values emerge from the Negro Left." [24]

Cruse had a good argument, although he probably focused his critique too narrowly. Other reasons, beyond the ones Cruse indicated, also led to the demise of *Negro Quarterly*. Surely the war took its toll, as costs rose and supplies dwindled. Given the challenges of the day, it is somewhat to the journal's credit that it survived four numbers, a feat not matched by countless other little magazines either before or after. The publication was not particularly successful, but it had more to its advantage than Cruse would admit. It said nothing memorable about the war, but it did have contributors who deserve acknowledgment, as they included Sterling Brown, Waring Cuney, Frank Marshall Davis, Owen Dodson, Langston Hughes, Alfred Kreymborg, and J. Saunders Redding. A noteworthy piece, from a literary standpoint, came from Ralph Ellison in his review of William Attaway's novel, *Blood on the Forge*. The essay is revealing not for what it claims about Attaway but for what it reveals about Ellison. He could praise the novel only so far: "Conceptionally [*sic*], Attaway grasped the destruction of the folk, but missed its rebirth on a higher level. The writer did not see that while the folk individual was being liquidated in the crucible of steel, he was also undergoing fusion with new elements. Nor did Attaway see that the individual which emerged, blended of old and new, was better fitted for the problems of the industrial environment." [25] In 1942, as the review suggests, Ellison was refining ideas he would make basic to his own novel, *Invisible Man* (1952). He would show in the book that "the destruction of the folk" did lead to a "rebirth," however agonizing the process.

Ellison and other young writers also appeared in *Negro Story*, which was issued nine times from May–June 1944 to April–May 1946. The journal became the most important black little magazine published during the war, although it has not been given such credit. Robert Bone simply stated that "for a brief time *Negro Story* ... attempted to provide an outlet for creative writing, but it has not managed to survive." John Henrik Clarke said even less about the magazine. In 1960, he published an essay in *Phylon* called "Transition in the American Negro Short Story." [26] He never once mentioned *Negro Story*, not even when discussing writers and periodicals prominent during World War II.

Gwendolyn Brooks, among others, had hoped the magazine would do better in the annals of literary history. In 1945, she told Alice C. Browning, editor of *Negro Story*, that the publication deserved lasting recognition for its encouragement of young writers.[27] Nick Aaron Ford felt a similar enthusiasm as his letter to the editor reveals: "There is no other magazine that is devoted entirely to experimental treatment of Negro life in fiction and poetry. There is no other national magazine so completely open to the contributions of young and daringly original writers." [28] Those who were old hands at little magazines also thought *Negro Story* worthy of support. Alain Locke declared that he was "very much interested" in the venture,[29] and Fenton Johnson, erstwhile editor of *Champion* and *Favorite*, penned a compliment along with his reminiscence. He clearly remembered the immense challenge of a small journal, as he mentioned to Browning: "I have been in the magazine publishing business, and I know what a difficult task it is." He urged her to go ahead, though, because "your magazine is an oasis in the desert." He added: "I also like it because it *avoids propaganda* and recognizes that art transcends race, creed and dogma." [30]

The most prominent novelist of the times had been an advocate for *Negro Story* from its very inception. Richard Wright, frustrated after two unsuccessful attempts to begin his own journal, helped Alice Browning get started. He introduced the Chicagoan to Jack Conroy, who shared with her the valuable experience he had gained as an editor of *Rebel Poet* (1931–32), *Anvil* (1933–37), and *New Anvil* (1939–41). He also gave Browning the publication rights to "Almos' a Man," which she included in the first number of *Negro Story*.[31]

Browning felt confident in establishing her magazine in Chicago. The city was the home of *Negro Digest*, which she defined as "THE important Negro magazine of the times" and then added, "we are proud that it is a product of Chicago." [32] The first series of *Negro Digest*, founded by John H. Johnson, ran from 1942 to 1951 and reprinted some of the best contemporary black literature, including influential Afro-American novels in monthly installments. The city spawned small journals as well, which Browning identified in part as *New Vistas* and *Expression*, two ephemeral magazines which were integrationist in emphasis. Such publications suggested to Browning that Chicago was significantly challenging Harlem for preeminence in Afro-American literary and artistic happenings. "It looks," she wrote in *Negro Story*, "as if Negro Chicago is trying to be the literary center of America. Look out New York!" [33]

Negro Story began in the honored tradition of little magazines, with no money. Browning revealed, in her editorials, that the magazine "was started from an *idea* with no capital even in sight," and that it had been maintained subsequently by "continual fighting" and by "sheer courage and will power." In the penultimate issue, she confessed with a hint of self-pity that "our editor does ALL the work and I mean *all*." [34]

Beholden to none, at least financially, Browning felt free to shape her magazine in the direction she felt best. She bucked considerable opposition in labeling the journal according to her wishes: "Many people objected to the title *Negro Story* but we ignored them. We love it." She thought Du Bois was on her side, and that seemed sufficient, she told the persistent grumblers: "*W. E. B. Du Bois* expresses our opinion when he says, 'The word Negro today is no longer an epithet. It has become the proper designation of approximately 213 million people who stand for a series of culture.' "[35]

Browning was basically optimistic. She envisioned a magazine about blacks which would interest people of varied backgrounds. Thus, she subtitled the journal first as "A Magazine for All Americans" and later as "Short Stories by and about Negroes for All Americans." She thought the curtain should come down on protest literature, which she believed had served its day but was unsuited to contemporary needs. In articulating another emphasis, she characterized the protest tradition, saying that it had been more propaganda than art, and that it had stressed the negative, which was proper in earlier decades but not in the 1940s. The black writer, she noted, "has used fiction as a vehicle for shouting aloud his problems" and reflecting a "bitterness of attitude." [36]

She believed that a new drama was unfolding. Discerning signs of integration everywhere, Browning told her readers that "there is a wide change in conditions. The Negro is achieving status and consciousness in all phases of his life." She pointed to outstanding white leaders—"the Eleanor Roosevelts" and the "Lillian Smiths," among others—and concluded that "many whites and blacks are striving to solve their common problems." She pledged *Negro Story* to a united effort, explaining that "our desire [is] to publish creative writing which would reflect the struggle of the Negro for full integration into American life as well as the many aspects and aspirations of his life." Hence, she urged black writers to adopt a more positive note, to stress cooperation rather than protest.

She urged them, as well, to take the time to develop their craft, to make art rather than polemics their primary interest: "We are urging young writers to study story techniques in order to present effectively the wealth of dramatic material at hand." [37] She thought, too, that the time was right for the opening of a "Negro Story" magazine to white writers as well as black. In her early editorials, she invited contributions from white authors "who treat the Negro subject honestly and objectively." In her later editorials she reshaped the invitation, observing that *"we will accept for publication a limited number of any type of story about or by any nationality."* She ultimately urged white contributors, who had not been forthcoming in significant numbers, to consider material from their own backgrounds: "By the way, we haven't received any recent contributions from white writers not dealing with the Negro—How about it! Our policy has been broadened to include them, you know." [38]

Despite the open door policy, *Negro Story* was clearly a black magazine. The staff was primarily black, with Fern Gayden as co-editor for the first three issues, and with Ralph Ellison, Nick Ford, Chester Himes, and Langston Hughes as advisors. The exception was

Earl Conrad, who served as associate editor of *Negro Story* for the last issues and who was also on the staff of *PM* and the author of *Harriet Tubman,* among other books. In a letter to Browning, which she termed a "magnificent letter," Conrad gave his understanding of *Negro Story,* a periodical he believed "one of the most welcome development[s] in the recent period, in the sphere of Negro and white culture." He considered the magazine firmly integrationist: "By and large, Negro writers will write about Negro-white relations, and white writers who contribute to your pages will write about Negro-white relations, and I believe that material, in its very nature, will be of a highly social sort. Whatever it is, we need it." [39] White writers did publish in the magazine, but the majority of contributors were Afro-American.

Most of the contributors cast a hopeful eye on "Negro-white relations," according to the expressed wishes of Browning, Conrad, and others. There was another aspect to the magazine, however, one that surfaced in occasional stories that were clearly in the protest tradition and in a few comments by Browning herself. "Negroes should unite," she once asserted, "work in a solid whole—stick together— no *Uncle Tom* stuff. *Demand your birthright. Demand your freedom.*" [40] Such inclusions indicate characteristics of black literature in the 1940s as well as the 1950s, but there was no more unanimity among Afro-Americans on aesthetic matters than in previous decades. Influential black writers and editors could not simply break with the protest tradition, having been with it for so long. Some did not desire a break and searched instead for a means of reshaping protest literature to contemporary modes of expression.

The main theme of literature dealing with the war, as published in *Negro Story,* stressed the positive, with writers like Owen Dodson urging white "Brothers" to "Bury that agony, bury this hate, take our black / hands in yours." Others addressed universal considerations, thereby suggesting that humanity rather than race was the essential issue. In "Gay Chaps at the Bar," Gwendolyn Brooks viewed the ultimate, with soldiers suddenly realizing that "No stout / Lesson showed how to chat with death." The minor note sounded during the war was militant and emerged, for example, in Langston Hughes's "Private Jim Crow," a collage of vignettes showing Jim Crow—"Caw Caw!"—at work in the United States Army, among other places: "From San Diego to Maine, Mobile to Seattle, this bird flies." [41]

There was a continuity in the literature on the war published in *Negro Story* and in *Crisis* and *Opportunity.* Generally, it came from the same group of authors, old and new, who examined the same basic topics. They wrote occasional pieces addressed to the times, rather than lasting stories and poems. There were exceptions, of course, and when these exceptions emerged they were heralded by Browning. She applauded, for instance, the talents of Gwendolyn Brooks and Ralph Ellison,[42] but she cheered especially for Chester Himes, who contributed seven witty stories to her magazine, five of which examined situations shaped by the war. She revealed in an editorial that "his stories have been our most popular." She enjoyed his "rare sense of humor" as much as did anyone: "After all, people like to laugh, in these nerve-trying times. Soldiers write that Himes' stories have everyone in the camps in 'stitches' so to speak, which is certainly good for morale." She saw his fiction as something new, representing "a definite break with the stereotypes of Negro literature."[43]

The Himes stories published in Browning's journal are like those included in *Crisis*, only they are better, showing more audacious humor and more imaginative uses of language. Clearly Himes felt freer when writing for the audience of a little magazine than he did when addressing the followers of an organizational periodical. Not only were the readers of *Negro Story* more receptive to literary experimentation than were the supporters of *Crisis*, but Alice Browning was more open to controversial literature than were the editors of the more established magazines. When Himes considered war-related topics in his stories, he felt free to write facetiously and often of characters on the fringe rather than in the mainstream of society. In "Let Me At the Enemy—An' George Brown," for instance, George Brown—"strictly an icky, drape-shaped in a fine brown zoot with a pancho conk"—dupes High C—complete with "forty-inch frock and . . . cream colored drapes"—into believing he can dodge the draft by picking "uh tun uh cotton ev'y day" up in Bakersville.[44]

"A Penny For Your Thoughts," one of the best Himes pieces in *Negro Story*, details the unsuccessful attempt of a Southern mob to lynch a black soldier for supposedly raping a white woman. In building suspense, Himes focused not on the prisoner but on the whites, led by the improbable Bobbie Barber, who is an inventive cross between a gun moll of the old West and a sex queen: "She was a thin, sun-burned, long-boned woman with slick red hair and slitted gray eyes; but her breasty body in sweater and slacks was raw with sex—she looked like a broad who could line them up."[45] Set in Texas during 1944, the story brought some comedy to a subject customarily given in tragic tones. *Crisis*, with its long and often bitter campaign against lynching and its historic call for respectable literature, would have stepped out of character in carrying such a narrative.

Neither would it have readily published "My But the Rats Are Terrible," a sex farce and the tour de force among Himes's contributions to *Negro Story*. The narrative, like many of the better inclusions in the magazine, has nothing at all to do with the war. It takes its cue from another tragic situation, the rape of a black woman by a white man. Here, however, trouble is caused because the encounter never occurs. Harriet, a black "maid" of redoubtable age, encourages Eberhard, a timid white gardener forty-nine years old, to consummate his urges with her. As Eberhard plots his attempt, the sentences become longer and longer, eventually reaching some forty-eight lines. Then, as he finally approaches his goal, his desire collapses, as do the sentences: "And then, as he bent toward her, his slight body shaking with a desire that had accumulated in him over almost half a century, it went." The story ends with Harriet still unsatisfied: "You just ain't got no nerve, Eberhard. My first husband just came into my room one night and just took me. . . ." [46] The story has no overt moral, surely no explicit political purpose. Himes was not promoting interracial sex, but more probably laughing at sexual stereotypes. During the war, *Negro Story* was the only magazine publishing such fiction from a black writer. The journal realized an important function in giving Himes an outlet for his refreshing humor.

In the first half of the 1940s, *Negro Story* alone among contemporary magazines featured the work of Richard Bentley, a black writer of short stories. It took courage to advance the fiction of Bentley, since he penned graphic portraits of sexual encounters designed to titillate readers. Moreover, he would not restrict himself to descriptions of black lovers. Of his five stories included in the journal, one is about a black couple, two are about interracial, and two about white couples. Browning not only published Bentley, but she went out of her way to endorse his efforts. In a biographical note on the writer, she announced that "*Negro Story* intends to be *experimental* and will print stories dealing frankly with sex as well as those dealing with any other phases of life. We are open for the unusual at all times. We do not have the inhibitions necessary for the slick magazine." [47] By taking such a stand, she recalled the boldness of Wallace Thurman, who had included Bruce Nugent's "Smoke, Lilies and Jade" in *Fire*. Since *Fire*, and during the Depression and the war, editors of black little magazines veered away from fiction so sexually suggestive.

"Tomorrow," Bentley's first piece in the journal, came as something of a shock to the more staid readers of *Negro Story*. The narrative follows the white corporal, Jack Bryant, as he tries initially to seduce and finally to rape his reluctant sweetheart Helen, also white. Provocative ellipses predominate in the climax of their struggle: " 'Please Jack—don't—don't let me go. . . .' he heard her mumble through his fingers. He felt hot and ill. He tore at her viciously. He had her now. A little more and he would . . . if he just could . . . his arm was across her throat . . . she couldn't move . . . he fumbled in the front of his trousers . . . shoved his big body toward her . . . now . . . now . . . He could. . . he must . . . somehow he would. . . ." [48]

The story offended many, who wrote indignantly to Browning. She included several of their letters, plus a defense of "Tomorrow," in her next editorial, published in the March–April 1945 issue. Seemingly only the "sedate and prim" sent in notes. One protested that he could no longer put *Negro Story* in his children's library. Browning answered: "After all, we are an adult magazine." A young woman asked the editor to warn her of any such inclusions in the future so she could avoid the issue. Browning replied: "We wonder." Another thought the story morally useful only in showing young women how they might maintain their virginity. Browning then revealed that "Tomorrow" was the first contribution to *Negro Story* "to be requested for reprint." A brief defense of the story followed, as Browning compared the piece to *Lady Chatterly's Lover* and claimed it aroused similar responses. "You either like a frank and bold treatment of sex or you do not," she reminded the outraged portion of her audience.[49]

Not to be intimidated, she included another Bentley story, "The Slave," in the March–April 1945 issue and three other Bentley narratives in the succeeding three numbers. She tried to tantalize her audience into perusing "The Slave": "Richard Bentley, a young gentleman who aspires to realistic writing, has written another sensational story for this issue, one dealing with . . . but read it yourself!" The plot considers the daughter of a wealthy Virginia planter who seduces one of her father's handsome slaves. She becomes pregnant by him only to discover through her Mammy that he is her half-brother. Bentley stressed the sexual encounters in this story, but not as explicitly as in "Tomorrow." He was attempting to be more respectable by couching a message within the narrative. As Browning explained to her audience, "he is sincerely attempting to break down some of the fixed ideas in the minds of many people concerning miscegenation." [50] Despite such an avowal, Bentley never came across as a man attempting to right historic wrongs, as Browning probably realized. She liked his work because it broke, as did Himes's in a different way, with fixed types of black writing, especially with fiction advancing the black middle classes.

As an editor of independent mind, Browning secured contributions from the young Ralph Ellison. He sent her four stories, three of which had appeared initially in other magazines, including *Common Ground*, a liberal publication, and *New Masses*, a leftist periodical. Of the four narratives, the first three—"Mister Toussan," "If I Had the Wings," and "Afternoon"—give episodes in the lives of two clever and mischievous little black boys, Riley and Buster. "The Birthmark," published originally in the May–June 1945 issue of *Negro Story*, takes part in the protest tradition as a powerful and disturbing narrative about a lynching. It portrays the horror of a black family upon discovering the castrated and lynched body of their Willie, a younger brother.[51] The story offsets the tone of Himes's "A Penny For Your Thoughts," published one issue earlier, in the March–April number. In so doing, it suggests the diversity and the balance of styles and approaches included in the journal.

Negro Story flourished during the war, even though it was not devoted exclusively or even largely to the conflict. It became, in those days, a magazine where young writers—Ralph Ellison, Chester Himes, Gwendolyn Brooks, and Margaret Walker, to name a few—could experiment with their trade. It served, too, as a showcase for older writers, such as Langston Hughes and Frank Marshall Davis. After the war, it tried to continue in the same way. It could not, however, with Alice Browning doing "all the work" and receiving minimal financial aid. Less than a year after the war's end, the journal collapsed. For a little magazine, *Negro Story* had had a good run, surviving nine issues, and publishing some fine contributions.

An end came for other journals as well in the years immediately following the war. *Crisis* and *Opportunity*, both plagued by financial difficulties, reordered their priorities and brought an era to a conclusion. They continued to function as house organs and general magazines, but they discarded the historic role both had played for several decades as literary magazines. John Henrik Clarke noted the change, saying that *Opportunity* and *Crisis*, "once the proving ground for so many new Negro writers, were no longer performing that much needed service. The best of the new writers found acceptance in the general magazines."[52]

In his article on *Crisis* from 1934 to 1949, Roy Wilkins discussed the problems of his magazine in the postwar years. He noted that the journal did not have wide appeal among the larger audience, since the "vast majority" of readers came from NAACP members. During the period, rising prices necessitated a modest increase in rate for combined membership and subscription. The modified fees were not exorbitant, totaling $3.50, but they exceeded the limits of many supporters who dropped both membership and subscription.[53]

The editors, Wilkins until 1949 and then James Ivy, tried to lure them back. They developed new departments, including at various times "Fashion Hints," "Health Hints," "Recipes," "College and School News." Creative literature essentially disappeared, as a quick glance at tables of contents clearly shows. Occasionally, a literary essay of some significance did materialize. One such article was "The Importance of Georgia Douglas Johnson," by Cedric Dover. Published in 1952, the discussion testified to the continued influence of a woman who had emerged in the initial black magazines of the twentieth century. Dover identified with Johnson's preoccupations because, in his words, "she has faced and resolved the psychological and social complications of being a near-white." He gave her a title, as "the first and still the most prolific poet of the 'half-caste.' " Her only rivals for the post were, according to Dover, Langston Hughes and George Walker, "both of whom have had the advantage of an intellectual climate influenced by herself." [54] Johnson's books had been reviewed in *Crisis* and elsewhere, but her career had not previously been discussed in a separate literary essay published in an Afro-American magazine. Dover's article represents a first in the commentary on a poet who had the distinction of extraordinary survival. It also stands as one of the few literary contributions published in *Crisis* from 1945 to 1960.

Opportunity, until its demise in 1949, paralleled the career of *Crisis*. Literary works saw print, but only occasionally. Usually those pieces came from established authors, if they were not written about such figures. Advice from Langston Hughes, for example, appeared under the title, "Langston Hughes Speaks to Young Writers." He talked with Stella Kamp about the advantages of small and large journals. In the early stages of his own career, he "gave" his poems to little magazines, he explained, since no one else seemed much interested. As a reward, he saw his name in print and came in contact with other editors who soon wanted some of his work for their own periodicals. "After the experimental magazines," he remembered, " 'New Republic' and other magazines began to ask for and publish my poetry and so it went, until publication was no longer a problem." [55] Interestingly, Hughes did not recall the role that *Opportunity* and *Crisis* had played in his own career. Neither did he recommend the two magazines to aspiring authors. The latter omission was, however, understandable, since *Opportunity* and *Crisis* had little left to offer young creative writers.

Before it expired, *Opportunity* succumbed to nostalgia. A twenty-fifth anniversary issue appeared in late 1947, complete with reminiscences from Charles S. Johnson, Elmer Carter, and Dutton Ferguson, who had become editor earlier in the year. The latter two felt, along with many others, that *Opportunity* had reached its glory in the 1920s. "What has been long recognized as 'the Golden Age of OPPORTUNITY,'" recalled Ferguson, "came during the mid-1920's, when, beginning with 1925 the *Journal of Negro Life* sponsored a series of Literary Contests. From this effort, which won national and international attention, there emerged on the American cultural scene a phalanx of short story writers, poets, essayists, and playwrights whose creative gifts ushered in the Negro Renaissance and won a secure place for hitherto unknown artists in the world of literature." [56] The last issue, published in the winter of 1949, heralded the same period both in the essays and with the poems contributed by Langston Hughes, Countee Cullen, and Claude McKay.

In the postwar period, *Phylon* assumed the literary function formerly performed by *Opportunity* and *Crisis*.[57] The magazine had its origins much earlier, though, years before the beginning of the war. W. E. B. Du Bois had come to Atlanta University in 1934 with plans for establishing, in his words, "a scholarly journal of comment and research on world race problems." [58] These plans met the approval of John Hope, president of the University, and of Du Bois's distinguished friends, as a sampling of correspondence indicates. In a letter to Du Bois, dated April 8, 1936, Edwin Embree contrasted the "brilliant" days of *Crisis* and *Opportunity*, when Du Bois and Johnson had been editors, with the dismal contemporary scene: "Both [magazines] have now fallen into the doldrums and there is not left a single journal of Negro expression that is even respectable, to say nothing of excellent." He was not sure the situation could be remedied, but he thought Du Bois should at least try: "There is some responsibility on your head simply because you have proved what can be done." [59]

Du Bois had been attempting to act on the responsibility he fully accepted, but he was consistently blocked by Florence Read, the influential white president of Spelman College, the school for women in the newly integrated Atlanta University system. Her opposition, Du Bois explained in his autobiography, delayed the establishment of *Phylon* from 1934 to 1940. When he finally did found his magazine, he sent Read an acid note. "I recall," he commented, "how your determined opposition to any university periodical has cut five irreplacable years from my creative life, despite John Hope's previous promises and his repeatedly expressed desire to have such a journal." [60] Read did not respond in kind, but she had her day later. At a meeting of Atlanta's trustees in 1944, she moved, and the new president of the University, Rufus Clement, seconded the dismissal of Du Bois from the institution.

With considerable reluctance—"without a word of warning I found myself at the age of 76 without employment and with less than $5,000 of savings"—Du Bois retired from Atlanta University in 1944.[61] He went out with praise. The editorial board of *Phylon* described him in mythical terms, saying "at 76 he remains Man and Symbol, at once the fragile human and the oracular savant." The concluding line approached biblical phrasing, as it called Du Bois an "individualist, possessor of a rare, broad and restive intelligence which permits him to move on and on even until THE END." [62]

At Du Bois's retirement, the board consisted of Ira De A. Reid as editor and seven other members, among whom were Mercer Cook and Rufus Clement. The contributing editors numbered seven and included William Stanley Braithwaite, Allison Davis, Harold Jackman, and Rayford Logan. Reid, who had started as managing editor of *Phylon* in 1944, continued as editor-in-chief until the fall of 1948, when Mozell Hill succeeded to the position. Hill served as editor until 1958.

Upon assuming office, Hill reviewed the career of *Phylon*. He noted that the magazine, from the very beginning, "staked out its claim as a scholarly journal." Du Bois had originally intended the magazine as an organ for scientific discussion of race. The title itself established the tone of the publication, for "Phylon" comes from the Greek word meaning race. Very soon, the journal also became a medium for creative literature, as Hill noted: "Today there is no need for an *apologia* or a restatement of rationale; *Phylon* can stand on its record of ten years of publication of high-level comment and *belles-lettres*." He pledged that the journal would persist in the same vein. "The editors," he promised, "will continue to seek out high-quality contributions— scientific articles, essays, humane letters, short stories, poems, photographs, selected reviews, and appropriate art forms—that describe and analyze the factors that affect societal balance and cultural integration." [63] Under Hill, the contributing editors included those well versed in creative writing, such as Langston Hughes and Hugh Gloster, a scholar knowledgeable about Afro-American literature. Alain Locke joined the group at the end of 1950.

The literary direction of *Phylon* began to emerge during the war. The focus was tentative, since the journal did not publish much literature in those years which either established or reflected trends.

There was a poem by Georgia Douglas Johnson, however, which did have a sensor on the times. The theme appeared in the title, "Interracial," and in the final couplet: "Oh, let's build bridges everywhere / And span the gulf of challenge there." [64]

The emphasis came with more clarity after the war, particularly in the retrospective reviews of Locke. He captured the accents of other literary critics published in *Phylon*, such as Charles Glicksberg, Lewis Chandler, and Blyden Jackson, and he advanced his own understanding of the best approaches to integration in black literature. From 1947 to 1953, he contributed seven reviews and one article in the same mode to *Phylon*. After his death in 1954, the reviews were continued by Blyden Jackson, 1954–55; John Lash, 1956–59; Nick Aaron Ford, 1960–63; and Miles M. Jackson in 1964. They provided an overview of recent literature, but they exhibited neither the larger insight nor the stylistic flair of Locke. Seen in comparison, Locke emerges as a real master of the retrospective review.

Editor Hill praised him as such. In a statement published in 1952, he noted the scope of the reviews, saying the titles alone "summarized trends and laid bare current issues." He praised Locke particularly for his commitment, for completing his annual task frequently "when time and health considerations would have stayed men of less genius and modesty." To the end of his career, as Hill revealed, Locke pursued his work with zest, finishing exacting assignments way ahead of schedule: "For the past six years, *Alain Locke's* annual review of the previous year's literature of the Negro has been the Editor's harbinger of Spring-Issue-time. When our secretary says, 'Dr. Locke's paper is in!' we get a warm glow. That is our cue. And we bend straightaway to the task of getting another issue of *Phylon* ready for the printers." [65]

Locke went on as he had in the past when contributing annual reviews to *Opportunity*. He made thorough surveys of contemporary literature, discussing recent publications in fiction, poetry, drama, literary criticism, film, history, and sociology. He paid attention to his style. Each essay had a predominant metaphor, usually revealed in an eye-catching title. "Dawn Patrol," issued in two parts during 1949, developed the military imagery Locke had used so frequently in the 1930s. It first appeared in the thesis statement for the essay, given clearly at the end of paragraph one: "Many of us are deeply concerned to discover whether we are a death-watch or a dawn patrol," Locke declared.[66]

Some of the titles indicated Locke's understanding of his own role as reviewer. As his career drew toward an end, he suggested that his task devolved around not only the last year, but the past several decades. In 1951, he entitled his essay, "Inventory at Mid-Century." He continued the assessment in 1952, calling his article "The High Price of Integration" and introducing himself with modesty as a bookkeeper of sorts. "Year by year," the opening sentence read, "our cultural bookkeeping becomes more difficult; not primarily because of increased volume of production, but because of added complications in the computing of net gains or losses." The last essay, "From *Native Son* to *Invisible Man*," began with a long view: "In the thirty years' span of my active reviewing experience, there have been in my judgment three points of peak development in Negro fiction by Negro writers"—the publication of Jean Toomer's *Cane* in 1923, of Richard Wright's *Native Son* in 1940, and of Ralph Ellison's *Invisible Man* in 1952.[67]

He looked forward too, searching for a workable aesthetic he could recommend to young writers. At the beginning of his *Phylon* reviews he had no new formulas, but rehashed the old art and propaganda issue under the label of art and sociology: "And as surely as in a previous decade [the 1920s], art was in the saddle, now it is sociology that sits, for better or worse." The better meant that the "sober and searching" contemporary style would bring a reformation to black literature. It would be "good medicine," however bitter the taste. The worse came from those writers, black and white, who were so concerned with sociological issues that they altogether forgot artistic considerations. Locke cited authorities, foremost of whom was Aristotle. In Locke's words, he had said "that in a work of fiction, the truth must be more than possible or even probable, it must seem inevitable." Then came the reminder Locke offered in various guises for some two decades: "The best sociological intentions often make the worst dramas and novels." He once again posited the example of Zola, saying he had successfully "reconcile[d] good sociology with good art." He thought contemporary black novelists ought to reread Zola, "since they are all sociological realists."[68]

In his *Opportunity* reviews of the 1930s, Locke had given grudging acceptance to literature which was sociological in import, which analyzed the distinct characteristics of races and socioeconomic classes. All along, he was awaiting a renaissance of beauty, which he thought would occur as Afro-American literature issued into "the ocean of great universalized art" and as it became pleasing aesthetically as well as challenging intellectually. In the late 1940s, he thought the long-awaited development was in sight. He was not unique in so thinking, since a majority of his associates expressed similar attitudes.

As had been the case in the past, Locke stood out among his contemporaries not for the novelty of his ideas but for the uniqueness of his approach as it appeared in his retrospective reviews for *Phylon*. No other individual or journal traced on a yearly basis the emergence of a literary aesthetic based on integration.

The titles of the first three reviews indicate when Locke became aware of a significant new emphasis in postwar literature. "Dawn Patrol," the third essay, followed "Reason and Race" and "A Critical Retrospect of the Literature of the Negro for 1947," the only nondescript label in the grouping. Locke sensed a new beginning in the volume of poetry issued by Robert Hayden and Myron O'Higgins, called *The Lion and the Archer*. He declared that the two had proclaimed "proudly . . . the permanent emancipation of the Negro poet from the shackles of racial verse" and that they had thereby "issued what at first blast sounds like a poetic manifesto ushering in a new dawn in Negro poetry." Another year clarified matters for Locke. After studying the poetry of Gwendolyn Brooks, M. Carl Holman, and Margaret Walker, among others, he became convinced of new stirrings. Excited by the development, he proclaimed in his 1950 review "the rise of the universalized theme supplementing but not completely displacing the poetry of racial mood and substance." The tendency seemed proper, "sound in principle, morally as well as artistically." He applauded the young writers by complimenting them in the title of his 1950 essay, "Wisdom *de Profundis*." [69]

Six months later, a very confident Locke appeared in the special issue of *Phylon* devoted to Afro-American literature. In a featured article, he gave the answers he would state again in the reviews to follow. He expressed his ideas, however, with more clarity and force than he would do in subsequent discussions. He had been vindicated, he told readers. *The New Negro* had "forecast" the theories about a universalized race literature elaborated in a "new criticism," offered by Hugh Gloster and others. And so he said, "I agree. In fact, have always agreed, though this is neither the time nor place for self-justifying quotations." He proceeded with epigrammatic comments: "The necessary alchemy is, of course, universalized rendering, for in universalized particularity there has always resided the world's greatest and most enduring art." He rephrased the declaration: "Give us Negro life and experience in all the arts but with a third dimension of universalized common-denominator humanity." A few black writers had reached the "third dimension," he believed. They included Jean Toomer with *Cane* and Richard Wright with the first two chapters of *Native Son*, before the book became "more and more involved in propagandist formulae." Other writers could realize that dimension by first understanding "that in all human things we are basically and inevitably human, and that even the special racial complexities and overtones are only interesting variants." Such an insight could release black authors to pursue great themes hitherto avoided: "about the ambivalences of the Negro upper classes, about the dilemmas of intra-group prejudice and rivalry, about the dramatic inner paradoxes of mixed heritage, both biological and cultural, or the tragic breach between the Negro elite and the Negro masses, or the conflict between integration and vested-interest separatism in the present-day life of the Negro." [70]

The special issue highlighted Locke's essay, listing it as the sole entry in a category dubbed, "Summary." The essay was a summary, for it reflected the mood of the entire issue, which was devoted to the work of twenty-three writers. It particularly expressed the tone of articles labeled as "Symposium: Survey and Forecast." Contributions to the symposium came from eight authors: Hugh Gloster, J. Saunders Redding, Nick Aaron Ford, Charles H. Nichols, Jr., L. D. Reddick, G. Lewis Chandler, N. P. Tillman, and Ira De A. Reid. With the exception of Ford, they all stressed the type of integration endorsed by Locke. Hugh Gloster, for example, asserted that the Afro-American writer "should consider all life as his proper milieu, treat race from the universal point of view, and shun the cultural insularity that results from racial preoccupation and Jim-Crow esthetics." [71] The poets went along with the critics. Included in another category, "The Negro Writer Looks At His World," Langston Hughes was decidedly in no mood to "épater le bourgeoisie." "The most heartening thing for me," he confessed to the editors, "is to see Negroes writing works in the general American field, rather than dwelling on Negro themes solely. Good writing can be done on almost any theme—and I have been pleased to see Motley, Yerby, Petry and Dorothy West presenting in their various ways non-Negro subjects." [72]

In their essays, contributors addressed questions posed by Mozell Hill and M. Carl Holman, who had edited the issue. The questions were rhetorical, thereby suggesting that the editors felt there was basic consensus on the direction of black literature. Among the other queries were two of particular pertinence: "Does current literature by and about Negroes seem more or less propagandistic than before? Would you agree with those who feel that the Negro writer, the

Negro as subject, and the Negro critic and scholar are moving toward an 'unlabeled' future in which they will be measured without regard to racial origin and conditioning?" [73]

The answers satisfied the editors, who had high hopes for the issue. As indicated in their preface, they wanted the number to make a major contribution to the body of criticism on Afro-American literature. In retrospect, many believed it had done just that. Locke singled the number out for praise in his "Inventory at Mid-Century": "From its careful perusal anyone should know where we are on the literary highway, and approximately where we are heading. As a thorough account of our literary accomplishments and an incisive analysis of our objectives, the issue merits listing as an outstanding achievement of the year." [74] Although Locke was no objective bystander, his praise carries weight because he understood the mainstream of Afro-American literature.

There was a minority report, too. It came from Lloyd Brown, black associate editor of *Masses & Mainstream*, a Marxist publication. In "Which Way for the Negro Writer?" an essay published in the March 1951 number of *Masses & Mainstream*, he gave a resounding "nay" to the second query posed by Hill and Holman. He thought the special issue of *Phylon*, and the trend it represented, threatened "the very *existence* of *Negro* literature": "For nearly all Negro writers throughout American history the question of what to write about was compellingly simple: the pen was an essential instrument in the fight for liberation. This concept was not arrived at through any wringing and twisting; nor through any high-flown debates about Art-For-Art's-Sake *versus* Art-As-a-Weapon. Spontaneous and inevitable, it arose from the conditions of life—slavery and oppression." The conditions remained basically the same, contrary to the optimism voiced in *Phylon*: "Ironic and tragic it is, that at a time when, as never before, the attention of the whole world is focussed upon the stark truth of Negro oppression and struggle in our country, so many of *Phylon's* contributors and editors direct the Negro writer away from his people." He was "dismayed" over the seeming defection of Langston Hughes and Margaret Walker, "whose works, in form and content, have been notable contributions to Negro literature." [75] The direction of Brown's argument was clear: out of the mainstream and back to expressions of protest.

Brown did not alter the course of *Phylon* editors or the major contributors. In the last issue of the magazine for 1951, Blyden Jackson answered Brown in his essay, "Faith Without Works." Brown's arguments, Jackson posited, were more a matter of politics than aesthetics: "The plain fact remains that Mr. Brown is demanding that literature be judged for its political and social expediency." The special issue of *Phylon*, he noted, concentrated on the basic requirements for all good literature as well as the special responsibility of black writers: "At the same time that *Phylon* contributors press home their profound conviction that Negro writers should have full and free suffrage in the republic of letters they also make clear their feeling that these same writers have the duty to represent the life of their own people in work that can, as it were, stand on its own feet artistically." [76] In essence, he countered Brown by saying that black writers could not work or be judged by standards different from those applicable to any other authors.

Throughout the 1950s, *Phylon* never again stirred up such explicit controversy. As integration seemed ever more imminent, protest literature faded further from view. Many hailed the change, while some experienced a sense of loss. Arthur P. Davis, in "Integration and Race Literature," called protest literature the "oldest and most cherished tradition" of a black writer. "It was," he went on, "part of his self-respect, part of his philosophy of life, part of his inner being. It was almost a religious experience with those of us who came up through the dark days of the 'Twenties and 'Thirties." The "change" in the nation's climate was "radical," Davis noted, and it came with such "startling swiftness" that some of the older writers were left with "a spiritual numbness." A few of them, whom he declined to name, had not been able to adapt and had become silent. [77] The Davis essay offered another perspective on the issues addressed by Alain Locke and in the special number of *Phylon*. In the postwar years especially, the journal was important because it focused discussions among Afro-Americans on the literary aesthetics of integration.

In one of his reviews, Locke mentioned "the high price of integration." He weighed the gains for American literature against the loss for specifically black literary interests. He did not, however, talk about black little magazines. Nor did he broach the topic in his other essays for *Phylon*. The omission is significant, since Locke had in previous decades devoted much attention to small magazines. In the postwar period, Locke could not find much to say about such publications, even though he had tenuous connections with the *Harlem Quarterly*. There were only a few of these periodicals and the few were largely ineffective, including no really significant editorials, position papers, or creative compositions. Clearly, the emphasis on integration had taken its toll on black little magazines.

"Enforced interracialism," in the words of Harold Cruse, spawned one black literary journal at the end of the 1940s. During that period, the Committee for the Negro in the Arts formed as the cultural voice of the political left in Harlem. The CNA, as it was popularly called, was an interracial organization consisting of white communists and liberals along with some young black creative writers and social scientists, including Cruse. Early on, the communists gained control of the group and dictated literary policies, among other matters. The proscriptions allowed only "socialist realism," meaning "in Negro terms" a literature dealing with the race and class struggles and preferably showing "a triumvirate of Negroes, white workers and white Communists" joined in their fight against oppression. "Socialist realism" with its political demands wearied some of the black intellectuals, who broke away and formed the Harlem Writers Club. According to Cruse, who became chairman of the club, "we were certainly not against integration of the Negro in the arts; but at the time, it struck us that since Negroes had no flourishing ethnic cultural arts institutions in their own community, pursuing this integration theme was like launching a campaign with no thought of building a starting base." The new organization was significant, he continued, because it "manifested the first ideological split within the Harlem left-wing movement." [78]

To provide that necessary base, the club founded the *Harlem Quarterly*. Cruse was not so helpful on the journal itself as he had been on the politics surrounding its inception. "There were not even any independent Negro magazines devoted to cultural problems published until the 1960s, although there was a dire need for same," he stated simply. "When Benjamin Brown, one of the members of the Harlem Writers Club, did attempt to launch *The Harlem Quarterly* in 1949, it failed, for lack of financial support, after a few issues." [79]

The magazine appeared three times from 1949 to 1950. As editor, Brown had a distinguished cast of contributing editors, including Herbert Aptheker, Frank Marshall Davis, Owen Dodson, Shirley Graham, Langston Hughes, Ernest Kaiser, and Alain Locke. He did not, however, attract funds sufficient to maintain the journal. The *Harlem Quarterly* also foundered for other reasons.

In the first place, the politics of the magazine never became clear. The founders had broken with the CNA, but they allowed a supporter of the CNA into the last issue of the journal. Isobel Johnson, in a letter to the editor, urged Afro-Americans to support the combined efforts of the CNA and the ASP (National Council of the Arts, Sciences and Professions) in, among other matters, their "campaign for jobs for Negroes in publishing." The Harlem Writers Club had shaken off the communists, but it nevertheless gave Benjamin Davis a prominent position in a symposium on civil rights, published in the first issue. He forcefully portrayed the Communist Party as "the most uncompromising fighter for Negro rights." [80] The group showed ambivalence toward the white left as well. Herbert Aptheker could serve, for example, as a contributing editor, but he could not be accepted on equal terms with black historians. In an article for the journal, Ernest Kaiser listed the names of several white writers concentrating on black subjects. He included Aptheker, only to say that "while these white writers have made substantial contributions to the understanding of the Negro question in America, it is abundantly clear that the Negro question . . . has made them!" [81]

Then, too, the magazine never jelled around any consistent aesthetic issues, Cruse to the contrary. Cruse said the Harlem Writers Club revolted "against the aesthetics implicit in cultural integration" and "posed pertinent, creative questions not fully answered to this day." Club members most probably raised those questions, but they did not incorporate such matters into the magazine itself. In his "Prospectus" to the journal, editor Brown showed neither opposition to "cultural integration" nor a new understanding of Afro-American literature. "Our purpose in publishing *Harlem Quarterly* is," he declared, "to bring to our readers short stories, poetry and articles on all aspects of Negro life and history. We feel that not enough portrayals of Negro life and interracial relations have been reaching the American people." He suggested that the journal would be unique in the history of Afro-American periodicals: "We feel that up to our date of publication no other magazines, Negro or white, gave full expression to the needs and aspirations of the majority of the Negro reading public. In this respect we are proud to bring to our readers a broad cross section of opinions on problems facing American Negroes, West Indians, Africans and our white allies today." [82]

Formed in revolt, the *Harlem Quarterly* spent its life essentially as a general magazine. It offered a considerable quantity of creative work, generally three stories and nine poems in each issue, along with book reviews and feature articles. The poets covered a wide variety of topics, with Arnold Kramer on slave life in the old South, Langston Hughes on profiteers in the war, and Theodore Stanford on the tragedy of Dachau. The fiction writers exhibited no more consistency in outlook. Benjamin Brown, in probably the best story in the series, told the story of a black youth who cleaned for a white woman and stole books from her library. In "Within the Haze," the least successful story, John Lee Weldon used stream-of-consciousness to focus momentarily on interracial sex: "I saw black struggle against white, white press black, blacksweat whitesweat becoming plainsweat. White against black white forced within black is no longer white but blacker than black." [83]

The articles ranged widely as well, from "Africa," to "Youth," to "The Basis of Bop," to "The U.N. and the Italian Colonies." The most intriguing pieces were Shirley Graham's "Eighty-Two Years Alive! W. E. B. Du Bois," and Hughes's "How to Be a Bad Writer," written especially for the *Harlem Quarterly*. "Bad" was the adjective, not black, and thus Hughes gave general advice about topic and style. Only once did he direct his ironic presentation specifically to the black writer: "If you are a Negro, try very hard to write with an eye dead on the white market—use modern stereotypes of older stereotypes—big burly Negroes, criminals, low-lifers, and prostitutes." [84] Hughes mentioned the formulae to avoid, but he never outlined new approaches for black writers. In a similar manner, all three numbers of the *Harlem Quarterly* had problems because of omission. The editors believed that black writers must meet the needs of Afro-Americans in the 1950s, but they could not be more specific.

Another example of the confusion wrought by the aesthetics of integration emerged in 1950. *Voices*, edited by Harold Vinal, published in that year a "Negro Poets Issue" which was edited by Langston Hughes. The special number featured twenty-six poets, among whom were Russell Atkins, Gwendolyn Brooks, Marcus V. Christian, Waring Cuney, Frank Marshall Davis, Owen Dodson, Robert Hayden, M. Carl Holman, Georgia Douglas Johnson, Effie Lee Newsome, Myron O'Higgins, and Melvin B. Tolson. Vinal apparently considered the number a gesture toward integration, an attempt to endorse the work of contemporary black writers. The number was, in actuality, an expression of cultural separatism, a presentation of black writers as a distinct, even an isolated, group. In his review of the *Voices* number, published in the *Harlem Quarterly*, Aaron Kramer urged white editors to include black writers in their magazines on a regular basis. "It is to be hoped," he stated, "that *Voices*, as well as other literary journals, will from now on welcome Negro poets and critics to their pages." He was not talking about special issues, as his concluding metaphor showed. The inclusion of black writers would, he said, "be like a blood-transfusion into an anemic arm." [85]

Kramer thought the arm had been "anemic" indeed. "Without doubt," he asserted, the special black number would give the "regular subscribers" to *Voices* "a refreshing treat," the opportunity to meet "the finest, liveliest, tenderest, bitterest group of poets ever to appear in their magazine." Kramer recommended the black poets in these terms, even though he felt only three of the twenty-six had "enhance[d] their reputations." Those three were all established figures, including Frank Marshall Davis with his character sketches, Langston Hughes with his brief lyrics, and Georgia Douglas Johnson with her traditional verses. The younger poets—especially Brooks, Hayden, O'Higgins, and Tolson—erred on the side of style, Kramer asserted. Concerned primarily with "brilliant" phrasing, they cluttered their lines and obscured their ideas.[86]

The older poets did indeed carry the day for the "Negro Poets Issue," as Kramer suggested. "Miss Samantha Wilson," by Frank Marshall Davis, is particularly notable because it breaks with the proletarian verse Davis had so often contributed to magazines. In her sixtieth year, Miss Wilson suddenly leaves the "wilted loneliness / Of her dejected-brown cottage" and becomes a ministrant to the ill. Her motives emerge in the last stanza, which reads well:

> Knowing death eyed her closely
> Dreading eternity friendless
> She was arranging for companions
> Among the fatally sick she'd tended
> To be watchfully waiting
> In that misty place
> Beyond the grave.[87]

"Miss Samantha Wilson" stays in the mind, as do the contributions by Hughes.

The "Negro Poets Issue" is not particularly memorable, nor has it been well remembered. Hughes reminisced fondly over *Fire*, but he said nothing in his later essays about the number of *Voices* which he had edited. Frank Davis was not much more forthcoming. In an interview published in the January 1974 issue of *Black World*, Dudley Randall asked Davis about the seeming lapse in his publications since 1948. Davis recalled that he had appeared in "a magazine" edited by Hughes, but that he had forgotten both the name and date of the journal. Randall replied: 'Do you have any idea about that? That is important bibliographical information." [88] Davis did recollect the title after he had located his own copy of the special issue.

As the 1950s continued, the color washed out of black journals. Only two small magazines—*Free Lance* and *Yugen*—had black editors and contributors in significant numbers. Neither of the publications, however, theorized in meaningful ways about black literature or consistently pursued subjects of special interest to Afro-American readers. Thus, they do not qualify in the fullest sense as small race journals. They were, though, the closest approximation to such publications in the decade.

Free Lance: A Magazine of Verse emerged in the 1950s in Cleveland, which had become an important center of black literary activity. The city had famous sons—Charles W. Chesnutt, Langston Hughes, Chester Himes—and a black little theater of national reputation, the Karamu House. It also had many active lesser lights, among which had been the January Club. Founded in 1929, this local group of writers published in 1934 the one and only issue of *Shadows*, a literary magazine developed in "the shadow" of the best black writers Cleveland had produced.[89] Some members of the club, most especially Ruby Baker Tillman and her husband Norman, a painter, surfaced again in *Free Lance*.

Founded and edited by Russell Atkins, a black musician and writer, *Free Lance* first appeared in 1952 with an introduction by Langston Hughes. In his one-page statement, Hughes never mentioned race or protest, thereby indicating the great distance traversed since he had first appeared in a literary magazine. "Regardless of quality or content," he intoned, "a poem reveals always the poet as a person. Skilled or unskilled, wise or foolish, nobody can write a poem, without revealing something of himself. Here are people. Here are poems. Here is revelation." [90]

In its early years, *Free Lance* seemed in the pattern of *Shadows*. It published primarily traditional verse written mostly by local writers, such as Harvey Leroy Allen, Finley Nix, Helen Collins, Mary B. Langrabe, and Vera Steckler. The difference lay in the exceptions, poems which considered social issues and anticipated themes prominent in the 1960s. In "The Music Teacher," for example, Finley Nix conveyed the ambivalence many blacks felt in a period emphasizing cultural integration:

> I was a teacher here in the village.
> For years I taught the youngsters of Darktown
> The prim classics of Chopin,
> Liszt, Mendelsohn, and the rest.
> How much they rebelled I never knew
> Until I came here to sleep the long, long sleep
> Of the dead, for all my prize pupils
> In winning the plaudits of the world,
> Won them through the Blues, Spirituals, and Lamentations

That rose out of the bewildered souls
Of our ancestors. . . .[91]

And then there was Russell Atkins, the most technically experimental writer included in *Free Lance*. He was so experimental in both
essays and poems that it was often difficult to trace his ideas. The
essays came with impenetrable titles, like "Abstract of the Hypo-
thetical Arbitrary Constant of Inhibition's Continuumization Becoming 'Consciousness', (Nervous System ETC.)." The poems, on
the whole, were no easier, as some characteristic lines from "Lisbon"
illustrate:

> / the fourth in wrath the tall l
> flames S s staggers s s S s upon
> crashes) th' / 'xo .x / " " " " " " " " " " !

Atkins did not believe he was placing an undue burden upon his
readers. Rather, he faulted others for doing just that, with their
"pounds of passion" and their "war of metaphors." In one of his
only discursive poems, "Notes on Negro Poets," he satirized the
obscurity he found in the work of Gwendolyn Brooks, along with that
of Countee Cullen, Owen Dodson, Robert Hayden, and Margaret
Walker:

> I cannot make heads or tails
> of the new poets among Negroes.
> But then why bother?
> Could anything be made of them
> would it matter?
> But some say that they
> cannot make heads or tails
> of ME! How can that be?
> I am so clear! not like
> Gwendolyn Brooks—
> all blear.[92]

Free Lance, along with Russell Atkins, slowly gained a small but
loyal following. From relative obscurity in the 1950s, it achieved national recognition in the 1960s by publishing such writers as LeRoi
Jones (later known as Amiri Baraka), Dudley Randall, and Conrad
Kent Rivers. In the process, it began to show itself as a journal with
a distinct black emphasis. It was this emphasis which won it the
respect of the staff at *Black World*. In 1972, editor Hoyt Fuller reminded his readers about the existence of *Free Lance*, and in 1973,

Black World published Leatrice Emeruwa's discussion of "Black Art & Artists in Cleveland." Emeruwa praised Atkins as a creative writer and musician, saying he "has been to poetic, dramatic and musical innovation and leadership what John Coltrane has been to jazz avant-gardism." She credited him too as founder and editor of "the oldest Black literary magazine extant." Longevity in itself was admirable. "At times," she noted, "Free Lance was the only Black literary magazine of national importance in existence—the high mortality of magazines being what it is! Indeed, magazines have come and gone, but Free Lance has maintained its viability for the last 22 years." [93]

Yugen, published from 1958 to 1963, was a last ephemeral note of the 1950s. It was in all its vital characteristics a small magazine. The editors, LeRoi Jones and his first wife, Hettie Cohen, had little money for a journal. They had to finance it out of Cohen's salary as a manager of the *Partisan Review*. They had neither staff nor much equipment, so Cohen prepared the pages on an old IBM electric typewriter. The magazine, as a result, looked like the modest operation it was. "The people in San Francisco said 'Oh, it's such a messy thing,'" Cohen later remembered.[94] Despite its limited circulation, the journal reflected a larger tendency, for it was part of the beat generation. As indicated on the table of contents page for the first issue, "Yugen" is a Zen term meaning "elegance, beauty, grace, transcendence of these things, and also nothing at all." [95] Poems by LeRoi Jones, Bobb Hamilton, and A. B. Spellman appeared with those of Gregory Corso, Allen Ginsberg, and Gary Snyder.

The magazine was avant-garde, and it was also integrationist, as evidenced by the two editors, one black and the other white, by the racial mix among contributors, and by the generally nonracial tone of the poems, stories, and essays included. Assembled in Jones's apartment, on 402 West 20th Street and then on 324 East 14th Street, the magazine originated not from Harlem but from the intellectual community gathering in the Lower East Side. It was not a race publication. *Yugen* was a natural outgrowth of the postwar years and the cooperation between black and white intellectuals. It represented the end of a period, the way in which many young, experimental writers adapted to a dominant tendency of the times. It was, in final analysis, the creation of LeRoi Jones in the days before he became a revolutionary writer.

In the 1940s and 1950s, an undercurrent troubled and at times ran counter to the mainstream, with its emphasis on integration and assimilation of blacks into the larger culture. The underlying movement, which became increasingly strong, resisted cultural integration and emerged as a source for Afro-American literary and political expressions of the next decade. Alice Browning, for one, rejected the idea of an easy and smooth movement into the larger culture with her occasional militant comments. Lloyd Brown raised further and more angry objections with his spirited criticism of *Phylon's* special issue. Harold Cruse and the Harlem Writers Club, among others, thought Afro-Americans should concentrate on defining and preserving the distinctive qualities of their own culture before they focused on the mainstream. Contemporary social and political occurrences reinforced the reservations some Afro-Americans had about cultural integration and the commitment of the nation to racial justice. Black migration to the cities had resulted in racial conflict, such as the race riots of 1943 in Harlem, Los Angeles, and especially Detroit. In the South, segregation remained intact and was at times brutally enforced. One year after the 1954 Supreme Court decision, Emmett Till was murdered for allegedly whistling at a white woman.

The tragedies were numerous, but they did not radically alter the course of the main current. Throughout the postwar period to the end of the 1950s, prominent black and white leaders continued to articulate the vision of an integrated society, which many could see on the near horizon. A majority of black writers and intellectuals joined in the contemporary emphasis as they developed in Afro-American magazines a literary aesthetic based on integration.

6. Black Aesthetic

Revolutionary Little Magazines,

1960–1976

The situation prevalent in the 1950s in Afro-American literature and magazines reversed itself in the 1960s. The politics and aesthetics of integration, which had been mainstream, appeared by mid-decade to be tributary, and the undercurrent of resistance to cultural integration developed into the dominant force. The larger and older periodicals spoke for integration with Western culture, while the new and smaller publications generally called for a rejection of Western values. The older journals dwindled both in number and influence, down to *Phylon* and *Crisis*. The climate was conducive to black little magazines, however, which proliferated as they never had before. They began in 1961 with *Negro Digest*, which sometimes labeled itself a little magazine, and *Liberator*. These were followed by many others, including *Umbra* in 1963, *Soulbook* in 1964, *Black Dialogue* in 1965, *Journal of Black Poetry* in 1966, *Nommo* in 1969, and *Black Creation* in 1970.

At the beginning of the 1960s, optimism prevailed. The majority among Afro-American leaders affirmed integrationist objectives and were largely unchallenged in so doing. The sit-in demonstrations and freedom rides of 1960 and 1961, which led to the formation of the Student Nonviolent Coordinating Committee (sncc), and the expanding theater of civil rights efforts encouraged hopes for the realization of a more just and open society. Enthusiasm climaxed in the August 1963 March on Washington, when Martin Luther King described his dream of an America united, black and white together.

The large and established black journals had been dreaming the same, since the postwar period. *Crisis* underscored its integrationist emphasis in the April 1963 issue of the magazine, which included

Herbert Hill, a white essayist, and his discussion of "The New Directions of the Negro Writer." Hill spoke with confidence, tracing directions which had been visible throughout the 1950s. "The greater part of contemporary American Negro writing is characterized," he generalized, "by a determination to break through the limits of racial parochialism into the whole range of the modern writer's preoccupations." He thought most black authors were achieving a new level of expression: "Now most often they use the concepts of 'Negro' and 'race' as universal symbols in a new concern with the problems of individual consciousness, identity, and alienation." In an issue of *Phylon* published also in 1963, Harold Pfantz considered the term made famous by Alain Locke back in the 1920s. "In many ways," he explained, "the new 'New Negro' is the first to bear legitimately the accolade, for in his essential cha.acter and conduct he is the first to belie genuinely the basic traditions of American race relations. Unlike his precursors he is, at long last and simply, an emerging American." [1]

Although *Negro Digest* changed its focus dramatically mid-decade, later becoming *Black World*, it gave popular expression to similar ideas in the first half of the 1960s. The June 1961 number was a reappearance for the journal, which had been issued on a regular, monthly basis from 1942 to 1951. Publisher John H. Johnson, who also originated *Ebony*, *Tan*, and *Jet*, had recognized a continuing need for *Negro Digest*, as he explained in the first number of the new series. He hoped to satisfy his old constituency, which had long requested a renewal of the magazine. He wanted to join in the presentation of "Negro" news, covered increasingly in periodicals with international circulation. He desired, as well, to provide an outlet for young Afro-American writers, as he recalled the journal had done in the past. [2]

Patterned after *Readers' Digest*, the new series reestablished itself in the mainstream. Until roughly 1965, it specialized in popular articles digested and reprinted from other magazines, many of them white in ownership and orientation. The June 1961 number included, for example, "A Negro President by 1999?" reprinted from *Esquire*; "Plain Girls Can Make It, Too," *Down Beat Magazine*; "My First Boss," *Atlantic Monthly*; and "The White Man's Future in Africa," *Foreign Affairs*.

Editorial comments underscored the general emphasis. A characteristic statement appeared as a headnote preceding "Three Friends," a story by Rosemary Kelly published in 1962. "One woman recalls three others," the note read, "who played crucial roles in her life— and it is merely a matter of coincidence that the writer is white and her friends were Negroes."[3] The observation could have come from Johnson, who named himself on the masthead of each issue as editor of the journal. On the other hand, it could have originated with Hoyt W. Fuller, the managing editor. In 1961 and 1962, Fuller's name preceded several statements with integrationist implications. Fuller and Doris E. Saunders, the associate editor, coauthored a monthly column entitled "Perspectives" until August 1962, when Fuller became sole author. In September 1961, "Perspectives" observed that "as far as we know, no Negro artist has ever had the good fortune to have his comic strip syndicated or, for that matter, to appear regularly in white newspapers." The telling expression was "good fortune." In both intention and tone, *Negro Digest* of the early 1960s was integrationist. It drew tributes accordingly. Speaking as many contemporaries felt, Dudley Randall applauded the journal in November 1963 for "taking the place of the old Crisis and Opportunity magazines in providing an outlet for Negro poets."[4]

Others saw *Umbra,* one of the first black little magazines of the period, as heir apparent to the larger Afro-American journals. The editor was Thomas Dent, a staff worker at the NAACP Defense Fund. With the help of Calvin Hernton and David Henderson as associate editors and Rolland Snellings as circulation manager, Dent issued a periodical more in the tradition of *Opportunity* than of *Crisis.* Writing in the July 1963 number of *Mainstream,* Art Berger, who was one of the *Umbra* poets, described the magazine as "the first major outlet for Negro poets since the days of Opportunity," with the exceptions of such "college reviews" as *Dasein* of Howard University and *Phylon* at Atlanta University.[5]

Dent and his associates profited from the advice of Langston Hughes, who had attended some of their poetry readings in the early 1960s at the Market Place Gallery of Harlem. Probably recollecting his own association with many previous journals, Hughes urged the young writers to establish a noncommercial magazine for the publication of their own work.[6] He might have advised them, too, to separate art from politics. Surely the "Foreword" to the first number of *Umbra,* issued in the winter of 1963, recalls statements made by Hughes and his contemporaries in the 1950s as well as in the 1920s. "We maintain," it read, "no iron-fisted, bigoted policy of preference or exclusion of material. *Umbra* will not be a propagandistic, psychopathic or ideological axe-grinder. We will not print trash, no matter how relevantly it deals with race, social issues, or anything else." The magazine would publish work of "literary integrity and artistic excellence," and it would encourage young, unknown authors who might be *"too hard"* on society" or present an aspect of "social and racial reality" which could be unpopular in terms of the larger culture.[7] Those writers, featured in succeeding numbers, included Julian Bond, Ray Durem, Calvin Hernton, Clarence Major, Ishmael Reed, Conrad Kent Rivers and, among others, Rolland Snellings. *Umbra* did not provide them with a consistent outlet, though, since it appeared irregularly and with divergent emphases: as an anthology in 1967 to 1968 and 1970 to 1971, and most recently as a "Latin Soul" number in 1974 to 1975. In 1967, Henderson became editor and moved the periodical to Berkeley, since California had become the locale for many of the newer publications. *Umbra*, meaning darkest shadow of an eclipse, materialized just before the emergence in the mid-1960s of the black arts movement, a label characterizing the activities of revolutionary black writers a..d artists of the day. Set in the pattern of earlier publications, the magazine did not take a major part in the movement. It did, however, provide an early exposure for writers who would emerge with influential essays and poems in the newer and much more radical black journals.

While the civil rights movement encouraged an aesthetics of integration, the violence of the 1960s stimulated a new literary politics, an aesthetics of separatism. The apex of the civil rights movement in 1963 underscored the tragic ironies in American life and made hollow, for many, the integrationist approach in many contemporary magazines, especially in *Crisis, Phylon*, and the early *Negro Digest*. Even as Martin Luther King affirmed a philosophy of nonviolence and peaceful change, a series of brutal murders shocked the nation. Medgar Evers was slain one month before the March on Washington in 1963, and in September four young black girls were killed in the bombing of a Birmingham church. President John Kennedy was assassinated in November, and the assassinations of Malcolm X and of King followed in 1965 and 1968.

A backdrop for the assassinations were the riots marking the period. The first of the decade took place in Harlem during July 1964 and was followed by seven other outbreaks in black urban and residential areas during the same summer. These outbreaks multiplied, occurring in Watts and five other cities in 1965, in twenty cities during the summer of 1966, and in twenty-two cities during July and August of 1967. The intensity of violence increased as well, culminating in the large-scale riots of 1967 in Grand Rapids, Michigan; Plainfield, New Jersey; Toledo, Ohio; and especially in Newark and Detroit. The assassination of King sparked widespread rioting in 1968, but the occurrences, serious as they were, did not approach the violence of the preceding year and seemed to designate the ending of a stage in American racial conflict.[8]

Many young black writers and intellectuals read only the tragedies of the day. They thought Martin Luther King's call to integration an echo in the wind, a repetition of views which had been long proclaimed but had done so little to change the reality for blacks in America. Their rage found expression in the little and noncommercial magazines they developed. The most important of those magazines, the ones basic to shaping a black aesthetic for the period, were, in order of their importance: *Negro Digest; Liberator* of 1965 and 1966, when influenced by Larry Neal and LeRoi Jones; and the three journals originating in California, *Soulbook, Black Dialogue,* and *Journal of Black Poetry.* Carolyn Gerald, writing in the November 1969 issue of *Negro Digest,* noted a relationship between separatism and the contemporary little magazines. "The revolutionary black journal," as she labeled the new periodical, "made its appearance at that moment in our history, somewhere in the mid-Sixties, when black people began to forsake civil rights and integration, and began to seek out a sense of self." She called the journals revolutionary because, to her way of thinking, they represented "the literary enactment of the crisis of the Sixties: the Break With The West." Gerald, like so many others, alluded to separatism, nationalism, and revolution in her article but did not explicitly clarify the terms. Her further commentary suggests, however, that she was equating separatism with cultural nationalism, or black arts by and for black people. Through the little magazines, she explained, "black literature reorganizes itself, serving the cause of blackness by analyzing its suppression and recreating its images and its myths."[9] As the periodicals indicate, a majority of participants in the black arts movement were making an equation similar to Gerald's, between a break with the West and cultural nationalism. Others talked, in addition, about economic separatism from the larger culture, and sometimes about a nation for Afro-Americans either within the boundaries of the United States or in Africa.

Those who identified with the black arts movement wanted their little magazines to go to the heart, or the essential reality, of blackness. Thus, they insisted the journals be black at all levels of involvement, from owner to reader. In the first issue of *Soulbook,* the editorial board indicated accordingly that "to further the cause of the liberation of Black peoples we feel that this Journal and all ensuing issues of it must be produced, controlled, published and edited by people who are sons and daughters of Africa." Contributors came under the same umbrella. Generally, there were exceptions to the de facto rule that contributors be black only in the early issues of the magazines. Ted Vincent appeared in the second number of *Soulbook*, dated Spring 1965, with his article on "W. E. B. Du Bois: Black Militant or Negro Leader?" According to Carolyn Gerald, a considerable amount of discussion and "many editorial reservations" preceded his inclusion.[10]

Whites occasionally gained access to the magazines through letters to the editors. In published comments, some of the correspondents denounced the journals' separatist policies. The June 1966 issue of *Liberator*, for example, included a letter from Eileen M. Wilcox, who had been active in civil rights while a student at the University of Kansas. She told editor Daniel Watts that she liked his assessment of the black establishment but not the commentary directed toward whites in the movement: "I can't welcome this trend of Black racism. Your terminology sounds as ridiculous as that of the Klan and George Lincoln Rockwell." In statements printed immediately following hers, Watts informed Wilcox that she spoke "in the name of [a] W.A.S.P. perverted version of 'ethics and humanity.' " [11] Watts and the others included such missives from whites because they showed that the journals were making their break with the West.

As they sought new approaches to race and culture, the supporters of black little magazines denounced the "white racist press," to use the words of Willard Pinn in *Soulbook*. They warned their audience away from what they called white magazines, which included *Atlantic Monthly, New Yorker, Saturday Review,* and other large publications, along with such small journals as *Angel Hair, Dust, Kumquat, Mundus Artium, Out of Sight, Trace,* and *Vagabond.* "They all," declared Pinn, "stand for the perpetuation of racism, genocide and outright lying. The purpose of the white oriented mass media is to *white* orient." Publishing houses managed by whites bore the same symbolism, as several of the other writers explained. In an essay printed in the *Journal of Black Poetry*, Ahmed Alhamisi challenged his colleagues to use their own publishing houses: "It is time we refuse to submit our creations to such publishers as Dial, Harpers and Row, William Morrow & Company, Bobb-Merrill Company, Grove Press, Inc., Merit Publishers, Marzani and Munsell, or International Publishers, to name a few." [12] The clear alternatives were black presses which had emerged in the 1960s, including the Free Black Press of Chicago, Journal of Black Poetry Press of California, Black Dialogue Press of New York, Jihad Press of Newark, and especially Broadside Press of Detroit, established by Dudley Randall, and Third World

Press of Chicago, developed by Don Lee, later Haki Madhubuti.[13]

A few other little and commercial magazines came under fire. One of them was *Studies in Black Literature*, a scholarly journal in the planning stages which was to be edited by Raman K. Singh, a native of India, and to be developed at Mary Washington College in Virginia. Hoyt Fuller took repeated aim at the journal partly because its editor, he claimed, had "adopted the white attitude toward black literature"— the idea that whites can understand and criticize black literature as well as can blacks. Richard Long, among others, seconded Fuller. Writing in the September 1970 number of *Liberator*, he described the proposed journal as "clearly an act of imperialism motivated by opportunism." [14]

Commercial black journals drew most of the criticism. To writers for the black little magazines, the publishers of the larger periodicals had sacrificed their own heritage to business interests. They had some trouble assessing John H. Johnson, since he issued *Negro Digest*, a primary instrument of the black arts movement. Larry P. Neal, an influential contributor to the little magazines, advised his contemporaries that "we must support existing firms like *Johnson* publications, force them to publish meaningful work by deluging them with the best that we have." [15] To Neal and the others, the worst of Johnson was *Jet*, which one writer called "a substitute for *Coronet*," and *Ebony*, labeled as "an imitation of both *Life* and *Playboy*." They focused particularly on *Ebony* and on *Essence*, published by the Hollingsworth Group and considered another of the "negative forces" or "isolated entries in the bowels of a decaying America." [16]

Ebony, as described in the little magazines, was headed distinctly in the wrong direction, straight into the pockets of white businessmen profiting off the delusions of many Afro-Americans. *Liberator* exposed the fallacies promoted by *Ebony* in a two-part article written by Eddie Ellis and called "Is *Ebony* a Negro Magazine?" Ellis based his criticism on a premise articulated in the initial segment of his discussion: "*Ebony* has no loyalties to the Negro people. If *Ebony* can't even be loyal to the 750,000 Negroes who read the magazine, we know *Ebony* has NO identification with, or loyalties to, the other 30 million BLACK captives in America." To support his claim, he surveyed the advertisements carried in the magazine. The products— for lightening the skin and straightening the hair—and the models looking like Anglo-Saxons encouraged readers to "de-identify" with blackness. The advertisers of Dr. Fred Palmer's Skin Whitener, among other items, were profiting off *Ebony*, and they were almost exclusively white.[17]

Essence was judged to be similarly guilty. All of the black little magazines, but especially the *Journal of Black Poetry*, lashed the publication. Askia Muhammad Toure, formerly Rolland Snellings, criticized *Essence* on three grounds. First, its ownership was tainted: "*Essence* was initiated by a group of negro businessmen (with reported white financial backing) in an effort to appeal to the needs of Black women throughout the country." Second, according to Toure, its editor was a cultural renegade. "Mister Gordon Parks is alleged to have remarked," Toure reported, "that 'Black people have no culture' . . . There is no 'Black' point of view . . . There are no good Black illustrators or photographers . . . We're not interested in 'color'; we're interested in quality. . . .'" Finally, the magazine's staff was integrated, as were its contributors. Toure ended his comments angrily, in capital letters: "Blackhearts!! we urge you to BOYCOTT *ESSENCE* MAGAZINE THROUGHOUT THE COUNTRY, AS ANOTHER 'GAME' BEING RUN ON BLACK PEOPLE BY SLICK NIGGAS HUSTLING 'BLACKNESS' FOR PROFIT; AIDED BY AN UNCLE TOM EDITOR WHO HATES AND DESPISES BLACK CREATIVE ARTISTS." [18] Joe Goncalves, as editor of *Journal of Black Poetry*, summarized the case that his magazine and the others presented against *Essence*. "We need," Goncalves declared, "land, fresh air, Black love, good food, freedom from the beast. *Essence* offered us cosmetics, the desire for the latest everything, and plain nonsense. In full color. Its intent was to move us further into consumption, and our direction, even now, should be production and a-way from this beast's goods." [19]

Critical of the larger culture and its periodicals, writers for the black little magazines tried in the 1960s and into the 1970s to establish a black literature founded on new aesthetic principles. At the prompting of Hoyt Fuller, along with a few others, they developed theories about the black aesthetic, as they called it, in their essays and poems contributed to the periodicals. The best definitions of the term emerged, in fact, from these contributions. In the introduction to his anthology of essays, entitled *The Black Aesthetic*, Addison Gayle identified black journals as the primary vehicle for discussions of the black aesthetic: "This anthology is not definitive and does not claim to be. The first of its kind to treat of this subject, it is meant as an incentive to young black critics to scan the pages of *The Black World* (*Negro Digest*), *Liberator Magazine*, *Soul-book*, *Journal of Negro Poetry*, *Amistad*, *Umbra*, and countless other black magazines, and anthologize the thousands of essays that no single anthology can possibly cover." [20]

The term itself, with its definite article, glossed over a considerable divergence of opinion, even among those writers who considered themselves revolutionaries. While some offered over and again their view of the black aesthetic, others declared that the term could not be defined, even while in the process of offering a definition.[21] The theorists did, however, share certain basic ideas, and they encouraged creative work based on those understandings. As a result, black literature of the period has qualities distinguishing it from that of other decades, even though it is part of the historic evolution of the black arts.

Spokespersons for the black aesthetic provided a new version of the old dialectic over art and propaganda. They too rejected art-for-art's sake, as had many before them, but they were more complete and angry in their rejection. They talked contemptuously of art-for-art's sake, seeing it generally as the standard of Western literature, with its emphasis on style and technique and its apparently elite audiences. The slogan of the day, raised in all the black little magazines, became art-for-people's sake. Expanding on the motto, the more extreme theorists claimed that concern for form was irrelevant, that it attracted the attention of only the highly literate, and that it distracted from the larger issue at hand, the health and happiness of black peoples.

Two men in editorial capacities further clarified the expression through their frequent and influential essays. As arts editor of *Liberator* in 1966, Larry Neal declared on several occasions that problems for black writers had originated historically over "a confusion about function, rather than a confusion about form." For Neal, the function of Afro-American literature was clear, "the only goal" being "the psychological liberation" of black peoples throughout the world, beginning with the United States.[22] Hoyt Fuller discerned a similar goal, as he revealed month-by-month in "Perspectives," his regular column for *Negro Digest*. In the last half of the 1960s especially, he stressed the function of black literature, declaiming in one way or another that "all our art must contribute to revolutionary change and if it does not, it is invalid." Like Neal, he fleshed out his theories by relating them to specific individuals and types of writing. In the process, he declared the blues "invalid," since "they teach resignation, in a word acceptance of reality—and we have come to change reality." Seeing himself as a cultural revolutionary, Fuller asserted that his contemporaries should shake off the shackles of the past in their literature as well as in other aspects of their lives. "Whatever we do," he advised them, "we cannot remain in the past, for we have too much at stake in the present." [23]

Advocating an art-for-people's sake, proponents of the black aesthetic emphasized the community, not the individual. The well-being of the collective group, of black persons everywhere, was more important than the needs of one person. In a similar manner, the evolving concerns of black literature were more significant than the artistic idiosyncracies and the reputation of the individual author. Ascribing to these ideals, contemporary black writers felt, at their best, an esprit de corps and endorsed each other's efforts with enthusiasm. In "Black Poetry: Which Direction?" an essay published in *Negro Digest* during 1968, Don Lee described the atmosphere existing within the community of black artists. His description conveys the excitement of the times, the feeling that great possibilities were at hand: "This atmosphere of beautiful days now exists among blk / poets. There is a feeling of cooperation and companionship rather than one of competition." [24]

A series of writers conferences fed the excitement. The gatherings occurred so frequently that *Negro Digest* carried a special column dubbed, "On The Conference Beat." The meetings originated in 1956 at the First Negro Congress of Writers and Artists, staged in Paris and attended by such major authors as Richard Wright and Chester Himes. Supporters for a black magazine in French, *Presence Africaine*, hosted the gathering. Inspired by the Paris assembly, the American Society for African Culture sponsored in 1959 the first black writers conference. Organized by different groups, the meetings came rapidly in the next decades, occurring in Berkeley, California, during 1964; in New York City, 1965; in Dakar, Senegal, 1966 (First World Festival of Negro Arts); in Detroit and Newark, 1966; in Detroit, 1967; in New York City, 1968; at Fisk University, 1966, 1967, and 1968; at Howard University, during 1974, 1976, 1977, and 1978; and in Lagos, Nigeria, 1977 (called the Second World Black and African Festival of Arts and Culture). These gatherings and others of the 1960s and 1970s gave considerable impetus to the black arts movement. They brought writers together, enhanced their sense of community, and provided a setting and forum for the debate over and celebration of the black aesthetic.

While proponents of the black aesthetic emphasized community or groups, individuals did emerge as prominent. In her essay for *Negro Digest*, Carolyn Gerald stressed the importance of key individuals and underlined the work of black writers in identifying such persons. "The work of the poets" is in part, she revealed, "to give us back our heroes and to provide us with new ones." Writers of the black aesthetic were chary of the past, but they retrieved a few heroes from earlier decades. In their contributions to the black little magazines and at the writers conferences, they headlined Marcus Garvey for his Back-to-Africa movement, Franz Fanon for his emphasis on the decline and imminent fall of the West, and especially Malcolm X for his outspoken celebration of blackness. Tributes to Malcolm, by way of essay, poem, and photograph, appeared frequently in the journals. Gerald gave the ultimate praise when she described him as "the epic hero of our struggle, of our journey toward a new consciousness, toward a new nation." [25]

The contemporary scene produced a new hero in LeRoi Jones, later Imamu Amiri Baraka. By the last half of the 1960s, he was clearly the charismatic leader of the black arts movement. With his concept of the revolutionary theatre and his Harlem Repertory players, he stimulated the movement in its early years. With his inflammatory essays, featured in all the black little magazines, he did much to shape the movement. With his well-circulated poems and plays, he gave quotable examples of the new writing. He also popularized its vocabulary, the use of both sacred and profane language.

Jones defined the black poet as priest. Hence, in an essay published in *Journal of Black Poetry*, he told his colleagues that "we must, in the present, be missionaries of Blackness, of consciousness, actually." He offered his message—dealing with the spiritual values of blackness—as the prelude to apocalypse, to a new and beautiful black community. In labeling the enemy, a decadent Western culture, he referred to the "beast," an expression from Revelations. The label reappeared frequently in the work of his contemporaries, as did reference to "missionaries of blackness" and explanations of the phrase. Inspired by Jones, Don Lee declaimed that "black poets will be examples of their poems, and if their poems are righteous the poet will be righteous and he will be a positive example for the black community." [26] In his afterword to *Black Fire* (1968), a poetry anthology he coedited with Jones, Larry Neal recalled another expression of his collaborator and described the black artist as "warrior," "priest," "lover," and "destroyer." [27]

When commenting later on the black arts movement of the 1960s and early 1970s, Neal referred to its "language of religious reform" and to "the new religiously inspired nationalism." He also noted the scatological vocabulary. Rather than conflicting with the religious language, it served the same end, cultural liberation. Neal explained that black writers used obscenity to "release tension" and to sever black literature from "its genteel moorings" and Western ways. [28] Maxine Elliston demonstrated the idiom in "Uncool Motherfuckers," a poem included in *Nommo*: "Why do you use words like / mother-fucker / cocksucker / son-of-a-bitch? / Because / You have to get un-cool to communicate with / uncool motherfuckers." Generally viewed as a prophet of the black arts movement, Jones encouraged other writers to adopt a profane terminology by his own example. He popularized "Up Against the Wall, Motherfucker!" a confrontationist slogan replacing the integrationist "We Shall Overcome." In "Black Revolutionary Language," an essay included in *Liberator*, Florence Turbee traced the history of the contemporary expression. Having first been used by white policemen in black communities, the slogan appeared in a well-known poem by Jones, called "Black People!" and published originally in a 1967 issue of *Evergreen Review*. One year later, it served as a motto for both the Black Panthers and dissident students at Columbia University.[29] For ascribers to the black aesthetic, the most influential usage of the expression came with Jones's poem.

As revealed in black little magazines, the theorists and practitioners of the black aesthetic focused on both the appearance and purpose of the new literature. The purpose determined all other aesthetic matters, considered secondary in importance. Stated in general terms, the literature was to be an instrument of separatism, a means of disengaging blacks from Western culture. Writers accordingly eschewed traditional literary forms, such as sonnets and odes, and patterned their work on jazz, an expression indigenous to their own culture. For the same reason, they attempted a distinct vocabulary. By obscenity, they illustrated their contempt for Western ways. They endorsed their own culture by repeating terms characteristic of it, such as "brother" and "sister," and by adopting African words when possible. Separatism, emphasized in contemporary literature, was not an end in itself. The larger goal was a new black consciousness and hence a new black community. As envisioned by their proponents, the revolutionary black arts were to prepare the way for such a goal. Inspired by their sense of purpose, writers of the black aesthetic presented themselves as missionaries of blackness, talked about art-for-people's sake, and dreamed of a literature exclusively by, about, and for, blacks.

Among black little magazines, *Liberator* developed into the first influential exponent of the black aesthetic. The advocacy came mid-decade, with the beginning of the black arts movement, but it lasted for only about two years. Throughout the course of the magazine, editor Daniel Watts concentrated not on literary-politics but essentially on politics itself, particularly on matters involving African independence. In pursuit of his main interests, he had established the

Liberation Committee for Africa in 1961. The committee, never more than Watts and a few associates, founded *Liberator* in the same year and published the journal monthly from its office on 244 East 46th Street, New York City. On the masthead of each issue, the magazine announced itself as "the voice of the new Afro-American protest movement in the United States and the liberation movement in Africa." In his editorials, Watts spoke in the same vein. "*Liberator* is dedicated," he stated in the January 1963 issue, "to uncompromising participation in the liberation struggle both in America and in Africa, thus serving as a bridge for unity between the two movements which must eventually become one." From first issue to last, *Liberator* seemed a platform for black nationalism. Watts reinforced this impression in August 1969, when he told readers of the journal that he had established *Liberator* as "a public forum" for blacks to discuss matters important to blacks. "At no point," he added, "have I or my associates considered turning *Liberator* into a magazine for the 'enlightenment' or entertainment of whites." [30]

Appearances did not tell the whole story. Watts may have talked with confidence about his views, but in reality *Liberator* had no clear ideological position. Harold Cruse, who had contributed to the magazine before 1965, claimed rightly that Watts as editor either would not or could not define such basic terms as integration, nationalism, and Marxist Communism.[31] Because Watts did not formulate his own ideas with clarity, he did not attract people to the journal who shared consistent understandings of politics and literature. In the early issues, the contributors were interracial, involving black integrationists, black nationalists, white liberals, and black and white Marxists, some of whom belonged to the Communist Party.

The advisory board, which Watts established with the first issue and disbanded finally in March 1967, represented widely divergent interests. Originally involving twelve persons, it included George B. Murphy, who was a Communist politician and one of the chief editors of *Freedom* (1950–1955), a newspaper edited by Paul Robeson and Marxist in orientation; Richard Moore, a West Indian who had formerly been a member of the Communist Party but who had become, in the words of Cruse, "very critical and bitter against the Communists"; and James Baldwin, who was an integrationist and a supporter of Martin Luther King.[32] While the board was not given a major role in the magazine, the influence of such persons, listed on the masthead of each issue, blunted Watts's support of black nationalism. Looking at the magazine during its first five years, Cruse declared that Watts had achieved only a "surface pro-nationalism." He found Watts specific only in his criticism of Martin Luther King: "The only Negro leader the *Liberator* ever attacked consistently was Martin Luther King—and in a most unconstructive way—for the editorial attacks on King were based on the editor's bias against passive resistance." In general, Cruse concluded, *Liberator* had "the most inept, naive, and politically unimaginative editorial leadership with which a journal of this was ever cursed." [33]

Cruse is perhaps the angriest critic of *Liberator*. Having contributed essays to the magazine in its formative years, he had hoped Watts would free himself of any communist influences and address the issues at hand. When Watts appeared incapable of such a task, Cruse withdrew his support of the periodical. Cruse knew the journal well, even though he gave his opinions in a highly subjective manner. Watts did not, as Cruse stated, develop either a political or cultural approach to his magazine. He expended many editorials attacking the head of the Southern Christian Leadership Conference rather than recommending viable alternatives to integration.

Watts was not alone in his denunciation of King. Most of the editors of black little magazines and many of the contributors to the same publications criticized him as well, along with Roy Wilkins, the NAACP, the Urban League, and any other race leader or race organization espousing integration. The distinctive qualities of Watts's comments lay in their vituperative tone and their persistence. The critical editorials followed a pattern, emerging after a significant happening involving the larger black community. "Dream and Reality" appeared in October 1963, one month after the bombing of the Sixteenth Street Baptist Church in Birmingham, Alabama: "These brutal murders of defenseless young Afro-Americans horribly point up the reality of the American scene in contrast to the dream which Rev. Martin Luther King recently revealed on the steps of the Lincoln Memorial in Washington." Watts arraigned King for "false leadership of the black people" and Afro-Americans "for tolerating the misleadership of Rev. Martin Luther King." [34]

In subsequent editorials, Watts used epithets, thereby indicating that his anger and frustration had increased. In a September 1965 editorial, penned after the riots in Watts, Los Angeles, the editor called his favorite target a "pork chop 'preacher' " and addressed the head of the NAACP as " 'uncle' Roy." Both leaders, he claimed, supported the police in their use of force to quell the rioting and thus both were "negro anglo-saxons" and "poor excuses for men." In his May 1967 editorial, penned after King had gone on record opposing the Vietnam War, Watts complained: "No matter how much we in the Black community shift our focus, demands or programs, we are constantly being saddled with King as *our* leader either by the white left, the middle-of-the-road pork chop preachers or the white establishment itself." Watts thought King was currying favor and dollars from white liberals by his stance.[35]

As the editorials show, Watts was becoming progressively more militant. He made some of his most extreme statements in 1967 and 1968, the very years marking a strongly nationalistic phase in other black little magazines. In his September editorial, "The Eve of Revolution," written four months after his last criticism of King, Watts claimed that it was no longer practical for Afro-Americans to think of returning to Africa or of setting up a separate country within United States borders. "Finally, and it seems to me inevitably," he concluded, "we can prepare for the final confrontation at the barricades. When that moment arrives, we at *Liberator* shall lay down our pens and take up the sword." [36] Watts could envision cataclysm and express his opinions with energy. He was not so effective, as his editorials show, in hewing out a rational and consistent political ideology for his magazine.

He had similar difficulties in determining the cultural and literary role of *Liberator.* Cruse regretted that "neither the *Liberator* nor the Afro-American nationalists have yet developed their own cultural critique on literature, art or drama within the context of American culture." [37] Afro-American nationalists had not, as he noted, formulated theories showing the Afro-American arts as part of American culture. As nationalists, they were opposed to integrationism both politically and artistically. Cruse missed one very important development. Just as he was concluding work on his book, *Liberator* was beginning to attract young critics who would bring the magazine to its high point in literature and the other arts.

In 1964, Larry Neal had met Daniel Watts. They were introduced by Clayton Riley and Clebert Ford, both on the editorial board of *Liberator.* Through that introduction, Neal became involved in the magazine. He contributed several important essays to *Liberator* in 1965 and 1966, served as arts editor for the journal during 1966, and attracted other young writers to the periodical, the most important of whom was LeRoi Jones.

With articles he published in *Liberator,* Neal did much to define the black arts movement. He wrote a series of essays entitled "The Black Writer's Role," each number of which concentrated on one author. The philosophy underlying these articles appeared in the first discussion, a consideration of Richard Wright: "The central thesis of this series is that the Black Writer's problem really grows out of a confusion about function, rather than a confusion about form." [38]

In the first essay of the sequence, published in December 1965, Neal explained that Wright knew much about the role of the Afro-American writer. His "Blue Print for Negro Writing," published in the 1937 *New Challenge*, showed his understanding. Specifically, Wright realized that the black author had special responsibilities since he was a member of an oppressed group. Wright, in other words, saw the connection between literature and politics. Neal faulted the author on his politics, however. He criticized Wright for his membership in the Communist Party and for an attempted "reconciliation," in "Blue Print for Negro Writing," "between nationalism and communism." Neal went on to make the type of statement Cruse was looking for in *Liberator*. He declared that "American Communism" had helped develop some black writers, but that it had ultimately forced their creative energies into "areas that have proved particularly uncreative. . . ." Communism, he continued, "proved to be harmful to the long range development of an organized and cohesive outlook among Black people." [39] With such a statement, Neal helped direct young black nationalists away from the Communist Party. It is ironic that the commentary appears in a journal supported in its early years by several Communists. By the mid-1960s, those individuals had generally been removed from the advisory board and from influence in the magazine.

In the next and last two essays of the series, Neal developed estimates of Ralph Ellison and James Baldwin that would be affirmed in the other black little magazines throughout the period. Neal declared, in the January 1966 article, that Ralph Ellison had not lived up to his potential. Addressing Ellison directly, he claimed that "we" still remembered the words "you" spoke in an editorial comment for the 1943 issue of *Negro Quarterly*. "The problem is psychological," Ellison had explained; "it will be solved only by a Negro leadership that is aware of the psychological attitudes and incipient forms of action which the black masses reveal in their emotion-charged myths, symbols and war-time folklore." From beginnings so auspicious to Neal, Ellison had developed his work on the ideas of white writers, including Kenneth Burke, T. S. Eliot, André Malraux, and Ezra Pound. "And thus," concluded Neal, "another vital mind has been lost in the graveyard that is America." [40]

He was not as hard on James Baldwin, since Baldwin had attempted a synthesis of literature and politics. In the essay published in April 1966, Neal commended Baldwin for the attempt but criticized him for his politics. Baldwin, a great admirer of Martin Luther King, had become "the conscience" of the civil rights movement. That movement, Neal went on, "has as its goal integration into a dying system; instead of the destruction of the *white* idea of the world." [41] As Neal's article shows, cultural revolutionaries were setting the tone for black little magazines by the mid-1960s, and Baldwin was losing some of the influence he had formerly enjoyed among young black writers. Baldwin was still on the advisory board of *Liberator*, but he did not have the ear of Daniel Watts.

Besides his series, Neal published another influential essay in *Liberator*. Entitled "Development of LeRoi Jones," the twofold discussion appeared in the January and February issues of 1966. It traced Jones's progression from Howard University, where he had been a student, to Greenwich Village and *Yugen*, and to Harlem, where Jones was attempting to establish a revolutionary black theater. As Neal explained, Jones was searching for "a unified identity . . . that is in tune with the following exigencies: the spiritual demands of Black people, revolutionary tendencies in the social order, the Black community, the Third world; and a necessity to bring aesthetics in line with ethics." [42] Neal's essay was important primarily because it explained and publicized Jones's evolution as a theorist and writer.

Neal did more than talk about Jones. During the two years when he was associated with *Liberator*, Neal secured several contributions from his friend for the journal. The most significant piece, "The Revolutionary Theatre," had been published originally in *Black Dialogue*. Appearing early in the black arts movement, in July 1965, the essay helped provide a theoretical base for the new writing. In an influential statement, one quoted later by many authors, including Neal, Jones emphasized the function of black literature: "Wittgenstein said ethics and aesthetics are one. I believe this." He went on with expressions considered outrageous by the larger society but quotable within the movement. The theatre would be political, "a weapon to help in the slaughter of these dimwitted fat-bellied white guys who somehow believe that the rest of the world is here for them to slobber on." He devised a label for the struggle ahead: "Even as Artaud designed The Conquest of Mexico, so we must design the Conquest of White Eye, and show the missionaries and wiggly Liberals dying under blasts of concrete." The "sound effects," as he imagined them, would include "wild screams of joy, from all the peoples of the world." [43]

Jones provided an example of the revolutionary theater with his *Black Mass*, a one-act play published in the June 1966 *Liberator*. The drama is a version of *Frankenstein*, as an overly ambitious black magician called Jacoub creates "The Beast," who is the other main character and the antagonist. The Beast identifies himself with his first utterances: "I white. White. White. White." His actions are meant to portray the essential qualities of whiteness. Immediately after his first speech, he "begins to vomit terribly, licking his body where the vomit lands." Before the play concludes, he turns the entire cast, which includes two other black magicians and three women, into beasts. The last words go to a narrator, who indicates that the work was not devised to produce a catharsis but to spur blacks into action: "And so Brothers and Sisters, these beasts are still loose in the world. Still they spit their hideous cries. . . . Let us find them and slay them. Let us lock them in their caves. Let us declare the Holy War. Or we cannot deserve to live. . . ." [44]

Jones contributed one other piece to *Liberator* which merits commentary. "Black Art," a poem included in the January 1966 number, established characteristics for the new black poetry. In so doing the poem became, in the words of Eugene Redmond, the "embodiment of the black aesthetic." The opening lines called for poems of meaning. They would both destroy, as "teeth" suggests, and provide, as "trees" and "lemons" imply:

> Poems are bullshit unless they are
> teeth or trees or lemons piled
> on a step.

The poems would destroy Western culture, symbolized by the Irish policeman:

> We want 'poems that kill.'
> Assassin poems, Poems that shoot
> guns. Poems that wrestle cops into alleys
> and take their weapons leaving them dead
> with tongues pulled out and sent to Ireland.

Jones called, as well, for poems that would destroy whiteness in the minds of Negroes, a term he used for satire:

> Black poems to
> smear on girdlemama mulatto bitches
> whose brains are red jelly stuck
> between 'lizabeth taylor's toes. Stinking
> Whores!

"Black Art" should, Jones concluded, reconnect readers with their essential blackness:

Let Black People understand
that they are the lovers and the sons
of lovers and warriors. . . .[45]

Jones and Neal both disappeared from the pages of *Liberator* after
1966. Neal exited because he wanted to concentrate on *Black Fire*,
which was then in a formative stage and demanding increasingly more
of his time and energy. With Neal gone, there was no one to secure
contributions from Jones, who gave his work to other magazines.
Watts did not mourn their departure, for he wanted to be in control
of his journal. During 1965 and 1966, Neal and Jones had sounded
the dominant note.

The years 1961 to 1966 marked an important period in the history
of *Liberator*, which survived until March 1971. In its first years the
periodical reached an audience of around two hundred persons. Circulation figures multiplied in 1963. In January of that year, Watts told
his readers that he would increase the printing order and would dis-
tribute the magazine "throughout the country." He considered "this
venture into mass distribution" as "a kind of public opinion poll." [46]
The public responded, with some twelve hundred subscribers to the
magazine by 1964.[47] The periodical reached its largest circulation in
the mid-1960s, when it was distributed in radical bookstores in Harlem, Greenwich Village, and in major cities throughout the United
States. Surely Larry Neal's involvement accounted for much of the
magazine's popularity. He captured the imaginations of young angry
blacks by the essays he wrote and by the contributors, especially
Jones, he attracted to the journal.

With the departure of Neal, Jones, and a few others, including
Clayton Riley, *Liberator* went into a decline from which it never
recovered. In the late 1960s and in the early 1970s, some of the
editors of other little magazines began to criticize the journal. Joe
Goncalves focused briefly on *Liberator* while reviewing Don Lee's
Dynamite Voices in *Journal of Black Poetry*: "*Liberator*, perhaps first,
which Don regards as important for the rise of Black poetry (and it
was not) began to open its pages to Black (actually Black) writers, but
lacking the adeptness (or money or whatever) of *Negro Digest*, *Liberator* could not pull the co-option off." [48] The truth about *Liberator*
lies somewhere between the estimates of Lee and Goncalves. *Liberator* was important to the black arts movement, but only in the
mid-1960s. Watts himself was not a creative writer, nor was he
particularly interested in literature. When Neal resigned from the
journal, Watts could not reestablish the primacy *Liberator* had en-

joyed among black little magazines and in the black arts movement.

The 1960s saw the furtherance of a process Alain Locke had noted in 1928, when he described the spread of beauty to the provinces. Black little magazines showed by their locations that New York was not the focus of the black arts movement. Among the most influential of the small black journals, *Liberator* alone originated in New York City. The other periodicals appeared to the west, *Negro Digest* in Chicago, and *Soulbook, Black Dialogue,* and *Journal of Black Poetry* in California. Chicago had been the scene of some notable Afro-American journals, especially in the 1930s and 1940s, but California had never before hosted any of the significant black little magazines. Many Easterners were discouraged by the move westward. Askia Toure, who had been associated with the *Umbra* poets, also of New York City, declared it "a shame that our main journals . . . are all located on the West Coast!" [49]

The California magazines, influential as they were, did not alone constitute the "main journals." They were, however, perhaps the most outspoken of the small magazines, and hence they attracted considerable attention to themselves and to the black arts movement in the 1960s. Modestly excluding mention of his own periodical, which merits the same appellation he gave the others, Goncalves claimed that the early issues of *Soulbook* and *Black Dialogue* were "bombshells." [50]

Soulbook especially seemed a bombshell, and from the title page of the first number, published in the winter of 1964. As noted on that page, the journal had no one editor but rather an editorial board comprised of Donald Freeman, Isaac Moore, Ernest Allen, Jr., Carroll Holmes, Kenn M. Freeman, and Bobb Hamilton, who was also listed as the "east coast representative." The young editors identified themselves as revolutionaries, working out of "berkeley, calif. (racist u.s.a.)." Their magazine would be "the quarterly journal of revolutionary afroamerica." Their dream, as mentioned in the opening editorial, was "a radical socio-economic transformation within the United States" and the consequent liberation of black peoples everywhere. The editors dedicated their first issue to the "child-martyrs" of the Birmingham church bombing, to Medgar Evers, to Patrice Lamumba, and to other "Black Freedom Fighters who have been gunned down by the imperialist oppressors in Afroamerica, Africa, Latin America and Asia." [51]

Intended as a quarterly, *Soulbook* appeared only nine times from 1964 to 1972 and irregularly thereafter. The seventh issue, published in the summer of 1969, showed a change in management. As the masthead indicated, the original board had disappeared, with Mamadou Lumumba becoming editor-in-chief and Bobb Hamilton becoming senior editor. The 1972 number was pivotal, indicating a new and exclusively political orientation for the journal. It was fifteen pages long, which was less than a fourth the size of previous issues, and it featured three political articles, excluding all creative literature.

Until the 1972 *Soulbook*, about one quarter of each number had been devoted to literature, especially poetry, and the rest to political discussions. The journal published the same black writers who appeared in the other black little magazines, including Marvin Jackman, LeRoi Jones, Clarence Major, Sonia Sanchez, and Askia Toure. These writers liked to talk about *Soulbook*, but they did not send it their best poems, stories, and essays. Thus, none of the creative inclusions was particularly influential or memorable.

The editorial statements, especially those by Bobb Hamilton, made a greater impact, largely because of their anger and harshness. The second issue of the magazine, released in the spring of 1965, indicated the importance of Hamilton, along with one other editor: "Only the articles by Bobb Hamilton and Kenn M. Freeman necessarily represent the views of the Editorial Board of *Soulbook*." [52] The same number suggested that Hamilton's was the dominant voice, as it included three articles by him and one by Freeman. The most significant of the essays came in his debate with Langston Hughes over LeRoi Jones's *The Toilet*—"is it a masterpiece, or is it trash?"

Hughes considered the play to be trash spilling over with "bad language, obscenities of the foulest sort, and basic filth." Punning on the title, he characterized the effort as "pure manure" and "verbal excrement." As an integrationist, Hughes disagreed with the politics of the drama. "What all this does for race relations (as if it mattered at this late date) I do not know," he declared. He ended prayerfully: "God help us all!" [53]

Hamilton quickly labeled Hughes an "old head," just as Hughes and former associates had designated the critics of *Fire*. He dismissed him with epithets, calling him "Unca" Hughes, and one of the "house niggers," "prissy puritans," and "left-over Lazaruses." He applauded Jones's imagery and claimed nothing else could emerge from "this crappy society": "If LeRoi spouts verbal excrement, consider the fact that this culture is mired in manure, and that the role of the artist is to hold up a lens so that his society might better see itself." "'Racistly' yours," Hamilton ended his "Reply." [54]

In his various contributions to the magazine, Hamilton advanced radical heroes, such as Malcolm X, and derided anyone associated with the mainstream. He satirized the head of the NAACP in "A Letter to

Boy Wilkins": "You live in that / Piss-puddle / That the white folks / Told you to call, / 'The Mainstream.' " [55] Hamilton represented *Soulbook*, and Hamilton showed that the periodical had indeed burned its bridges to the past. In so doing, it became one of the most controversial journals on the contemporary scene, and it stimulated the development of other similar magazines.

Black Dialogue, the second of the California little magazines to materialize, emerged from a rivalry its supporters had with the editors of *Soulbook*. In the fall of 1964, black students at San Francisco State founded their own campus organization and decided that one of its primary objectives would be the creation of a revolutionary little magazine. Many of the students disagreed with some of Bobb Hamilton's and Kenn Freeman's understandings of black journals. Wanting a periodical which could serve a wide variety of opinions, they labeled their own effort "Black Dialogue" in an attempt to provide a forum for open discussion of literary and political questions. They secured the following staff, which released the first issue of *Black Dialogue* in the spring of 1965: Arthur A. Sheridan as editor; Abdul Karim (Gerald Labrie), as managing editor; Edward S. Spriggs as New York editor; Joseph Seward as African editor; Aubrey Labrie as political editor; Marvin Jackman as fiction editor; and Joe Goncalves as poetry editor. Goncalves was the only one of this group to have had editorial experience, and he consequently devoted long hours to production and distribution of the magazine.

The initial three issues of *Black Dialogue* established a format which continued for the duration of the journal's publication. After a lead editorial, an article would follow which focused on a literary-political matter, as in the opening number with LeRoi Jones's "The Revolutionary Theatre" or in succeeding issues with contributions from other influential figures, such as Larry Neal and playwright Ed Bullins. The third installment of the journal, released in the winter of 1966, captured well the enthusiasm and emerging focus of the publication. Its editorial and one of the essays were directed specifically toward the evolving black aesthetic. In his article, "Revolutionary Black Artist," James T. Stewart detailed the editorial call for a "new direction" in black writing based on "a thorough assessment of our cultural heritage and our present position" in American society. He answered affirmatively to the rhetorical question he had posed: "Can the black revolutionary artist rid himself of the oppressive aesthetics of the white society in this country?" The rest of the number featured creative work consonant with Stewart's conclusion, that a new black literature must unfold from the "very rockbed of the Negro experience." [56] Poems, short stories, a one act play, and an "open letter" to black women—"My Queen, I Greet You," by Eldridge Cleaver—reflected the editorial staff's effort to meet the outlook presented by Stewart.

Published in the winter of 1967–68, the sixth issue of *Black Dialogue* contained a strong reminder of the premise upon which the magazine had been founded. A staff reorganization had occurred in 1967, and Abdul Karim emerged as editor of the journal with Spriggs, Goncalves, and Askia Toure as associate editors. Toure, despite his displeasure over the concentration of black artistic happenings in the West, arrived in California one year later to become an instructor in the black studies department of San Francisco State, where LeRoi Jones taught in 1967. Prior to his move, Toure had inaugurated his involvement with *Black Dialogue* by urging inclusion of his "Letter to Ed Spriggs: Concerning LeRoi Jones and Others" in the sixth number. The letter was printed, but only after heated debate among members of the editorial board. "He has been approached by brother Abdul and others to modify some of the more caustic remarks of the text," Toure revealed, speaking of himself in third person. He refused to alter the letter, even though he had written it prior to the "Newark Rebellion" and had since become concerned over the safety of Jones, who had been arrested: "When it comes to the attacks of the Beast, the bourgies, or other nigger-lackeys, I will defend 'Roi with my life if necessary. However, between us nationalists, I believe these words should be spoken."

Toure emerged as one of the few revolutionary blacks who would challenge Jones. In sharply worded statements, he accused the writer of "Reactionary Super-Blackism, a dogmatic nihilism—in Black literature as well as politics. . . ." Using *Slave Ship* as an example of Jones's work, he faulted the man for his antiwhite bias and for a failure to develop positive perceptions of Afro-American culture. He also stressed the need for "internal self-criticism" among black writers and advocated a "militant, iconoclastic criticism that would be directed toward the 'sacred cows' within our group." [57]

Over a year and a half passed before *Black Dialogue* surfaced again. When it did appear in the spring of 1969, the journal bore a New York City address. In the months following the last publication, the supporters of the magazine had dwindled to Edward Spriggs. Hoping to revitalize the enterprise, he had moved it East and had attempted to involve other writers in the effort. As indicated on the masthead of the 1969 issue, the journal had an editorial board consisting of Spriggs, Nikki Giovanni, Jaci Earley, Elaine Jones, Sam Anderson, and James Hinton, in addition to a group of regional editors, including Joe Goncalves for the West Coast, Ahmed Alhamisi and Carolyn Rodgers for the Midwest, Julia Fields and A. B. Spellman for the South, and Ted Jones and K. W. Kgositsile for Africa.

"Our determination," the editors declared in the 1969 issue, "is still Black. Our printer is still Black. We are still distributed and sold (where possible) Black. *Black Dialogue* remains 'a meeting place for the voices of the Black community—wherever that community may exist.' " With the same number, they accordingly tried to mediate among differing perceptions of Afro-American politics. The lead editorial called for an end to the hostility between the Black Panther Party and Ron Karenga's U.S. organization and urged reconciliation between the two groups.[58] The number, like its predecessors, did not succeed as a "meeting place," as Carolyn Gerald indicated when characterizing the journal as being less consistent in tone and format and less militant than was *Soulbook*.[59] Without strong support for the magazine, Spriggs could not sustain the publication. In 1970, he produced the last issue of *Black Dialogue*.

Journal of Black Poetry emerged from the foundation established by *Black Dialogue* and *Soulbook*. Joe Goncalves, editor of the *Journal*, traced its lineage: "First came *Soulbook*, then *Dialogue*, and then the Journal. That is important because the Journal in many ways was born of *Soulbook* and *Dialogue*." [60] The *Journal* came right on the heels of its forerunners, the first number issued in San Francisco during the spring of 1966. "Published for all black people everywhere," as stated on the table of contents for each number, the magazine originated and, unlike the others, continued as a quarterly.

The *Journal* involved many of the same persons connected with the other California magazines. In the spring of 1967, Goncalves secured Clarence Major, Marvin Jackman, and LeRoi Jones as contributing editors. He brought Larry Neal to the group in the summer of 1967, just months after Neal had left *Liberator*. The only contributing editor to resign from the journal was Clarence Major, whose place was taken by Ernie Mkalimota. Goncalves secured, as well, the services of Ed Spriggs and Ahmed Alhamisi as corresponding editors, and Ed Bullins and Askia Toure as editors-at-large. He also appointed guest editors, who selected all the materials for special issues. They included, among others, Major, Alhamisi, Spriggs, Don Lee, and Dudley Randall.

Goncalves kept his editorial staff through the demise of the *Journal*, in the summer of 1973, and into the beginning of a new magazine. Published in San Francisco and edited by Goncalves, *Kitabu Cha Jua*, meaning "book of the sun," emerged in the summer of 1974. Like the

Journal, it was "for all Black People everywhere." "When possible," it would appear as a quarterly.[61] The qualification, which had not been seen on the masthead of the *Journal,* was necessary. Funding has been more difficult to obtain in the 1970s than it was in the 1960s. *Kitabu Cha Jua* has, as a result, been an irregular publication, with the most recent issue having appeared in 1975. The magazine has published many of the poets included in the *Journal,* but it is a child of the times. It talks about the decline of black nationalism and it lacks the exuberance of the *Journal. Kitabu Cha Jua* is not, then, a mere reappearance of the *Journal* under a different name.

Joe Goncalves assumed his most outspoken stance in the *Journal of Black Poetry.* In editorial comments, he mentioned his heroes, all of them among the most forceful and blunt of black speakers. He identified Marcus Garvey as "perhaps the greatest black man who ever lived." Malcolm X was also high on his list. "If you want to grasp the importance of Malcolm," he instructed his readers, "compare the late writings of Sonia Sanchez or Imamu Baraka with their early, pre-Malcolm works." [62]

Goncalves's prose could be as hard-hitting as the poetry of Sanchez. The Summer-Fall 1969 issue affords a good example of Goncalves at work, as it featured his interview with Ishmael Reed. In fielding queries, Reed had been so lengthy in his responses that Goncalves could not add his views. He consequently appended his "Afterword" to the printed interview.

As the interview shows, Reed was one of the few young writers who dared attack the black arts movement. He labeled the black aesthetic as "a goon squad aesthetic," and he described the leaders of the movement as "fascists" "flying around the country in . . . dashiki[s] talking about" what black writers were supposed to do and doing very little. Malcolm X, he proferred, would not have sanctioned such actions because he was, in his last days, "a universalist, a humanist, a global man." "This tribalism is for the birds," Reed concluded.[63]

Goncalves thought Reed had gone white and thus could not see how "whitenized" other cultures had become. Reed, he declared, had published in white magazines—"always serving some white man's purpose"—and had been attracted to white women—"Reed, drunk, sniffing white girls, dependent, lays [*sic*] dead about the white man's fort." [64]

After reading *Dynamite Voices,* Gonclaves feared for Don Lee as well. He criticized both book and author soundly in the last issue of the *Journal,* even though Lee had been a frequent and desirable contributor to the magazine previously. Lee, he asserted, had "white problems," and *Dynamite Voices* "is ultimately a restatement of the white aesthetic." He faulted the writer on several counts: for quoting from a "white nationalist," T. S. Eliot; for having a full-page advertisement for *Dynamite Voices* in *Poetry* of Chicago; and for appearing in anthologies of black poetry coming off white presses. "Talk about creative prostitution!" Goncalves exclaimed, using an image he favored when denouncing blacks for supposedly white ways. He criticized Lee once more for comparing the *Journal* to *Poetry*, which Goncalves considered a "mournful . . . activity." Giving a definition of his own periodical, he explained: "The Journal, despite its name is not a 'poetry' magazine. It is a means of communication, and poetry is one of the ways we communicate."[65]

The use of poetry as a primary means of communication was borne out by the flood of contributions that came in from the young writers published in all the other contemporary black little magazines. Despite a general consistency in the tone and emphasis of the creative offerings, a minority of the poems were somewhat diversified in subject and style. Clarence Major, for example, celebrated the existence of a three-year-old girl in "My Child." Only her curls, "like black sparkling things," suggested her racial identity. "My Child" stands out among the other poems because of its quiet, precise statement. The pieces usually rendered in the *Journal* spoke in loud tones of racial matters. Sonia Sanchez represents the emphasis in "on seeing pharoah sanders blowing," a writing which rejoices in the destruction of the United States:

> it's black/music/magic
> u hear. yeah. i'm fucking
> u white whore.
> america. while
> i slit your honkey throat.[66]

The essays, including editorials, were another primary means for communication in the *Journal*. The most influential essayist was Baraka, who made an impact on his peers with two particular contributions. It was in "Statement" that he urged his contemporaries to be "missionaries of Blackness." He popularized some of the imagery characteristic of the black arts movement with "The Fire Must Be Permitted to Burn Full Up," a piece recalling the foreword to *Fire* of the 1920s. "The fire is hot," Baraka chanted; "Let it burn more brightly. Let it light up all creation. . . . Let the fire burn higher, and the heat rage outta sight." As "firemakers," black writers were destroyers and creators, he concluded: "Ahhhh man, consider 200,-000,000 people, feed and clothe them, in the beauty of god. That is where its at. And yeh, man, do it well. Incredibly Well." [67]

Larry Neal, in his 1976 discussion of the black arts movements, called the *Journal of Black Poetry* "the first and most important" of the West Coast little magazines.[68] The *Journal* was not the first to emerge, but it was the "most important" of the three publications. It appeared regularly, unlike the others, and it lasted longer. Since the periodical did not include political articles, it could provide a greater outlet for the young writers. It consequently gained the endorsement of *Negro Digest*. "The *Journal of Black Poetry* should receive," declared Hoyt Fuller, "the immediate and enthusiastic support of everyone who loves poetry and is concerned about supporting black writers." The *Journal* made a place for itself in the black arts movement. That place was not, however, so significant as the one occupied by *Negro Digest*, viewed by Neal as the magazine having "had the most consistent effect on contemporary black letters." [69]

Participants in the movement thought *Negro Digest* an "exception," to adopt Carolyn Gerald's expression. Compared to the other small black journals, it had more tangible marks of outward success: a longer history, a larger circulation and readership. At the same time, it functioned as a revolutionary periodical. Before the other magazines had even been conceived, Gerald noted, *Negro Digest* "began considering the nationalist alternative." It continued in the same vein, publishing the most radical writers of the decade. *Negro Digest* started as a copy of *Reader's Digest* but emerged as a pacesetting little magazine. Hoyt Fuller once noted that the publication "certainly qualifies as a 'little' magazine in terms of its efforts at seeking out and publishing the creative work of talented Negro writers." [70]

Through his work with *Negro Digest*, Hoyt Fuller emerged as the most influential editor of a contemporary black journal. He drew testimonials accordingly from writers familiar with periodicals of the day. Don Lee, for one, asserted that "the extraordinary editorship" of Hoyt Fuller brought *Negro Digest* to "the vanguard in terms of publishing black writing." Loften Mitchell highlighted Fuller when stressing the significance of black magazine editors in general. "I suspect very strongly," he predicted, "that in the very near future someone is going to declare that Hoyt Fuller and other black editors 'mid-wifed' the present Black Renaissance." Larry Neal credited Fuller for stimulating the discussion over the black aesthetic which flourished in the 1960s and persisted into the 1970s.[71] Given this interpretation, it is appropriate that Addison Gayle began his edition of *The Black Aesthetic* with Fuller's essay entitled, "Towards the Black Aesthetic."

It took some years for Fuller to move toward the black aesthetic. As his ideas evolved, so did the black arts movement. Fuller's development into a spokesperson for the movement deserves brief examination, then, since it tells much about the period. Having directed his magazine into the mainstream in the early 1960s, Fuller began in 1964 to introduce a new militancy into his basically integrationist approach. From the very title of his essay published in the June issue, "Ivory Towerist vs. Activist: The Role of the Negro Writer in an Era of Struggle," he emphasized the inseparable connection he had come to see between politics and the black arts. Like many of his colleagues at that time, he advanced James Baldwin as a model for the young writer, since Baldwin had involved himself in the civil rights movement. He furthered his objections to the isolated artist by publishing "A Poet Apologizes to His Critics," a poem by Zack Gilbert included in the same issue. Gilbert pledged to sing of Birmingham, Little Rock, and "Ole Miss," even though his detractors would claim, "It's crude." The concluding couplet advocated, in so many words, art-for-people's sake: "Forgive me critics then if I should cry aloud; / Sing out with gusto, join the artless crowd." [72]

The September issue continued in the integrationist mold, although it did show Fuller moving toward a position that would become prominent in years following. In an essay highlighted in this number, "The Negro Writer in the U.S.: Assembly at Asilomar," he summarized meetings at a recent writers conference and provided photographs of the participants. Along with black authors, including Gwendolyn Brooks, Ossie Davis, and Baraka, he pictured several white critics, such as Robert Bone, Herbert Hill, Kenneth Rexroth, and Harvey Swados. He never again featured pictures of white writers in *Negro Digest*. Nor did he let Bone off again with mere passing commentary as: "Prof. Bone delivered a scathing attack on novelist James Baldwin." [73] The only criticism of the scholar was implicit, couched in the word, "scathing."

For the rest of the decade, Fuller thundered away at Bone. His statements, extreme as they might have seemed to some readers, represented the opinions of his colleagues and traced, thereby, the descending curve of Bone's reputation among writers of the black aesthetic. Fuller saw the critic as an intruder into territories about which he knew nothing and for which he had not even a map. As a white man, he could not understand black literature, according to Fuller. The proof, explained the editor, was that Bone kept advising black writers to forget about function or politics and to concentrate on form or art. Fuller tried to wither Bone with such epithets as: "the good 'expert' on Negroes and Negro literature," "author of the 'authoritative' *The Negro Novel in America*" and, especially, "the Great White Father of Negro Literature." He directed similar labels to other whites, most notably Richard Gilman and Louis Simpson, who tried to criticize black literature. "Playing politics with black poetry is a dangerous game," he warned them.[74]

While Fuller scattered his comments on several fronts, he concentrated his verbal attacks on influential writers who seemingly represented misguided approaches to black literature. Bone became the model of the white critic as colonialist or intruder into enemy territory. Ralph Ellison emerged in *Negro Digest* as a type of traitor, as the sort of black man who would not pay his debt to his own culture. Fuller's repetitive criticism of Ellison, which continued throughout the decade, began in 1965, or one year before Neal published similar opinions of Ellison in *Liberator*. Appearing as early as they did, Fuller's comments helped solidify a growing reaction among revolutionary black writers against Ellison. The negative appraisal came "not because of anything" Ellison wrote in *Shadow and Act* or *Invisible Man*, but because of what he said to white audiences, and Fuller emphasized the word white. On the lecture circuit, Ellison chastized revolutionary black writers for placing politics before art, or in place of art. Fuller responded by scoring Ellison for "his above-it-all pose relative to the racial conflict" and by labeling him a mainstream writer and a universalist—"No need to feel responsible for the degradation of Negroes. It's just the way life is. Universal, you know." [75]

The irony vanished when he considered Baraka. He began to endorse the increasingly controversial writer with scattered commentary in 1965, a few months before Neal published his influential articles on the same subject in *Liberator*. In the process, Fuller showed that he had reached a more outspoken radicalism than he had ever revealed before in the magazine. When describing the Black Arts Repertory Theatre/School, he asserted that Baraka "is doing what Negro *playwrights absolutely must do* if they are to survive and grow and give voice to the anguish and hopes and joy of Negro people." The statement most revealing of Fuller's evolution came when he posed two alternatives: "Negro playwrights must break free or else follow the route of degradation. Black nationalism? Race hatred?— Well, call it what you will." [76] Fuller underscored his own choice by publishing several of Baraka's works, including *Slave Ship*, a "historical pageant" similar in tone and idea to *The Beast*, and "In Search of the Revolutionary Theatre," an essay very like the one on the black theater Baraka contributed to *Black Dialogue* and *Liberator*.

As Fuller became increasingly radicalized, he began to explore new definitions of black writing. He furthered his effort by polling Afro-American authors on various questions relating to black literature. The results appeared in two symposiums, one published in April 1965 and one in January 1968. Larry Neal credited the second symposium with exciting the conversations over the black aesthetic.[77] Of the two, the second did encourage more discussion, partly because it came at the height of the black arts movement and partly because it was more structured than the first collection of opinions. By 1968, Fuller was surer of his new ideas than he had been, and he understood better how to express them within the confines of a survey. The first symposium is significant, nevertheless, in that it initiated early considerations of the black aesthetic and laid a basis for the second gathering of opinions in 1968.

The initial symposium showed that Fuller was not always the black nationalist he appeared to be when discussing Baraka in 1965. As indicated in prefatory remarks, he had polled thirty-six writers who were "famous and relatively unknown, black and white." At the time, he still felt that the opinions of some whites were worth consideration. The question embodied a preoccupation central to Fuller's thought by mid-decade: "What is the task of the Negro writer concerned with creating a work of art in a segregated society and how does his task differ from that of the white writer—if it differs at all?" [78]

Several of the authors surveyed described black literature as a weapon for revolution, as did Baraka, John Killens, and Ossie Davis who wrote that the black writer "must make of himself a hammer, and against the racially restricted walls of that society he must strike, and strike, and strike again, until something is destroyed—either himself—or the prison walls that stifle him!" Others, including William Demby, William Kelley, and Frank Yerby, stated that black writing should not be used as a political or propagandistic tool. In a time of freedom marches and sit-in demonstrations, Demby saw the Afro-American author as "free from the need to make propaganda, free from the need to protest, free from the need to dramatize sociological theses." Still another, Langston Hughes, reaffirmed the need for a literature of propaganda, saying that his colleagues had to offset by their own work the negative pictures of blacks he believed fostered by the revolutionary writers. He criticized "the graffiti" of

The Toilet and "the deathly behavior" of a *Slow Dance On the Killing Ground*, both by Baraka, and he asserted that "the Negro image deserves objective well-rounded (rather than one-sided) treatment, particularly in the decade of a tremendous freedom movement in which all of us can take pride." A clash between the older and younger generations showed clearly in the contrasting statements of Hughes and Baraka, which were published side by side on one page. Baraka, who took no pride in the civil rights movement, claimed that "the Black Artist must draw out of his soul the correct image of the world" and that "the Black Artist must teach the white eyes their deaths. . . ." A further contrast appeared between white and revolutionary black critics. Harvey Swados, representing the first group, prefaced his response with a cautionary statement. "It would be presumptuous," he declared, "for any white writer to offer gratuitous advice to any Negro writer." [79] He went on and offered the advice anyway, observing that the first responsibility of a black author was to himself and his own artistic needs rather than to society.

Harvey Swados did not surface in the second symposium, nor did any other white critic. By 1968, Fuller had shaped a consistent image of himself as a cultural revolutionary. When he polled authors, then, he selected thirty-eight who were both "famous and unknown," as with the 1965 survey, but he chose only black writers. Having considered Afro-American literature at greater length than he had by 1965, Fuller was able to direct twenty-five queries to his sampling of writers. Most of the questions were not obviously political, as they asked for the identity of the three greatest writers of all time, the three most important white writers, the three most important black writers, and, with other queries, the most promising of young black writers. Among the last questions, a few dealt specifically with the black aesthetic:

19. Do you see any future at all for the school of black writers which seeks to establish 'a black aesthetic?'
20. Do you believe that the black writer's journey toward 'Art' should lead consciously and deliberately through exploitation of 'the black experience?'
25. Should black writers direct their work toward black audiences? [80]

Such questions were the most difficult to answer for some respondents, for they challenged writers either to identify with the black arts movement or to disassociate themselves from it and expose themselves to the charge of being reactionary.

Fuller declared his own position, as he had not in the 1965 symposium. In an extended prefatory statement, he boiled down the twenty-five questions to one rhetorical query: "The essential question, it would seem, is this: Are not black people in America systematically and literally murdered and degraded by white racism, and are not rage and bitterness and hatred perfectly natural and legitimate responses to this murder and degradation?" He stated, moreover, that black writers were seeking a black aesthetic since the white aesthetic, as he described it, had been imposed upon them to their detriment.[81]

The results of the survey were not as revolutionary as Fuller might have anticipated or desired. In the "greatest writer of all times" category, William Shakespeare topped the list, with Dostoevsky and W. E. B. Du Bois coming in a close second and third. As the most important black writer ever, "more than half" selected Richard Wright, which could have been expected. The second choice was Langston Hughes, who had a few more votes than the "evenly matched" James Baldwin and Ralph Ellison, the latter of whom would not respond to Fuller's surveys. Having scored well in the greatest writer area, Du Bois fell behind Baldwin and Ellison in the black writer listings. Baraka emerged as the "most promising" black author, but he "edged out" John A. Williams by only one vote.[82]

Commenting on the diverse responses among the writers surveyed, Fuller explained that many Afro-Americans did not like progress towards "Black Consciousness" because it seemed to them a simultaneous turn to segregation. Persons who were not involved in the black arts movemenet were critical, or as Fuller stated, "less sympathetic" regarding the twenty-five queries. Generally, the most outspoken of the critics were older than the other responders, despite Fuller's disclaimer that "angle of vision" rather than age accounted for the wide differences in commentary.[83] Feeling secure in their own careers and identities, they could speak their opinions freely. Saunders Redding replied "No" to question nineteen and stated that "aesthetics has no racial, national or geographical boundaries." Becoming impatient with the queries, he burst out: "Again, you're asking for absolutes, and, damn it, in this business there are no absolutes, except in a negative sense." Robert Hayden was of like mind. He, too, answered negatively to question nineteen, observing that a black aesthetic would be feasible only in a "predominantly black culture," which the United States was not. He considered the black aesthetic to be merely a new form of "racist propaganda," and he noted that Baraka, for all his power as a writer, was a spokesperson for "black nazism," an expression "I deplore," he added. In essence, Hayden staked out a universalist position. "Segregation in any form is stultifying," he declared. "Let us direct our work toward human beings."[84]

A majority of the writers espoused varying definitions of the black aesthetic, as did Gwendolyn Brooks, Julia Fields, Don Lee, and Larry Neal. The most extensive response came from Neal, who contributed a four-page essay on the black aesthetic. As the most protracted statement, being two or three times longer than the others, the Neal essay dominated the symposium and, in so doing, stressed the literary-political stance of *Negro Digest*. Neal wrote partly in an incantatory style, probably because he was not defining but celebrating the generally understood tenets of a movement: "Kill the Beast of a fetid literary tradition. Blow them away. Open up. Link up with the struggle. . . . Your own magazines and journals. Your own films and playhouses. Your own critique." [85]

By 1968, *Negro Digest* was clearly a revolutionary magazine. As such, its purpose clashed with its name, since "Black" had replaced "Negro" in the vocabulary of the new writers. The title of the magazine, which offended many, remained intact until May 1970, when it was replaced by *Black World*. With a statement published in the March 1970 issue, Fuller announced that the change would reflect the spirit of the journal, which differed considerably from that of the 1940s series. "The new magazine," he noted, "sought to reflect the new black spirit wafting gingerly across the land and to provide it room in which to expand and mature." During the decade, that tentative "black spirit" had "fomented a full-fledged revolt, and Black Consciousness flashed like lightning into every corner of America." To those who had wondered about the name of the journal, Fuller offered no explanation, stating merely that "the moment has come to do the bidding of the magazine's friends." Supporters of the periodical welcomed the step, which they had promoted for the past several years. "We thank you," Don Lee wrote to Fuller, "not just because it's of a positive nature or an ultimate objective . . . but because we feel that the decision to do that will force questions from those who don't traditionally question; therefore, it will also force answers— right or wrong, the new name, *Black World*, will force answers." [86]

Black World came tardily, for the name marked not the height but the waning of original emphases in the black arts movement. The movement itself continued, but participants sought for new directions as they became increasingly disenchanted with nationalism and revolution and the accompanying focus on separatism. This change was not immediately apparent, as the 1970s ushered in a host of black little magazines, including *African Progress*, *Black Review*, *Black Lines*,

Focus in Black, Proud Black Images and, among many others, *Wakra*
("Have you awakened?"). Developed in the mold of their immediate
predecessors, the new magazines generally rejected cultural integration. For example, Mel Watkins, editor of *Black Review*, informed
his readers in the journal's first number that the broadening "hiatus
between American rhetoric and deeds" had "exposed as a cul-de-sac"
"the traditional quest for integration—which has meant the eradica-
tion of one's blackness." [87] *Black World*, as it unfolded issue by issue,
showed the mood underlying the ostensible flurry of journalistic
activity and renewed enthusiasm. It traced and illustrated in its own
course the ending of a period in Afro-American literature.

Poems and reports first suggested a shift in the climate. In "Did
I Dream Them Times? Or What Happened?" a short poem included
in the May 1972 issue of *Black World*, Jo-Ann Kelly observed that
"Everybody talkin bout / What happened to the Revolution / And
the 'mean-bad-militant-children of the Sixties' / . . . Who let 'they-
hair' grow." Considerable talking about the sixties took place at the
first National Annual Conference of Afro-American Writers at
Howard University in November 1974. As Carol Parks reported in
Black World, many of the participants declared, in one way or another,
that the decade was nothing but "jive." Askia Toure upheld the
record of the decade and credited *Soulbook, Black Dialogue,* and
the *Journal of Black Poetry* as the main organs of the black arts movement. Like others, he saw division and confusion in the present decade.
He directed his criticism at Baraka, who he believed had separated
art from politics by talking about cultural nationalism. Continuing
his rivalry with Baraka, he followed up his commentary by saying
there had been "no father or prophet" of the movement. A young
man who introduced himself as a member of the Congress of Afrikan
People, an organization numbering Baraka among its members, stood
up at the conference and asked Toure to identify the person to
whom he was alluding. Toure immediately shot back: "Imamu Amiri
Baraka." [88]

A transformation in Baraka's thought was the most dramatic sign
that the cultural revolution initiated in the 1960s was ebbing. Questioned frequently about his recent conversion, Baraka chose to explain his views in *Black World* with an essay entitled, " 'Why I
Changed My Ideology': Black Nationalism and Socialist Revolution."
In the article, he identified the Congress of Afrikan People as "a
revolutionary communist organization" and as a black group, "which
makes it a revolutionary nationalist organization." He showed himself to be a Marxist, declaring that the real enemy of the people was

not white colonialism but capitalism. From history, especially from reading Du Bois, he had learned that capitalism fostered the slave trade and the development of a bourgeoisie, comprised not only of whites but also of "Black bureaucrats, with Mercedes Benzes, afros, hip sideburns, Cardin suits, humpback high heels, Lincolns. . . ." The bourgeoisie had oppressed workers of all backgrounds, including the white. A reoriented Baraka asserted that "it is fantasy to think that we can struggle for our own liberation and be completely oblivious to all the other struggling and oppressed people in this land. Or throughout the world for that matter."

Baraka faulted black nationalists, including himself in earlier years, for an indiscriminate emphasis on Africa, for trying "to impose continental Afrikan mores and customs, some out of precapitalist feudalist Afrika, upon Black people living in North America, whose culture actually is that of Afrikans living in America for three centuries, Afro-American." He criticized them, too, for attempting to reject everything white. Baraka advised his contemporaries that they could profit from studying Marx, Lenin, and Engels, even though they were Europeans. After all, he interjected, the most militant blacks still used the telephone, an invention of the white Alexander Graham Bell. With the last three lines of the essay, all stated as slogans, Baraka summarized his new position: "Victory to Black people! Victory to the strugglers! Victory to all oppressed people!" [89]

Succeeding issues of *Black World* underlined the alteration in black literature and politics. Nathan Hare, former editor of *Black Scholar*, contributed "Division and Confusion: What Happened To The Black Movement" to the January 1976 issue. He claimed that the focus on Africa had been extreme, even "pathological," and that the emphases of the 1960s had been more form than substance: "We soon arrived at an ultra-nationalism that was mystical, messianic and hence dysfunctional. Our symbols, our dashikis (where, oh where, did they go?) and our bushy Afros became Black badges of militancy which required no acting out or actualizing." The movement, he explained, had lacked a viable combination of race and class struggles. As had Baraka, he praised Marx, describing him as "probably the most creative social scientist the world has yet projected and, regardless of what a narrow-minded Black nationalist might proclaim, his white skin alone should not prevent us from learning from him, if possible." Hare saw his contemporaries going from Marxism to integrationism once again, and thus he advanced a cyclical view of Afro-American literature and politics: "We have a cycle—integrationism, then nationalism, then Marxism, then integrationism again." [90]

The last issue of *Black World,* dated February 1976, included a transcript of Richard Long's interview with George Schuyler, then eighty-one years old. During the conversation, Schuyler glanced briefly at contemporary Afro-American literature and dubbed much of the poetry "crap" and many of the novels "dribble." The charge went unanswered in *Black World.* In the mid-1970s, Fuller featured writers who criticized the 1960s and tried to analyze the mood of the new decade, but he generally held back his own opinions on the subject. An occasional statement showed that he no longer saw the world in simple terms of black versus white and that he, along with the others, was groping for fresh understandings. "It is sadly ironic that, on every front," he noted in the November 1975 issue, "the state of well-being of ordinary Black people diminishes at the same time as the number of BEO's [black elected officials] increases." [91] Such a comment heralded the end of *Black World.* As nationalism diminished among black writers, and as the revolutionary fervor subsided, there was no longer a vital need or solid support for *Black World* and the other radical black magazines.

They either expired or entered a phase of irregular appearance by commenting on the decade passed and the promises not met. The March 1971 editorial of *Liberator* provided one of the more memorable statements. Entitled "Slogan's End" and occupying one page, it pictured, in cartoon form, a billboard advertisement for "ATCO supreme gasoline" which read: "ALL POWER TO THE PEOPLE!" Shown standing before the billboard, one white hippie declared to another that "I guess it was bound to happen . . . sooner or later. . . ." [92] The summer 1975 number of *Kitabu Cha Jua* featured two pieces by Baraka which paralleled the comments given in his essay for the July 1975 issue of *Black World.* In "A New Reality Is Better Than a New Movie!" a one-page statement, he used biting satire to propagandize "the new socialist reality." He employed the same technique in "Today," a poem ridiculing "reactionary middle class idealists": "Where is the revolution brothers & sisters? / Where is the mobilization of the masses led / by the advanced section of the working class?" The same issue of *Kitabu Cha Jua* included Aubrey Labrie's essay, "The Decline of Black Nationalism & What Can Be Done About It," and thereby underscored the differences among contemporary black writers. Labrie would not endorse Marxism, nor would he, as the title indicates, accept passively any fading of revolutionary ideas. Instead, he advocated a separatism somewhat along the lines of that advanced by Du Bois in the 1930s: "We must begin the exceedingly difficult and painstaking task of creating and maintaining distinct, compatible and independent institutions. Primary emphasis should be placed on economic and educational institutions." [93]

Several factors contributed to the "decline of black nationalism" and the black little magazines endorsing nationalism and cultural separatism. Money problems came high on the list of the primary causes. Very few of the journals included discussions of their financial difficulties, probably in part because straitened budgets were endemic to little magazines and were not considered worthy of public consideration. *Black Creation,* a journal founded on the New York University campus and edited by Fred Beauford, was an exception in its frankness about money, as related to its own production and the larger picture of the black arts. Established in 1970 as a quarterly, *Black Creation* made its last appearance as an annual in 1974–75: "Due to financial exigencies that face all publications today, we have become an annual." [94] The issue included "Arts Organizations in the Deep South," a report by Tom Dent, formerly editor of *Umbra.* Dent noted that the mid-1970s was not a period of expansion but of retrenchment, of holding on "if only in memory" to the work accomplished in the previous decade. "Most of the recent movement towards Black community cultural organizations" in the South and throughout the nation "has come to a halt now," he observed. "The same factors," he went on, were responsible for "this dismal period." More specifically, the federal government and private foundations had withdrawn "almost all" of the money and other support given to creative programs, including magazines, in black communities. Thus, the artist and organizer suffered as "the accumulation of personal and economic pressures" caused them to accept positions more rewarding financially if not personally.[95] Dent did not so explain, but the national recession and a disenchantment with activities seen as separatist caused public and private agencies to forego such involvements.

Changes in leadership further undermined black nationalism and cultural separatism. Baraka, former prophet of the black aesthetic, brought confusion to the black arts movement and its magazines as he turned toward Marxism and as he used revolutionary black periodicals to help publicize his newly adopted ideology. Other leaders, one of the most notable of whom was Larry Neal, added to the disorder as they too accepted other views of literature and politics. In "The Black Contribution to American Letters," published in 1976, Neal criticized Addison Gayle, Ron Karenga, and Don Lee, saying that their ideas about literature made sense "only on the level of emotional rhetoric." He still felt that the black writer's difficulties lay in a confusion about function and form, but he interpreted the problem differently than he had in the old *Liberator* days. He had come to believe in the importance, even the primacy, of form, and to substantiate his views he quoted from Kenneth Burke, a white critic whom he formerly would have denounced. "When the appeal of art as method is eliminated and the appeal of art as experience is stressed," Burke had commented in *Counter-Statement*, "art seems futile indeed. Experience is less the *aim* of art than the *subject* of art; art is not *experience*, but something added to experience." If art and experience were identical, Neal explained, there would be no reason for art. "In other words," he postulated, "if a man can make real physical love to a woman, what's the sense in writing a love poem?" Artistic methods or techniques were significant, then, because they ordered experience and thus made possible new understandings. Neal had radically altered his definition of the function of the arts, as one statement particularly illustrates: "Literature can indeed make excellent propaganda, but through propaganda alone the black writer can never perform the highest function of his art: that of revealing to man his most enduring human possibilities and limitations." In conclusion, he asserted that the black writer, as is true of "any serious writer," must deal with the entirety of human experience, with "the accumulated weight of the world's aesthetic, intellectual, and historical experience." [96] By his comments, Neal offered universal artistic concerns in place of cultural separatism. This emphasis, along with the renewed appeal of Marxism, dimmed remaining enthusiasm for the black aesthetic.

The black arts movement might better have sustained significant losses, both in leadership and money, had it established itself on a firm and secure ideological base. It did not, however, create such a foundation, largely because participants could not achieve a consensus on the meaning of separatism, nationalism, and revolution, all expressions central to the movement. As a result, the political implications of art-for-people's sake, a slogan used as a partial definition of the black aesthetic, never became sufficiently clear.

Writers of the movement did not explicitly differentiate between art-for-people's sake and the expression popularized by Du Bois in *Crisis* of the 1920s, art for the sake of propaganda. They were not ahistorical or antihistorical, as evidenced by the many magazine articles and special issues devoted to previous literary periods, especially the renaissance of the 1920s, and authors prominent in those periods, such as Du Bois, Alain Locke, and Richard Wright. They bypassed, though, the debates over art and propaganda which had surfaced among black writers and journals in every decade of the twentieth century, and in preceding years. Occasionally Du Bois's famous expression emerged, as it did in John Killens's remarks at the 1966 writers conference at Fisk. After a few comments about Du Bois, Killens had declared that "all art is propaganda." [97] In his discussion of the conference in *Negro Digest*, David Llorens did not explain that the statement had originated with Du Bois; nor did he indicate whether Killens had expressly acknowledged his source.

Because they were not involved in the historic implications of art and propaganda, many of the young writers of the 1960s failed to credit their forebears. Some of their statements suggested that black literature had emerged full-blown in the 1960s and that it owed little debt to the past. Don Lee, for one, explained that "black literature, as we know it, is relatively new. This is not to negate the contributions of Du Bois, McKay, Wright, and other blk / literary greats, but to realize that these men were primarily addressing themselves to white audiences." [98] Considering themselves cultural revolutionaries, writers of the black aesthetic focused on the present and future, rather than on the past. They could have planned better for the future, however, had they concentrated more on the past. Specifically, they could have defined the black aesthetic in more detail if they had directly compared their theories with the aesthetic understandings of previous generations.

One other factor, perhaps the major one, discouraged the literary politics of the 1970s. Stated in general terms, the political climate of the larger society experienced a significant change. The last half of the 1960s had seen an unprecedented enlargement of the black middle class, as Fuller and Baraka noted in their disparaging commentaries. Black spokespersons appeared prominently in all areas of public concern, including the fields of education, business, and politics. The voting rights act of 1965, which was extended in subsequent years, greatly expanded the numbers of black voters by the turn of the decade, particularly in the South. The statistics on black elected officials rose concurrently, especially as black mayors emerged in big cities across the land, including Cleveland, Newark, Atlanta, Detroit, and Los Angeles. A majority among the black electorate felt a new power and sensed more than ever that it would be possible to accomplish their goals through the system, that integration was far superior to separatism as an approach to race relations in the United States. Such a feeling discouraged cultural revolutionaries in their hopes for a larger constituency. They had not been able to popularize their movement widely after the deaths of Medgar Evers, Malcolm X, and Martin Luther King, and after the urban violence of the 1960s.

Surely, they realized in the 1970s, their chances for success lessened each year as black politicians like Thomas Bradley, Kenneth Gibson, Richard Hatcher, Maynard Jackson, Carl Stokes, Percy Sutton, and Coleman Young wielded increasing power in major urban centers of the nation.

The black arts movement initiated in the 1960s encouraged nationalism among blacks who felt alienated from the cultural mainstream, but it did not foment revolution or radicalize the broader Afro-American population. The movement did, however, aid in altering the status quo. By adopting a revolutionary stance in their magazines and elsewhere, writers of the black aesthetic drew attention to the unresolved questions of racial and social caste in the nation. In the process, they advanced the civil rights movement, even though they did not support its tenets and leadership. Their extreme statements pushed many whites into accepting the positions articulated by relatively moderate blacks, such as Martin Luther King, Bayard Rustin, Roy Wilkins, and Whitney Young. Talk about "assassin poems" and "the Conquest of White Eye" made the historic black call for full civil liberties seem quite reasonable. By urging revolution, the black arts movement of the 1960s and early 1970s dramatized the need for change and helped secure some long-needed reforms.

Epilogue

More Than Mere Magazines

In comparison to journals issued by the culturally dominant groups in the United States, Afro-American magazines as a whole have been more committed to social and political expression. Throughout the twentieth century and earlier, they have provided an essential platform for black Americans and thereby articulated the needs of a minority and historically oppressed people. The editors of such publications have pursued their ends through various types of literature—scholarly articles, essays of persuasion, and creative literature in all the genres. Customarily, the large race journals have featured a sizeable amount of creative writing, while the small literary magazines highlighted political statements. Since black writers represent no monolithic body, there has always been resistance to the idea and practice of creative work used for social and political ends. Factions opposing each other over art and propaganda, as the issue came to be known, argued for their positions in the periodicals. As a result, the function of the black arts became a central theme running through the journals, as well as in black literature generally, from the beginning of the century to the present.

As conditions in the larger society evolved, so did the approaches of the magazines. At the beginning of the century, a significant number of black intellectuals and artists directed their periodicals, which carried both creative and critical work in the protest tradition, away from the compromising efforts of Booker T. Washington and into the struggle for fundamental civil liberties. The end of World War I ushered in a heady sense of freedom, and New Negroes set about developing black little magazines which talked of universal concerns in literature and which challenged both the politics and aesthetics of a previous generation. As the Depression unfolded, black periodicals renewed the protest theme, with newer Negroes bearing a fresh accent as they considered the needs of both black and white workers. The conclusion of the Second World War again encouraged universal themes, which appeared with greater prevalence in Afro-American publications than had previously been the case. The climate of the 1960s led many young writers to reject the concerns of their elders and of Western culture altogether. In the process, they took the idea of art-as-propaganda further than had any of their predecessors. They utilized their periodicals, along with other efforts, not to gain admittance into the broader society but to attempt separation from Western ways. In so doing, they captured headlines and demanded attention from the wider literary community as Afro-American creative writers had not done since the 1920s. Although significantly different in artistic and political direction, the two decades were more fertile than other periods in the twentieth century for the development of Afro-American magazines.

The most influential editor of black journals in the century reached the height of his power in the 1920s. The career of W. E. B. Du Bois stretched longer than that of any other editor of an Afro-American magazine, from the establishment of *Moon* in 1905, to *Horizon* in 1907, to *Crisis* in 1910, to *Phylon* in 1940, and to *Freedomways*, which he encouraged in the early 1950s. His impact was more extensive as well, particularly with his outspoken editorials and his support of creative writers in the 1920s series of *Crisis*. Du Bois brought to completion the policies articulated by his distinguished forebears, Pauline Hopkins of *Colored American Magazine* and Max Barber of *Voice of the Negro*. Having seen how Hopkins and Barber were hamstrung by their editorial boards and publishers, Du Bois established himself as the voice of *Crisis*. He became the first black editor who was able to emphasize with regularity in a periodical the beauty of blackness, the richness of the Afro-American and African heritage, and the worldwide unity of black peoples. Charles S. Johnson was the next most important editor of a large black journal, second to Du Bois because his editorial career was so much shorter than that of his rival. In his work with *Opportunity*, and especially through the literary contests sponsored by that magazine, Johnson did much to further the outlets for black writing, the careers of many New Negroes, and the evolution of Afro-American literature.

Little magazine editors deserve recognition as well. Prominent among them was Wallace Thurman, who goes down in history as one of the most daring among small journal editors, a group customarily willing to take risks. With *Fire*, he published the first influential black little magazine of the century. The publication shocked the contemporary bourgeoisie because it appeared obscene and revolutionary. By screaming "FIRE" and airing "Smoke, Lilies and Jade," Thurman challenged middle-class codes of respectability, rejected the prevailing notion of art and propaganda, and offered another approach to aesthetics. In so doing, he prepared the way for others who could build on the precedents established by *Fire*. One of the beneficiaries was Alice Browning, who found it not so difficult to include Richard Bentley after Thurman had published Bruce Nugent. Browning could insist on freedom as editor partly because Thurman before her had indicated the way to such freedom, as well as the concomitant risks. The editors of the 1960s and early 1970s also benefited, even though they never admitted as much. As editor of the *Journal of Black Poetry*, Joe Goncalves felt at liberty to publish Baraka's "The Fire Must Be Permitted To Burn Full Up." To a certain extent, his independence rested on a foundation strengthened some four decades earlier when Thurman and associates had described fire "melting steel and iron bars, poking livid tongues between stone apertures and burning wooden opposition with a cackling chuckle of contempt."[1]

The same editors also owed a debt to the *Challenge* periodicals, which were the first black little magazines to attempt an explicit fusion of literary and political concerns. From the onset of her periodical, in 1934, Dorothy West struggled toward the ideas articulated later by Richard Wright in *New Challenge*. As she became more radical politically, she found it increasingly difficult to issue her journal, and when the ideas finally coalesced in *New Challenge*, her publication disappeared altogether. The career of the *Challenge* magazines illustrates the historic difficulty of developing and maintaining an Afro-American periodical on a literary-political base.

The black magazines of the 1960s and early 1970s provided similar lessons. When they encountered financial difficulties, as had *New Challenge* before them, they could not tap the wider literary audience for aid because their aesthetics seemed essentially political and far too revolutionary. The publication lasting the longest survived on the largess of its publisher, John H. Johnson. Existing on a relatively stable base of support, *Negro Digest / Black World* became not only the oldest but the most significant of such journals. Much credit goes to Hoyt Fuller, who can be numbered among the most influential editors of black little magazines. By his involvement in the black arts movement, he transformed *Negro Digest* from a popular commercial publication to a pacesetting small journal.

Unlike most of his predecessors, Fuller could not profit from the advice of Alain Locke, who had died in 1953. One wonders how Locke would have braced himself for the revolutionary magazines of the 1960s, had he lived a few years longer. As it was, his career as a contributor to black periodicals reached over more decades than that of anyone else, save for Du Bois; he made a first appearance in the *Colored American Magazine* during 1909, and a last one in *Phylon* during 1953. With *Stylus* of Howard University, he began the first black college literary journal, which gave a boost to several young writers, most especially to Zora Neale Hurston. His editing of the special Harlem number of *Survey Graphic* resulted in *The New Negro*, the book which defined and publicized the literary movement of the 1920s. The Harlem number also encouraged other predominately white magazines to publish special issues of Afro-American literature. Among Locke's greatest accomplishments were his retrospective reviews, which appeared in *Opportunity* from 1929 to 1942 and in *Phylon* from 1947 to 1953. The reviews are invaluable partly because they record for over two decades the various expressions in Afro-American literature of art-as-propaganda. They provide, then, information which makes more understandable the emergence of the theme, with a revolutionary turn, in the 1960s.

Afro-American magazines of the twentieth century have carried a double function. They have provided black writers with an outlet for their work and have thereby participated in the shaping of black literature and culture. At the same time, they have recorded basic concerns of each period and become historical documents in their own right. The editors and many of the contributors to the publications have recognized the importance of their work all along. Speaking for her contemporaries in the late 1960s, Carolyn Gerald testified that "the direction and developing quality of black literature can be but imperfectly seen if these journals [the revolutionary magazines] are ignored." Similar statements can be traced back through the decades to Max Barber. In an editorial for January 1904, Barber expressed a wish that *Voice of the Negro* would become a valuable cultural index: "We want it to be more than a mere magazine. We expect to make of it current and sociological history so accurately given and so vividly portrayed that it will become a kind of documentation for the coming generations." [2] He achieved just such an end, as did many subsequent editors. As a result, Gerald's statement can be rephrased so as to emphasize a point often obscured in literary history. The evolution of Afro-American literature becomes more clear if one has a sound understanding of twentieth-century black magazines: of the high drama, the historic dialogues, and the aesthetic traditions recorded in their pages.

Notes

Chapter 1

1. "The Morning Cometh," *Voice of the Negro* 1 (January 1904):38.
2. "The Rise of the Negro Magazine," *Journal of Negro History* 13 (January 1928):8. Mary Fair Burks includes a discussion of nineteenth-century Afro-American literary magazines in "A Survey of Black Literary Magazines in the United States: 1859–1940" (Ph.D. diss., Columbia University, 1975), pp. 10–90.
3. Johnson, "Rise of the Negro Magazine," p. 11; "The Way of the World," *Colored American Magazine* 7 (July 1904):471.
4. Arthur P. Davis, Sterling A. Brown, and Ulysses Lee, eds., *The Negro Caravan* (1941; rpt., New York: Arno Press, 1969), p. 139; "Our Greatest Want," *Anglo-African Magazine* 1 (May 1859):160.
5. *The Black Man: His Antecedents, His Genius, and His Achievements* (Boston: Robert F. Wallcut, 1865), p. 35.
6. R. S. Elliott, "The Story of Our Magazine," *Colored American Magazine* 3 (May 1901):47. It is impossible to determine the exact beginning of Hopkins's editorship. The staff neither announced her coming to the editorship, nor did it regularly list the name of editor on the masthead. William Stanley Braithwaite, a contributor to the magazine, recalled later that Hopkins had become editor during 1902. "Negro America's First Magazine," *Negro Digest* 6 (December 1947):24.
7. "Editorial and Publishers' Announcements," *Colored American Magazine* 1 (May 1900):60. William Stanley Braithwaite remembered that white publishers had patronized Chesnutt in a manner "which declared the traditional assumption of the inferior status of the Negro and his people": "Was I not told by a journalist friend, which gave me a shock, that it was common in literary and publishing circles, to refer to that superb and tragic artist, Charles Waddell Chesnutt, as 'Page's darky!' because Walter Hines Page, as editor of the *Atlantic Monthly*, had discovered and printed Chesnutt's earlier stories in the magazine, and persuaded Houghton, Mifflin to publish his books?" "The House Under Arcturus," *Phylon* 3 (2nd quarter 1942):188.

8. "John Mercer Langston," *Colored American Magazine* 3 (July 1901):177; "Toussaint L'Overture," *Colored American Magazine* 2 (November 1900):24; "Heroes and Heroines in Black," *Colored American Magazine* 6 (January 1903):206.

9. "Robert Morris," *Colored American Magazine* 3 (September 1901):337.

10. Hopkins, "Robert Morris," p. 337; "Educators," *Colored American Magazine* 5 (June 1902):130.

11. "Editorial and Publishers' Announcements," *Colored American Magazine* 5 (May 1902):76; "Book Reviews," *Colored American Magazine* 4 (November 1901):73. Braithwaite had agreed to edit a regular column called "Book Reviews." The column appeared very infrequently, however, in the magazine.

12. "Me 'N' Dunbar," *Colored American Magazine* 3 (July 1901):163; "Juny at the Gate," *Colored American Magazine* 5 (May 1902):3–4; "An Awful Problem Solved," *Colored American Magazine* 6 (November 1903):793–95; "The Gift of the Greatest God," *Colored American Magazine* 4 (December 1901): 101–3.

13. "Black Is, As Black Does," *Colored American Magazine* 1 (August 1900):163; "The Quality of Color," *Colored American Magazine* 5 (May 1902):67–75.

14. "Editorial and Publishers' Announcements," *Colored American Magazine* 4 (Jan.–Feb. 1902):335.

15. *Contending Forces: A Romance Illustrative of Negro Life North and South* (1900; rpt. Miami: Mnemosyne, 1969), pp. 13–14. The italics in this and in all subsequent footnotes appear originally in the text.

16. *Winona: A Tale of Negro Life in the South and Southwest, Colored American Magazine* 5 (May 1902):29; "A Dash for Liberty," *Colored American Magazine* 3 (August 1901):246.

17. *Hagar's Daughter: A Story of Southern Caste Prejudice, Colored American Magazine* 3 (May 1901): 26.

18. "Editorial and Publishers' Announcements," *Colored American Magazine* 6 (March 1903):398–99.

19. "Editorial and Publishers' Announcements," *Colored American Magazine* 1 (September 1900):262; "Editorial and Publishers' Announcements," *Colored American Magazine* 4 (Jan.–Feb. 1902):335.

20. "Sojourner Truth," *Colored American Magazine* 4 (December 1901):127; "Munroe Rogers," *Colored American Magazine* 4 (November 1902):22.

21. "Publishers' Announcements," *Colored American Magazine* 7 (November 1904):700; "Editorial," *Colored American Magazine* 8 (May 1905):342.

22. "The Colored Magazine in America," *Crisis* 5 (November 1912):33; Johnson, "Rise of the Negro Magazine," p. 13.

23. "Editorial and Publishers' Announcements," *Colored American Magazine* 6 (May–June 1903):466.

24. August Meier, "Booker T. Washington and the Negro Press: With Special Reference to the *Colored American Magazine*," *Journal of Negro History* 38 (January 1953):68–70; Moore to Washington, March 23, 1910, Container 51, Booker T. Washington Papers, Library of Congress (hereafter cited as Washington Papers).

25. "Publishers' Announcements," *Colored American Magazine* 7 (September 1904):606.

26. "In the Editor's Sanctum," *Colored American Magazine* 7 (November 1904): 693; Moore to Woodlee, March 28, 1907, Container 36, Washington Papers.

27. Moore to Washington, December 31, 1904, Container 29, Washington Papers.

28. "Editorial," *Colored American Magazine* 8 (May 1905):342; Moore to Scott, April 4, 1905, Container 29, Washington Papers.
29. "Editorial," *Colored American Magazine* 8 (May 1905):343.
30. Simmons to Washington, July 13, 1904, Container 25, Washington Papers.
31. "In the Editor's Sanctum," *Colored American Magazine* 7 (May 1904):382–83: Moore to Woodlee, March 28, 1907, Container 36, Washington Papers.
32. "In the Editor's Sanctum," *Colored American Magazine* 7 (November 1904): 693.
33. "Publishers' Announcements," *Colored American Magazine* 10 (June 1906): 435.
34. Washington to Moore, September 14, 1905, Container 29, Washington Papers.
35. Washington to Moore, June 5, 1905, Container 29, Washington Papers.
36. Washington to Moore, April 28 and April 9, 1906, Container 33, Washington Papers.
37. "Editorial," *Colored American Magazine* 9 (March 1905):157.
38. "The Way of the World," *Colored American Magazine* 10 (February 1906):75.
39. "The Month," *Colored American Magazine* 13 (October 1907):247–48; "Publishers' Announcements," *Colored American Magazine* 14 (January 1908):74.
40. Moore to Washington, March 23, 1910, Container 51, Washington Papers.
41. "Colored Magazine in America," p. 33.
42. "A Brief Sketch of Our New Company," pp. 4–5, Container 21, Washington Papers; "A Plucky Man," *Crisis* 5 (November 1912):16.
43. Barber, "The Morning Cometh," p. 38.
44. Barber to Du Bois, March 2, 1912, *The Correspondence of W. E. B. Du Bois* ed. Herbert Aptheker (Amherst: University of Massachusetts Press, 1973), vol. I: 176–77.
45. Barber, "The Morning Cometh," p. 38; "The Magazine with a Purpose," *Voice* 4 (May 1907):208. In November 1906, *Voice of the Negro* became *Voice*.
46. "The Healthful Growth of the Magazine," *Voice of the Negro* 2 (June 1905): 424; William Pickens, "Jesse Max Barber," *Voice* 3 (November 1906):486.
47. "In the Sanctum," *Voice of the Negro* 1 (October 1904):486.
48. "Debit and Credit," *Voice of the Negro* 2 (January 1905):677; "The Niagara Movement," *Voice of the Negro* 2 (September 1905):621.
49. "The Significance of the Niagara Movement," *Voice of the Negro* 2 (September 1905):600.
50. Du Bois to Ward, March 10, 1905, Aptheker, *Correspondence of W. E. B. Du Bois*, p. 96; Elliott M. Rudwick, *W. E. B. Du Bois* (New York: Atheneum, 1969), p. 91.
51. Du Bois, "A Plucky Man," p. 16.
52. Scott to Barber, April 14, 1904, Container 26, Washington Papers; Barber to Scott, April 18 and April 27, 1904, Container 26, Washington Papers.
53. Scott to Washington, July 23, 1904, Container 26, Washington Papers; Scott to Barber, July 23, 1904, Container 26, Washington Papers.
54. Scott to Hertel, Jenkins and Company, August 4, 1904, Container 21, Washington Papers; Jenkins to Scott, August 5, 1904, Container 21, Washington Papers.
55. Jenkins to Washington, August 10, 1904, Container 21, Washington Papers.
56. "Shall We Materialize the Negro," *Voice of the Negro* 2 (March 1905):194.
57. Washington to Jenkins, March 12, 1905, Container 29, Washington Papers; Hertel to Washington, March 22, 1905, Container 29, Washington Papers; Washington to Hertel, August 7, 1905, Container 29, Washington Papers.

58. Hertel to Washington, August 9, 1905, Container 29, Washington Papers.
59. Barber, "Significance of the Niagara Movement," p. 600.
60. Barber to Washington, April 6, 1906, Container 32, Washington Papers; Washington to Barber, April 14, 1906, Container 32, Washington Papers; Barber to Washington, April 23, 1906, Container 32, Washington Papers.
61. "Over-Look," *Horizon* 1 (February 1907):20; "The Atlanta Tragedy," *Voice* 3 (November 1906):474, 477.
62. "Why Mr. Barber Left Atlanta," *Voice* 3 (November 1906):470–72.
63. "Our Name Changed," *Voice* 3 (November 1906):464; "A Few of the Thousand Letters from Our Friends," Ibid., p. 500.
64. Hertel to Scott, June 1, 1907, Container 36, Washington Papers; Hertel to Scott, April 24, 1907, Container 36, Washington Papers; Scott to Hertel, May 29, 1907, Container 36, Washington Papers.
65. Du Bois, "A Plucky Man," p. 16.
66. "Inside with the Editor," *Voice of the Negro* 2 (July 1905):438.
67. "The Southern Conspiracy," *Voice of the Negro* 2 (May 1905):315–17; "Rough Sketches," *Voice of the Negro* 2 (November 1905):783.
68. "The Niagara Movement," *Voice of the Negro* 2 (November 1905):770; George W. Forbes, "Requiem Dirge for Atlanta's Slain," *Voice* 3 (November 1906):479; J. N. Samuels-Belboder, "And This, the White Man's Burden," Ibid., p. 516.
69. In 1937, when the reputation of *Voice* was clearly ascendant over that of the *Colored American Magazine*, Brawley mentioned to Arthur Spingarn the magazines which had published his early pieces. He recalled *Voice of the Negro*, but said nothing about *Colored American Magazine*, which had issued several of his poems: "My first writing consisted of a number of experimental stories and poems, some of which appeared in the Springfield *Republican*. I also made a few light contributions to *Lippincott's Magazine*, and several papers or poems appeared in *The Voice of the Negro*...." John W. Parker, "Benjamin Brawley and the American Cultural Tradition," *Phylon* 16 (2nd quarter, 1955):187.
70. Johnson, "Rise of the Negro Magazine," p. 13; " 'The New Negro Man,' " *Voice of the Negro* 1 (October 1904):447–52.
71. Paul G. Partington, "The Moon Illustrated Weekly—The Precursor of the *Crisis*," *Journal of Negro History* 48 (July 1963):213, 210.
72. Ibid., p. 206, Du Bois to Partington, March 31, 1961.
73. Chesnutt to Du Bois, June 27, 1903, Aptheker, *Correspondence of W. E. B. Du Bois*, pp. 56–57.
74. Du Bois to Schiff, April 14, 1905, Ibid., pp. 108–9; Partington, "Moon Illustrated Weekly," pp. 210–11.
75. New York *Age*, February 1, 1906, p. 2.
76. "Moonshine," *Horizon* 1 (January 1907):9.
77. "Burton," *Horizon* 2 (November 1907):3; "Socialist of the Path," *Horizon* 2 (February 1907):7.
78. "Literature," *Horizon* 5 (January 1910):4.
79. "The Song of the Smoke," *Horizon* 1 (February 1907): 4–6; "The Burden of Black Women," *Horizon* 2 (November 1907):3–4; "A Day in Africa," *Horizon* 3 (January 1908):5–6.
80. "My Country 'Tis of Thee," *Horizon* 2 (November 1907): 5–6.
81. "Subscriptions," *Horizon* 1 (January 1907):4–5; "The Race Magazines," *Horizon* 1 (February 1907):20–21.

82. "The Horizon," *Horizon* 4 (July 1908):1–3.
83. "Support," *Horizon* 5 (November 1909):1; "Subscribers," *Horizon* 5 (May 1910):1.
84. "Editorial and Publishers' Announcements," *Colored American Magazine* 4 (April 1902):411.

Chapter 2

1. "Editorial," *Crisis* 5 (November 1912):28.
2. "Ebony Flute," *Opportunity* 5 (January 1927):28.
3. "How the National Association for the Advancement of Colored People Began," *Crisis* 8 (August 1914):184.
4. "Editing 'The Crisis,'" *Crisis* 58 (March 1951):147.
5. "Editorial," *Crisis* 5 (November 1912):28.
6. Ovington, "How the National Association for the Advancement of Colored People Began," p. 187.
7. Du Bois, "Editing 'The Crisis,'" p. 148; "Editorial," *Crisis* 5 (November 1912):28.
8. "Editorial," *Crisis* 1 (November 1910):10.
9. Herbert Aptheker, ed., *The Autobiography of W. E. B. Du Bois* (New York: International Publishers, 1968), p. 261.
10. Du Bois to Ovington, April 9, 1914, *The Correspondence of W. E. B. Du Bois* ed. Herbert Aptheker (Amherst: University of Massachusetts Press, 1973), vol. 1, pp. 188–91; Du Bois to Spingarn, October 28, 1914, Ibid., 204, 207. Du Bois criticized Villard in his *Autobiography* as well (pp. 256–57).
11. "W. E. B. Du Bois in the Role of *Crisis* Editor," *Journal of Negro History* 43 (July 1958):224; *W. E. B. Du Bois: A Study in Minority Group Leadership* (Philadelphia: University of Philadelphia Press, 1960), p. 151.
12. "The Crisis, 1934–49," *Crisis* 58 (March 1951):154; Du Bois, *Autobiography*, p. 261.
13. Du Bois, "Editing 'The Crisis,'" p. 148; "Editorials," *Crisis* 11 (November 1915):25, 27.
14. Rudwick, "W.E. B. Du Bois in the Role of *Crisis* Editor," p. 234; Du Bois, "Editing 'The Crisis,'" p. 150. In his article, Du Bois asserted that *Crisis* reached a circulation of 100,000 in 1919 (p. 149).
15. Wilkins, "The Crisis, 1934–49," pp. 154–55.
16. "Report of the Crisis Committee," Series F, Container 1, NAACP Papers, Manuscripts Division, Library of Congress (hereafter cited as NAACP Papers); Rudwick, "W. E. B. Du Bois in the Role of *Crisis* Editor," p. 235.
17. "Report of the Director of Publication and Research for the year 1924," Series F, Container 1, NAACP Papers; "Department of Publications and Research: *The Crisis*," Series F, Container 1, NAACP Papers. James Weldon Johnson asked Du Bois to write another draft. "I think," he said, "that the tone of the report is too much of an apology, or an argument, or a defense, and will, I believe, be more hurtful than helpful to The Crisis. It seems to me that it induces the wrong psychology." "Memorandum from Mr. Johnson to Dr. Du Bois," March 13, 1926, Series F, Container 1, NAACP Papers.
18. "To the Crisis Committee," April 11, 1929, Series F, Container 2, NAACP Papers; "Negro Journalism," *Crisis* 36 (July 1929):244.
19. Ovington to Du Bois, December 20, 1930, Aptheker, *Correspondence of W. E. B. Du Bois*, p. 430.

20. Wilkins, "The Crisis, 1934–49," p. 154.

21. Du Bois, "Editing 'The Crisis,'" pp. 151, 213. Du Bois's departure became certain as he developed a plan for a segregated economy. See Rudwick, "W. E. B. Du Bois in the Role of the *Crisis* Editor," pp. 237–40.

22. *Dust Tracks on the Road* (1942; rpt. Philadelphia: Arno Press, 1969), pp. 175–76; *The Big Sea* (1940; rpt. New York: Hill and Wang, 1963), p. 218; *100 Years of Negro Freedom* (New York: Dodd, Mead, and Company, 1961), p. 229. These statements have influenced many recent critics, including S. P. Fullinwider and Patrick Gilpin. A former student of Bontemps, Gilpin made some of the more extreme claims, saying that Johnson was "the entrepreneur of the Harlem Renaissance" and that *Crisis* "never seemed to capture the spirit of the Renaissance." "Charles S. Johnson: Entrepreneur of the Harlem Renaissance," in *The Harlem Renaissance Remembered*, ed. Arna Bontemps (New York: Dodd, Mead, and Company, 1972), pp. 228, 223. Among the scholars giving chief credit to Du Bois is Arthur P. Davis, whose comments stand in direct opposition to those of Gilpin. He acknowledged that Du Bois "anticipated the Renaissance long before 1925" and that he emerged as "the chief Planter of the New Negro Renaissance." *From the Dark Tower* (Washington, D.C.: Howard University Press, 1974), pp. 18, 17.

23. "The Negro in Literature," *Crisis* 28 (September 1924):209. Francis L. Broderick noted that Du Bois's reputation as a writer would rest more on his editorials than on his poems, stories, and novels. *W. E. B. Du Bois: Negro Leader in Time of Crisis* (Stanford: Stanford University Press, 1959), p. 229. Elliott Rudwick recognized the impact of Du Bois's prose on his contemporaries: "No Negro author could help but have been stimulated by many of Du Bois's lyrical and plaintive editorials. "W. E. B. Du Bois in the Role of *Crisis* Editor," p. 233.

24. "Postscript," *Crisis* 35 (July 1928):239.

25. "Opinion," *Crisis* 26 (October 1923): 247; "Opinion," *Crisis* 27 (April 1924): 248; "The House of the Black Burgharts," *Crisis* 35 (April 1928):133–34; "The Shadow of Years," *Crisis* 15 (February 1918):169.

26. "Personal Journalism," *Crisis* 6 (May 1913):29.

27. "The Crisis for 1914," *Crisis* 7 (December 1913):93; Du Bois, "Editing 'The Crisis,'" p. 148; Du Bois, *Autobiography*, p. 295.

28. "Opinion," *Crisis* 22 (May 1921):7; "Robert E. Lee," *Crisis* 35 (March 1928):97; "The Browsing Reader," *Crisis* 29 (December 1924):81.

29. "Opinion," *Crisis* 19 (December 1919):46.

30. "As the Crow Flies," *Crisis* 36 (June 1929):187.

31. S. P. Fullinwider, *The Mind and Mood of Black America* (Homewood, Illinois: Dorsey Press, 1969), pp. 52, 54; "Editorial," *Crisis* 2 (September 1911):196.

32. "The Gospel According to Mary Brown," *Crisis* 19 (December 1919):41–43.

33. "Easter," *Crisis* 1 (April 1911):20; "The Gospel According to St. John, Chapter 12," *Crisis* 27 (December 1923); 55–56; "Steve," *Crisis* 17 (December 1918):62–63.

34. An excellent example of a piece containing all these elements is "Hopkinsville, Chicago and Idlewild," *Crisis* 22 (August 1921):158, 160.

35. "Editorial," *Crisis* 1 (April 1911):21; "The Future," *Crisis* 11 (November 1915):28; "The Looking Glass," *Crisis* 17 (November 1918):22; "Opinion," *Crisis* 19 (April 1920):299.

36. "Opinion," *Crisis* 19 (April 1920):298–99.

37. "The Beginning of Sorrows," *Crisis* 11 (March 1916):237–39; "The First

Stone," *Crisis* 13 (December 1916):68–70; "Ebon Maid and Girl of Mine," *Crisis* 13 (January 1917):118; "The Washer-Woman," *Crisis* 12 (June 1916): 90; "Africa," *Crisis* 17 (February 1919):166; "Black Sampson of Brandywine," *Crisis* 14 (September 1917):255.

38. "Negro Soldiers," *Crisis* 14 (September 1917):249; "Some Contemporary Poets of the Negro Race," *Crisis* 17 (April 1919):278.

39. W. E. B. Du Bois, "The True Brownies," *Crisis* 18 (October 1919):286. In *Crisis*, the most sustained publication for children came later with Effie Lee Newsome's "Little Page" of poetry, which appeared from 1925 to 1929.

40. "The People of Peoples and Their Gifts to Men," *Crisis* 6 (November 1913): 339–41; "The Drama Among Black Folk," *Crisis* 12 (August 1916):169, 171, 173; "Editorial," *Crisis* 10 (September 1915):230–31.

41. Fauset to Du Bois, December 26, 1903, Aptheker, *Correspondence of W. E. B. Du Bois,* p. 66.

42. "As to Books," *Crisis* 24 (June 1922):66; "Brawley's 'Social History of the American Negro,'" *Crisis* 23 (April 1922):260.

43. "The New Books," *Crisis* 27 (February 1924):177.

44. Marion L. Starkey, "Jessie Fauset," an interview, *Southern Workman* 61 (May 1932):220. In the interview, Fauset recalled the bewilderment of her own girlhood: "When I was a child I used to puzzle my head ruefully over the fact that in school we studied the lives of only great white people. I took it that there simply have been no great Negroes, and I was amazed when, as I grew older, I found that there were. It is a pity that Negro children should be permitted to suffer from that delusion at all. There should be a sort of 'Plutarch's Lives' of the Negro race. Some day, perhaps, I shall get around to writing it."

45. *A Long Way From Home* (New York: Lee Furman, 1937), p. 112; Hughes, *Big Sea,* p. 218.

46. In his *Autobiography,* Du Bois claimed that "most of the young writers who began what was called the renaissance of Negro literature in the 20's saw their first publication in *The Crisis* magazine" (p. 270).

47. "Postscript," *Crisis* 34 (December 1927):347.

48. Ibid.

49. "Opinion," *Crisis* 22 (June 1921):55; "Opinion," *Crisis* 30 (May 1925):9.

50. "Our Book Shelf," *Crisis* 31 (January 1926):141.

51. "Opinion," Ibid., p. 115.

52. "Opinion," *Crisis* 31 (February 1926):165.

53. "Criteria of Negro Art," *Crisis* 32 (October 1926):296.

54. "Books," *Crisis* 33 (December 1926):81–82; "The Browsing Reader," *Crisis* 35 (June 1928):202.

55. "The Negro in Art," *Crisis* 31 (April 1926):278; "The Negro in Art," *Crisis* 31 (March 1926):219.

56. McKay to Du Bois, June 18, 1928, Aptheker, *Correspondence of W. E. B. Du Bois,* pp. 374–75.

57. Guichard Parris and Lester Brooks, *Blacks in the City* (Boston: Little, Brown and Co., 1971), p. 171.

58. Gilpin, "Charles S. Johnson," in *Harlem Renaissance Remembered,* p. 297 n. 27.

59. Johnson to Locke, August 8, 1924, Literary Series, Alain Locke Collection, Howard University (hereafter cited as Locke Collection).

60. "A Contribution to American Culture," *Opportunity* 23 (Oct.–Dec. 1945): 192–93.
61. " 'Co-operation' and 'Opportunity,' " *Opportunity* 1 (January 1923):5; "Editorials," *Opportunity* 1 (February 1923):3.
62. "Editorials," *Opportunity* 3 (January 1925):2. In discussing this statement, Parris and Brooks noted that Johnson's "point of departure was decidedly different from that of editor Du Bois of the *Crisis* and purposely so" (*Blacks in the City*, p. 175).
63. "The Rise of the Negro Magazine," *Journal of Negro History* 13 (January 1928):15; "The Negro Renaissance and its Significance," in *The New Negro Thirty Years Afterward: Papers Contributed to the Sixteenth Annual Spring Conference of the Division of the Social Sciences*, ed. Rayford W. Logan, Eugene C. Holmes, and G. Franklin Edwards (Washington, D.C.: Howard University Press, 1955), p. 81.
64. "The Browsing Reader," *Crisis* 35 (May 1928): 165.
65. "1928: A Retrospective Review," *Opportunity* 7 (January 1929):9; Locke, "A Contribution to American Culture," pp. 193, 238.
66. "Public Opinion and the Negro," *Opportunity* 1 (July 1923):202, 206.
67. "Editorials," *Opportunity* 3 (May 1925):130; "Editorials," *Opportunity* 4 (June 1926):174; "Editorials," *Opportunity* 4 (August 1926):239.
68. "Editorials," *Opportunity* 4 (September 1926):270.
69. "Romance and Tragedy in Harlem—A Review," *Opportunity* 4 (October 1926):316.
70. "Ebony Flute," *Opportunity* 4 (September 1926):292; "Ebony Flute," *Opportunity* 5 (April 1927):122; "Ebony Flute," *Opportunity* 6 (April 1928):122.
71. "Award For Published Contributions," *Opportunity* 5 (January 1927):6.
72. Locke, "A Contribution to American Culture," p. 193.
73. Johnson to Locke, March 4, 1924, Locke Collection.
74. "The Debut of the Younger School of Negro Writers," *Opportunity* 2 (May 1924): 143–44.
75. Locke, "A Contribution to American Culture," pp. 238, 193.
76. "Contest Awards," *Opportunity* 3 (May 1925):142; "Contest Awards," *Opportunity* 4 (May 1926):156.
77. "The Opportunity Dinner," *Opportunity* 3 (June 1925):176–77; "The Awards Dinner," *Opportunity* 4 (June 1926):186.
78. "The Contest," *Opportunity* 5 (June 1927):159; "Editorials," *Opportunity* 5 (September 1927):254.
79. "Editorials," *Opportunity* 5 (September 1927):254.
80. "Editorials," *Opportunity* 4 (August 1926):241; "Ebony Flute," Ibid., p. 260.
81. "Editorials," *Opportunity* 4 (November 1926):337.
82. "Ebony Flute," *Opportunity* 4 (August 1926):261; "Dark Tower," *Opportunity* 6 (April 1928):120.
83. Nancy Joan Weiss, " 'Not Alms, But Opportunity': A History of the National Urban League, 1910–1940," (Ph.D. diss., Harvard University, 1969), pp. 337, 363–64.
84. "Editorials," *Opportunity* 6 (October 1928):292–93.
85. Hughes, *Big Sea*, pp. 236, 233.
86. *Messenger* 1 (November 1917):21.
87. "Who's Who," *Messenger* 2 (July 1918):27.
88. "Phases of Du Bois," *Messenger* 2 (April–May 1920): 10–11.
89. "Labor's Day," *Messenger* 2 (September 1919):31.

90. Hughes, *Big Sea*, p. 233.
91. "I Hate Myself," *Messenger* 8 (June 1926):182.
92. "Art and Propaganda," *Messenger* 6 (April 1924):111.
93. "A Thrush at Eve with an Atavistic Wound," *Messenger* 8 (May 1926):154.
94. "Editorials," *Messenger* 8 (August 1926):209.
95. "A Stranger at the Gates," *Messenger* 8 (September 1926):279.
96. "Shafts & Darts," *Messenger* 8 (October 1926):307.
97. Hughes, *Big Sea*, p. 234.
98. Theodore Kornweibel, Jr., "The *Messenger* Magazine: 1917–1928," (Ph.D. diss., Yale University, 1971), pp. 112–14. Kornweibel provided a basic quantitative study of *Crisis, Opportunity,* and *Messenger* as literary organs. He determined that while the three included comparable amounts of literary work, *Crisis* and *Opportunity* published more of the better known writers and more of their writings were later anthologized. For a full discussion of this comparison, see his Appendix no. 1, pp. 378–82.
99. Ibid., p. 123.
100. Locke, "1928: A Retrospective Review," p. 10.

Chapter 3

1. "Announcement and Prospectus of the *New Era Magazine*," and "Editorial and Publisher's Announcements," *New Era Magazine* 1 (February 1916):3, 60.
2. "Editorial and Publisher's Announcements," Ibid., p. 60.
3. "Editorial and Publisher's Announcements," *New Era Magazine* 1 (March 1916):124; "Announcement and Prospectus of the *New Era Magazine*," p. 1.
4. "Announcement and Prospectus of the *New Era Magazine*," p. 4.
5. "Editorial and Publisher's Announcements," and "John Trowbridge," *New Era Magazine* 1 (March 1916):124, 112.
6. "William Stanley Braithwaite," *New Era Magazine* 1 (February 1916):61.
7. "Announcement and Prospectus of the *New Era Magazine*," p. 2; "Topsy Templeton," *New Era Magazine* 1 (March 1916):77.
8. "Prize Contest," *New Era Magazine* 1 (March 1916):111.
9. *Crisis* acknowledged the death of Hopkins on August 23, 1930, at Cambridge, Massachusetts. The brief obituary noted only that Hopkins had been an "authoress and poetess" and that she had worked as a stenographer at the Massachusetts Institute of Technology. "Along the Color Line," *Crisis* 37 (October 1930):344.

Ann Allen Shockley says nothing of *New Era* in her brief article on Hopkins. "Pauline Elizabeth Hopkins: A Biographical Excursion into Obscurity," *Phylon* 33 (Spring 1972): 22–26.

If included anywhere, the magazine should have been mentioned in the dictionary of *Black American Writers*, compiled by Theressa Gunnels Rush, Carol Fairbanks Myers, and Esther Spring Arata. The editors did note Hopkins's association with the *Colored American Magazine*, but they made no reference to *New Era* (Metuchen, New Jersey: Scarecrow Press, 1975), vol. 1, pp. 389–90.
10. "Foreword," *Stylus* 1 (May 1921):6.
11. "The Stylus," *Howard University Record* 19 (May 1925):372; "Visions of the Dawn," *Stylus* (June 1934):1. The issues of *Stylus* following May 1921 were assigned neither a volume nor a number.
12. Gregory, "Foreword," p. 6.

13. "The Looking Glass," *Crisis* 12 (August 1916):182; *Dust Tracks on a Road* (1942: rpt. Philadelphia: Arno Press, 1969), pp. 175–76; Robert E. Hemenway, *Zora Neale Hurston* (Urbana: University of Illinois Press, 1977), pp. 18–20.

14. "Our Book Shelf," *Crisis* 31 (January 1926):141.

  Within the discussion, Du Bois essentially cast Kellogg and associates as inconsistent liberals who advocated social reform for all groups save for the black. He recalled that the editors had wanted, for a 1914 issue of *Survey*, a statement concerning the aims of the NAACP. Du Bois sent back a militant, but routine comment, as his conclusion indicates: "Finally, in 1914, the Negro must demand his social rights. His right to be treated as a gentleman when he acts like one, to marry any sane, grown person who wants to marry him, and to meet and eat with his friends without being accused of undue assumption or unworthy ambition." He never expected the subsequent uproar, the calls from *Survey* editors to the NAACP office, the demand that the offending passage be excised, if the piece was to appear in the magazine. Among the NAACP leadership, Du Bois remembered, "they found easily several who did not agree with this statement and one indeed who threatened to resign if it were published." The unnamed objectors must have included those trying to intimidate Du Bois into subservience to the organization. Du Bois, stubborn from the beginning of his editorship, would not comply and thus *Survey* rejected his entire statement.

  In 1923, Kellogg divided the *Survey* into two magazines: the *Survey Graphic*, which appeared on the first of each month and reached a popular audience with general information and analysis of social problems, and *Survey*, which served as a professional bulletin for the field of social work.

15. "The Negro Renaissance and its Significance," in *The New Negro Thirty Years Afterward: Papers Contributed to the Sixteenth Annual Spring Conference of the Division of the Social Sciences*, ed. Rayford W. Logan, Eugene C. Holmes, and G. Franklin Edwards (Washington, D.C.: Howard University Press, 1955), pp. 85–86. Clarke Chambers said nothing about the Civic Club Dinner but stressed Kellogg's own motivation for the Harlem number. He noted that Kellogg had always liked "folk," that he had previously published special issues on the Gypsies, the Irish, and the Mexican peasants, and that his "favorite artists were always those who worked with folk themes, especially when their styles reflected the primitive strength of the common folk." *Paul U. Kellogg and the Survey* (Minneapolis: University of Minnesota Press, 1971), pp. 112–13.

16. "Harlem," and "Enter the New Negro," *Survey Graphic* 6 (March 1925):629–30, 633.

17. "The South Lingers On," Ibid., 645, 644, 646.

18. "Enter the New Negro," Ibid., 631, 633.

19. "Youth Speaks," Ibid., 659.

20. "The Black Man Brings His Gifts," Ibid., 655, 710.

21. "The Negro Renaissance and its Significance," in *The New Negro Thirty Years Afterward*, p. 86; "The Negro Enters Literature," *Carolina Magazine* 57 (May 1927):48.

22. "Editorials," *Messenger* 7 (April 1925):156; Chambers, *Kellogg and the Survey*, p. 115.

23. The first issue of *Palms* appeared in October 1923 and the last in April 1927. Idella Purnell commented, in the last number, that *Palms* would emerge again in the fall: "The editors feel it necessary to bring forcibly to the attention of

Palms' readers that the magazine has continued and will continue." Despite such protestations, *Palms* never again reappeared. See "Notice," *Palms* 4 (April 1927):190.

24. "Poem," "The Song of America," and "Black Madonna," *Palms* 4 (October 1926):19, 18, 8.

25. In a letter dated September 27, 1925, Countee Cullen asked James Weldon Johnson if he would contribute a short article on black poets to the issue. Committed elsewhere, Johnson could not supply the essay; hence, the discussion by White. Cullen to Johnson, James Weldon Johnson Papers, James Weldon Johnson Collection, Yale University.

26. "Ebony Flute," *Opportunity* 5 (April 1927):123; "Ebony Flute," *Opportunity* 5 (January 1927):28.

27. "Contributors," *Carolina Magazine* 58 (May 1928): 48. Virginia Lay, acting editor of *Carolina Magazine* and also sister of Paul Green, had originally asked James Weldon Johnson either to write a survey of Afro-American literature for the May 1927 issue or to suggest someone else who could contribute the essay. Apparently, Johnson did not have time to author the piece and thus recommended Charles S. Johnson for the lead article. Lay to James Weldon Johnson, April 18, 1927, Series C, Container 83, NAACP Papers, Manuscripts Division, Library of Congress (hereafter cited as NAACP Papers).

28. "The Message of the Negro Poets," *Carolina Magazine* 58 (May 1928):11.

29. "The Hunch," *Carolina Magazine* 57 (May 1927):24.

30. "Boy," "Boy on Beale Street," "African Dancer in Paris," and "Once Bad Gal," *Carolina Magazine* 58 (May 1928):38, 36, 22.

31. "Comment," and "Plays of Negro Life," *Carolina Magazine* 59 (April 1929):4, 46.

32. "The Negro in Literature," *Crisis* 36 (November 1929):377; "Dark Tower," and "Ebony Flute," *Opportunity* 5 (June 1927):181, 183; "Dark Tower," *Opportunity* 5 (July 1927):211.

33. "Dark Tower," *Opportunity* 4 (December 1926):388. Starr and Fowler were still listed in their official capacities in the May 1927 issue of *Carolina Magazine*, even though Virginia Lay was serving as editor. In her letter to James Weldon Johnson, she indicated that Starr had to attend to business in New York for an indeterminate period. She also indicated that Starr had made plans and Lewis Alexander had gathered materials for the first special issue of black literature. Lay to Johnson, April 18, 1927, Series C, Container 83, NAACP Papers.

34. "Dedication," *Carolina Magazine* 58 (May 1928):4; Alexander, "Plays of Negro Life," p. 47.

35. *Harlem Renaissance* (New York: Oxford University Press, 1971), p. 29. John W. Blassingame called the Huggins's study "hardly definitive," saying that *Harlem Renaissance* "ignores the internal dynamics of the black community which fostered and nurtured the movement." Blassingame concluded that there still exists undiscovered "a different kind of renaissance than that which Huggins found. "The Afro-Americans: Mythology to Reality," in *The Reinterpretation of American History and Culture*, ed. William H. Cartwright and Richard L. Watson, Jr. (Washington, D.C.: National Council for the Social Studies, 1973), p. 69.

36. "The Twenties: Harlem and its Negritude," *African Forum* 1 (Spring 1966): 18–19; also see Hemenway, *Hurston*, pp. 43–50.

37. Hughes, "The Twenties," 19; Thurman to Hughes, December 8, 1927, Wallace Thurman Folder, James Weldon Johnson Collection, Yale University.
38. Hughes, "The Twenties," p. 19; *Fire* 1 (November 1926); introductory page.
39. Hughes, "The Twenties," p. 20; *Big Sea* (1940; rpt. New York: Hill and Wang, 1963), p. 237.
40. Thurman so autographed the copy of *Fire* in the Moorland-Spingarn Research Center of Howard University; "Foreword," *Fire*, p. 1.
41. "Fire Burns," Ibid., pp. 47–48.
42. "Cordelia the Crude," "Wedding Day," and "Sweat," Ibid., pp. 5, 25–28, 41.
43. "Smoke, Lilies and Jade," Ibid., p. 38.
44. "Elevator Boy" and "Little Cinderella," Ibid., pp. 20, 23.
45. Hughes, *Big Sea*, p. 237; "A Challenge to the Negro," *Bookman* 64 (November 1926):258–59.
46. "Dark Tower," and "Ebony Flute," *Opportunity* 5 (January 1927):25, 28.
47. Hughes, *Big Sea*, p. 237; Hughes, "The Twenties," pp. 19–20; "Looking Glass," *Crisis* 33 (January 1927):158.
48. "Fire: A Negro Magazine," *Survey* 58 (Aug. 15-Sept. 15, 1927):563.
49. Hughes to Locke, December 28, 1926, Literary Series, Alain Locke Collection, Howard University (hereafter cited as Locke Collection); Hughes, *Big Sea*, p. 237.
50. "The Negro Literary Renaissance," *Southern Workman* 56 (April 1927): 177–79, 183.
51. "Negro Artists and the Negro," *New Republic* 52 (August 31, 1927):37.
52. Hurston to Locke, October 11, 1927, Locke Collection.
53. Hughes, *Big Sea*, p. 238.
54. Thurman to Locke, October 3, 1928, Locke Collection; Locke to Thurman, October 8, 1928, Locke Collection.
55. "For Whom Shall the Negro Vote?" *Harlem* 1 (November 1928):5, 45.
56. "Art or Propaganda?" Ibid., p. 12.
57. "Editorial," Ibid., p. 21.
58. Ibid., pp. 21–22.
59. "High, Low, Past and Present," Ibid., pp. 31–32.
60. "Harlem Directory: Where To Go And What To Do When In Harlem," Ibid., p. 43.
61. "Editorial," Ibid., p. 22.
62. "Wallace Thurman Adores Brown Women Who Have Beauty Mark On Shoulder; Prefers Sherry to Gin," New York *Journal and Guide*, March 5, 1932. The article is included in the Wallace Thurman Folder, Vertical File, Schomburg Collection of Black History, Literature and Art, New York Public Library.
63. Ibid.
64. *Infants of the Spring* (New York: Macaulay Company, 1932), pp. 186–87, 180.
65. *Black Opals* 1 (Spring 1927): n.p. In a letter to Alain Locke, dated April 2, 1927, Langston Hughes noted the appearance of *Black Opals* and declared that he would submit some poems for publication in the magazine. Hughes to Locke, Locke Collection.
66. "Hail Philadelphia," *Black Opals* 1 (Spring 1927):3.
67. "Quicksand," *Black Opals* 1 (June 1928):19.
68. "Pardon Us for Bragging," *Black Opals* 1 (Christmas 1927):16.
69. "Far Horizon," *Crisis* 34 (August 1927):130; "Browsing Reader," *Crisis* 36 (March 1929):98.

70. "Dark Tower," *Opportunity* 5 (June 1927):180; "Ebony Flute," *Opportunity* 6 (February 1928):56.
71. In 1926, Helene Johnson was executive secretary for The Colored Poetic League of the World, an organization attempting to establish itself in Boston. The league tried to found the *Poets' Journal*, a magazine which apparently never materialized. In a circular letter sent to contemporary writers Thomas Oxley, President of the league and proposed editor of the *Journal*, outlined the intentions of the organization: "Our purposes are to increase and diffuse poetic knowledge; to sell and publish books; to criticise; and to help the young poet to recognition and fame. But this is not all—*The Poet's Journal*— the organ of the League will be published according to public subscription and for those interested in poetry" (Series C, Container 83, NAACP Papers).
72. Thurman, *Infants of the Spring*, p. 231.
73. "A Statement to the Reader," *Saturday Evening Quill* 1 (June 1928): front page.
74. "Abraham Lincoln," Ibid., p. 34.
75. "A Word in Closing: On Uncritical Criticism," Ibid., p. 72. Gordon had expressed like opinions in "Group Tactics and Ideals," *Messenger* 8 (December 1926):361, and in "The Contest Winners," *Opportunity* 5 (July 1927):204.
76. "The Negro's Literary Tradition," *Saturday Evening Quill* 1 (June 1930):6, 8.
77. "Excerpts from Comments on the First Number of *The Saturday Evening Quill*," *Saturday Evening Quill* 1 (April 1929):inside front cover; "The Browsing Reader," *Crisis* 35 (September 1928):301; "Excerpts from Comments on the Previous Numbers of the *Saturday Evening Quill*," *Saturday Evening Quill* 1 (June 1930): inside front cover.
78. In the years following, *Stylus* appeared in 1934, 1935, 1936, 1937, 1938, and 1941, which marked the twenty-fifth anniversary of the organization and the last number of the journal.
79. "Beauty and the Provinces," *Stylus* (June 1929):3–4.
80. Ibid., p. 4. In his *Opportunity* article, Locke mentioned that he had also used the expression "elsewhere." "1928: A Retrospective Review," *Opportunity* 7 (January 1929):10.

Chapter 4

1. *Blacks in the City* (Boston: Little and Brown, 1971), pp. 175–76.
2. "1928: A Retrospective Review," *Opportunity* 7 (January 1929):8.
3. Donald Ogden Stewart, *Fighting Words* (New York: Harcourt and Brace, 1940), pp. 58–59 quoting from Hughes's speech to the League of American Writers.
4. "Our Literary Audience," *Opportunity* 8 (February 1930):42.
5. Parris and Brooks, *Blacks in the City*, p. 176.
6. "Editorials," *Opportunity* 9 (October 1931):298.
7. "Editorials," *Opportunity* 13 (January 1935):7.
8. *Opportunity* published "The Literary Scene" on schedule from December 1930 to January 1933. From the spring of 1933 to December 1935, the column did not appear between March and September of each year. The last two installments of the column came in the July 1936 and the April 1938 issues.
9. "Imitation of Life: Once a Pancake," *Opportunity* 13 (March 1935):87; Hurst to Carter, and Brown to Carter, *Opportunity* 13 (April 1935):121–22; " 'Caroling Softly Souls of Slavery,' " *Opportunity* 9 (August 1931):252.

10. "The New Negro in Literature (1925–1955)," in *The New Negro Thirty Years Afterward: Papers Contributed to the Sixteenth Annual Spring Conference of the Division of the Social Sciences,* ed. Rayford W. Logan, Eugene C. Holmes, and G. Franklin Edwards (Washington, D.C.: Howard University Press, 1955), pp. 57–58.
11. "A Poet and his Prose," *Opportunity* 10 (August 1932):256; "Come Day, Go Day," *Opportunity* 13 (September 1935):280.
12. "The Negro: 'New' or Newer," *Opportunity* 17 (January 1939):4.
13. Locke, "1928: A Retrospective Review," p. 8.
14. Ibid.
15. Locke, "The Negro: 'New' or Newer," p. 5; "Black Truth and Black Beauty," *Opportunity* 11 (January 1933):14.
16. "Jingo, Counter-Jingo and Us," *Opportunity* 16 (January 1938):9.
17. "Deep River: Deeper Sea," *Opportunity* 14 (January 1936):6–7.
18. "The Negro: 'New' or Newer," pp. 4, 6.
19. Ibid., p. 6.
20. *From Slavery to Freedom,* 4th ed. rev. (New York: Alfred A. Knopf, 1974), p. 393.
21. "This Year of Grace," *Opportunity* 9 (February 1931):51, 48–49.
22. "Who and What Is 'Negro'?" *Opportunity* 20 (February 1942):36.
23. Locke, "Deep River: Deeper Sea," p. 7; Locke, "Black Truth and Black Beauty," p. 14.
24. "Of Native Sons: Real and Otherwise," *Opportunity* 19 (January 1941):5; "Of Native Sons: Real and Otherwise," *Opportunity* 19 (February 1941):48. Locke originally thought Wright's first name was Willard. Benjamin Brawley made the same mistake in *The Negro Genius.* Sterling Brown, when reviewing Brawley's book, noted the error and explained that Willard Wright was not the black writer but "a white author of detective novels." "Book Reviews," *Opportunity* 15 (September 1937):280.
25. Locke, "Who and What Is 'Negro'?" p. 36.
26. Ibid., p. 37.
27. "Dry Fields and Green Pastures," *Opportunity* 18 (January 1940):4–5.
28. "Freedom Through Art," *Crisis* 45 (July 1938): 227.
29. "The Du Bois Literary Prize," *Crisis* 40 (February 1933):45.
30. Letter from Mathews to Du Bois, reprinted in *Crisis* 38 (April 1931): 117; "The Donor of the Du Bois Literary Prize," *Crisis* 38 (May 1931): 157.
31. "The Crisis, 1934–49," *Crisis* 58 (March 1951):155.
32. John McKinley, "Hail!" *Reflexus* 1 (April 1925):3. For a short note on this journal, see "Reflexus," *Black World* 22 (February 1973):88.
33. "Editorials," *Opportunity* 8 (December 1930):358.
34. Roi Ottley, *The Lonely Warrior: The Life and Times of Robert S. Abbott* (Chicago: Regnery, 1955), pp. 291, 294.
35. The one number of *Metropolitan*, which was issued in New York during January 1935, was a blend of the popular and the literary magazine, and it used contributions of wide appeal from some of the best contemporary writers. *Champion,* edited by Fenton Johnson in Chicago from September 1916 to February 1917, had similar characteristics. Through his magazine, Johnson said he wanted to help "bring about a literary Renaissance" and "to be of service in the literary and artistic development of our race." At the same time he announced, "we want this to be the magazine of the masses, for after all one finds that the masses have the greatest intelligence." "To

Contributors," *Champion Magazine* 1 (September 1916):37; "A Confidential Talk," Ibid., p. 3.

36. "Editorials," *Opportunity* 8 (December 1930):358–59.

37. "Elderly Race Leaders," *Race* 1 (Summer 1936):87. The first issue of the magazine featured an article by E. Franklin Frazier, "The Du Bois Program in the Present Crisis," *Race* 1 (Winter 1935–1936):11–13. James Young considered Frazier's essay "perhaps the bitterest attack of the decade upon the older race men in general and Du Bois in particular." *Black Writers of the Thirties* (Baton Rouge: Louisiana State University Press, 1973), p. 47.

38. "Propaganda–or Poetry?" *Race* 1 (Summer 1936):73.

39. *The Negro Novel in America* (New Haven: Yale University Press, 1958), pp. 116–17; *The Crisis of the Negro Intellectual* (New York: William Morrow, 1967), pp. 185–86. A brief article on *Challenge* has recently appeared. See Walter C. Daniel, " 'Challenge Magazine': An Experiment That Failed," *CLA Journal* 19 (June 1976):494–503.

40. West to Johnson, October 23, 1933, James Weldon Johnson Papers, James Weldon Johnson Collection, Yale University (hereafter cited as Johnson Papers).

41. West to Johnson, October 30, 1933, Johnson Papers.

42. Johnson to West, no date, Johnson Papers.

43. West to Johnson, November 11, 1933, Johnson Papers; Johnson to West, February 7, 1934, Johnson Papers.

44. "Dear Reader," and "Barrel Staves," *Challenge* 1 (March 1934):39, 16–24.

45. "Dear Reader," *Challenge* 1 (September 1934):30, 29.

46. "Dear Reader," *Challenge* 1 (May 1935):45.

47. "Alabama Welcomes You," and "Song of a Song," Ibid., pp. 18, 43.

48. "The National Negro Congress," *Challenge* 1 (June 1936):32, 31; "Dear Reader," *Challenge* 1 (January 1936):38.

49. "Big Men" and "Voices," *Challenge* 2 (Spring 1937):38, 43, 42.

50. "Dear Reader," Ibid., p. 41.

51. "Report on the Second American Writers Congress," p. 9, Johnson Papers. This gathering, which met in New York City, represented a continuing effort of the Communist-dominated League of American Writers to advance party solutions among editors, journalists, and creative writers. The first congress, held in 1935, had established the league to carry forth the party's work in this area.

52. Michel Fabre, *The Unfinished Quest of Richard Wright* (New York: William Morrow, 1973), pp. 102, 128–29.

53. "Editorial," and "Letters," *New Challenge* 2 (Fall 1937):3–4, 5.

54. "Blueprint for Negro Writing," Ibid., pp. 56, 62, 58, 55.

55. Sharecropper letter and "Contributors," Ibid., pp. 92, 93.

56. "Snapshots of the Cotton South," "South Chicago, May 30, 1937," "Old Lem," and "Hounds," Ibid., pp. 43, 49, 46–48, 50.

57. "Creative and Cultural Lag," Ibid., p. 91.

58. "Spiritual Truancy," Ibid., pp. 81–85. Locke expressed similar opinions in an *Opportunity* review, where he claimed that *A Long Way From Home* is unbalanced and that it "exploits a personality." "Jingo, Counter-Jingo and Us," p. 11.

59. West to Johnson, December 1, no year, Johnson Papers; McKay to Johnson, November 28, 1937, Claude McKay Papers, Johnson Collection (hereafter cited as McKay Papers). Locke and McKay had their first real disagreement over

Locke's selection and edition of McKay's poems for *The New Negro* (1925). Locke had arbitrarily changed the title of "The White House" to "White Houses." He had also included "Negro Dancers" in the volume without first consulting McKay, who "would have vetoed their publication," he said. McKay protested to Locke, in a letter dated August 1, 1926: "You knew my address. You might easily have consulted me. That is the very ordinary and usual procedure among literary people. Besides, we—you and I—are something of friends and friendship calls for greater courtesy, I hold, than among strangers!" McKay to Locke, *The Passion of Claude McKay*, ed. Wayne F. Cooper (New York: Schocken Books, 1973), pp. 143–44. "The White House" still appears as "White Houses" in the latest edition of *The New Negro* (1925; rpt. New York: Atheneum, 1970), p. 134.

60. West to McKay, October 28, 1935, McKay Papers; West to Johnson, no date, Johnson Papers.
61. McKay to Johnson, November 28, 1937, McKay Papers.
62. Johnson to McKay, January 26, 1928, McKay Papers; Johnson to McKay, September 30, 1933, McKay Papers.
63. Cooper, *Passion of Claude McKay*, pp. 13–14, 18–20.
64. McKay to Gilmore, March 5, 1941, McKay Papers.
65. *Negro Americans, What Now?* (New York: Viking Press, 1934), p. 8; Johnson to Stewart, February 4, 1938, Johnson Papers.
66. McKay to Johnson, February 5, 1938, McKay Papers.
67. McKay to Johnson, August 8, 1935, McKay Papers; McKay to Johnson, April 8, 1937, McKay Papers.
68. McKay to Johnson, August 22, 1937, McKay Papers.
69. "The Negro Writers Guild," and "Constitution," two drafts of the group's constitution, n.d., McKay Papers.
70. "Constitution," McKay Papers; Brawley to McKay, November 12, 1937, McKay Papers.
71. McKay to Johnson, n.d., McKay Papers; McKay to Johnson, April 2, 1938, McKay Papers; Johnson to McKay, April 14, 1938, McKay Papers.
72. McKay to Johnson, April 22, 1938, McKay Papers.
73. McKay and Cullen to Johnson, May 14, 1938, McKay Papers.
74. Johnson to McKay, May 17, 1938, McKay Papers.
75. McKay and Cullen to Locke, May 14, 1938, Alain Locke Collection, Howard University.
76. "Announcement!" *African* 1 (May–June 1938):120; *African* 1 (July–August 1938):122.
77. Cullen to McKay, August 14, 1938, McKay Papers; Cullen to McKay, July 24, 1938, McKay Papers.

Chapter 5

1. "The Literature of Race and Culture," *Phylon* 5 (3rd quarter 1944):384; Langston Hughes and the Editors, "Some Practical Observations: A Colloquy," *Phylon* 11 (4th quarter 1950):308, 307.
2. *The Negro Novel in America* (New Haven: Yale University Press, 1958), p. 165.
3. O'Wendell Shaw, "Manuscript Revision," *Negro Story* 1 (May–June 1944):59.
4. In looking at the publishing industry, Theodore Peterson examined such

preferences in *Magazines in the Twentieth Century* (Urbana: University of Illinois Press, 1956), pp. 390–91.

5. *The Crisis of the Negro Intellectual* (New York: William Morrow, 1967), p. 209; "The Negro Writer—Shadow and Substance," *Phylon* 11 (4th quarter 1950):373.

6. "The Editor Says," *Opportunity* 20 (April 1942):99; "The Editor Says," *Opportunity* 20 (October 1942):291.

7. Dutton Ferguson, "Twenty-Six Years of *Opportunity,*" *Opportunity* 27 (Winter 1949):7.

8. "The Editor Says," *Opportunity* 20 (January 1942):2; "The Editor Says," *Opportunity* 20 (April 1942):98.

9. "Editorial," *Opportunity* 23 (Jan.–March 1945):3.

10. "Blackout," *Opportunity* 20 (March 1942):82; "Southern Negro Speaks," *Opportunity* 19 (October 1941):308.

11. "An Aspect of the Negro Renaissance," *Opportunity* 20 (October 1942):305; "Cosmos," *Opportunity* 23 (April–June 1945):65.

12. "Next Month," *Crisis* 48 (April 1941):102.

13. "We Take a Bow," *Crisis* 48 (June 1941):183.

14. "Twentieth Anniversary," and "ɴᴀᴀᴄᴘ," Ibid., pp. 187, 201.

15. "The Need for Heroes," Ibid., pp. 184–85.

16. "One Friday Morning," *Crisis* 48 (July 1941):216–18.

17. "On Saturday the Siren Sounds at Noon," *Crisis* 50 (December 1943):368.

18. "Ann Petry Talks About First Novel," *Crisis* 53 (February 1946):48–49.

19. "We Take a Bow," Ibid., p. 40. In an article published in 1951, Wilkins exhibited a similar progression of thought. He boasted that *Crisis* had discovered Petry and that it had, in so doing, continued "the Du Bois tradition of giving young writers a start." He then recalled Hughes and his debut in *Crisis*. "The Crisis, 1934–49," *Crisis* 58 (March 1951):156.

20. "Lunching at the Ritzmore," *Crisis* 49 (October 1942):314.

21. "So Softly Smiling," *Crisis* 50 (October 1943):315; "Two Soldiers," *Crisis* 50 (January 1943):29; "The Song Says 'Keep On Smiling,'" *Crisis* 52 (April 1945):103–4; "Heaven Has Changed," *Crisis* 50 (March 1943):83.

22. "Black Girl, Shouting," *Crisis* 49 (October 1942):327; "War Quiz for America," *Crisis* 51 (April 1944):114.

23. "Look Away, Dixie Land," *Crisis* 53 (June 1946):218–19.

24. Cruse, *Crisis of the Negro Intellectual*, pp. 187–88.

25. "Transition," *Negro Quarterly* 1 (Spring 1942):90.

26. Bone, *Negro Novel in America*, p. 165; "Transition in the American Negro Short Story," *Phylon* 21 (4th quarter 1960):360–66.

27. "Our Contributors," *Negro Story* 1 (Mar.–Apr. 1945):2.

28. "Editor's Mail Box," *Negro Story* 1 (May–June 1945): 94.

29. "What Should the Negro Story Be?" *Negro Story* 1 (Dec.–Jan. 1944–45):60.

30. "Editor's Mail Box," *Negro Story* 1 (May–June 1945):5.

31. Michel Fabre, *The Unfinished Quest of Richard Wright* (New York: Morrow, 1973), pp. 579–80 n. 24. *Negro Story* never again published a story by Wright, although Browning asked him for additional contributions: "We feel incomplete without stories by this great writer. If he reads his complimentary copy of *Negro Story*, we are hoping he will answer this plea for a story in our anniversary issue in spite of the vast demands on his time." "Just to Mention That," *Negro Story* 1 (Mar.–Apr. 1945):55.

Wright's attempts at magazines failed because he could not raise sufficient funds. In 1940 he had tried to counter reactionary stereotypes, as given in popular journals, with a magazine of his own. He sought in 1941 to begin another publication, a monthly issued along the lines of *PM*. Fabre, *Quest of Richard Wright*, pp. 258–59.

32. "Current Town Talk," *Negro Story* 1 (Dec.–Jan. 1944–45):61. Mary White Ovington, for one, thought highly of *Negro Digest*. She compared it "in form" to *Reader's Digest* and declared that "to anyone desirous of learning about the race today, it is indispensable." *The Walls Came Tumbling Down* (New York: Harcourt and Brace, 1947), p. 285.

33. "Just To Mention That," *Negro Story* 2 (Aug.–Sept. 1945):53–54.

34. "Just To Mention That," *Negro Story* 1 (May–June 1945); 86; "Just To Mention That," *Negro Story* 1 (Mar.–Apr. 1945):54; "Just To Mention That," *Negro Story* 2 (Apr.–May 1946):63; "Just To Mention That," *Negro Story* 2 (Dec.–Jan. 1945):64.

35. "Just To Mention That," *Negro Story* 1 (May–June 1945):87.

36. Alice Browning and Fern Gayden, "A Letter to Our Readers," *Negro Story* 1 (July–Aug. 1944):1.

37. Ibid.

38. "Negro Story," Ibid., p. 56; "Our Contributors," *Negro Story* 1 (May–June 1945):83; "Just To Mention That," *Negro Story* 2 (Aug.–Sept. 1945):56.

39. "Our Contributors," *Negro Story* 1 (Dec.–Jan 1944–45):62; Letters From Our Readers, "What Should The Negro Story Be?" p. 58.

40. "Just To Mention That," *Negro Story* 1 (May–June 1945):85.

41. "Open Letter," *Negro Story* 1 (Mar.–Apr. 1945):48 (rpt. from *Common Ground*); "Gay Chaps At The Bar," *Negro Story* 1 (Mar.–Apr. 1945):49, rpt. from *Poetry*; "Private Jim Crow," *Negro Story* 1 (May–June 1945):3.

42. For her poem, "Revision of the Invocation," which was published in the May–June 1945 issue of *Negro Story*, Gwendolyn Brooks won first place and two $25 war bonds in a poetry contest sponsored by *Negro Story* and funded by the Chicago District CIO United Electrical Radio and Machine Workers. See "Our Contributors," *Negro Story* 1 (Mar.–Apr. 1945):2.

43. Ibid., 57; "Current Town Talk," *Negro Story* 1 (Oct.–Nov. 1944):60.

44. "Let Me At The Enemy—An' George Brown," *Negro Story* 1 (Dec.–Jan. 1944–45):9, 11.

45. "A Penny For Your Thoughts," *Negro Story* 1 (Mar.–Apr. 1945):15.

46. "My But The Rats Are Terrible," *Negro Story* 1 (May–June 1945): 25, 32.

47. "Our Contributors," *Negro Story* 1 (Dec.–Jan. 1944–45):62.

48. "Tomorrow," Ibid., p. 36.

49. "Just To Mention That," *Negro Story* 1 (Mar.–Apr. 1945): 54–55.

50. "Our Contributors," and "Just To Mention That," Ibid., pp. 2, 55.

51. "Mister Toussan," *Negro Story* 1 (July–August 1944):37–41 (rpt. from *New Masses*); "If I Had the Wings," *Negro Story* 1 (Oct.–Nov. 1944):3–11 (rpt. from *Common Ground*); "Afternoon," *Negro Story* 1 (March–April 1945):3–8 (rpt. with permission of author); "Birthmark," *Negro Story* 1 (May–June 1945):20–23.

52. Clarke, "Transition in the American Negro Short Story," p. 366.

53. Wilkins, "The Crisis, 1934–49," p. 156.

54. "The Importance of Georgia Douglas Johnson," *Crisis* 59 (December 1952): 635.

55. Stella Kamp, *Opportunity* 24 (April–June 1946):73.

56. "Twenty-Five Years and Beyond," *Opportunity* 25 (Oct.–Dec. 1947):188.

57. In this context, two other university-related journals bear mentioning in that they fulfilled minor roles as outlets for black writers and literary critics. Between 1937 and 1939, Dillard University in New Orleans sponsored the *Arts Quarterly*, which attempted to function as a Southern black fine arts magazine. Then in 1948 Lincoln University in Jefferson City, Missouri, began publication of the *Midwest Journal*, "devoted to research and creative writing," and managed to keep the journal operating until 1956. M. Carl Holman, Melvin B. Tolson, Georgia Douglas Johnson, Arthur P. Davis, and Langston Hughes, among others, published in the *Journal* during its seven-year run.

58. *The Autobiography of W. E. B. Du Bois*, ed. Herbert Aptheker (New York: International Publishers, 1968), p. 301.

59. Embree to Du Bois, April 8, 1936, *The Correspondence of W. E. B. Du Bois*, ed. Herbert Aptheker (Amherst: University of Massachusetts Press, 1976), vol. 2, p. 132.

60. Du Bois to Read, May 6, 1940, Ibid., p. 235.

61. *The Autobiography of W. E. B. Du Bois*, p. 323.

62. "Persons and Places," *Phylon* 5 (3rd quarter 1944):279.

63. "Re-View of the Review—Editorial," *Phylon* 10 (4th quarter 1949):298–99.

64. "Interracial," *Phylon* 5 (2nd quarter 1944):188.

65. "This Quarter," *Phylon* 13 (1st quarter 1952):4.

66. "Dawn Patrol," *Phylon* 10 (1st quarter 1949):5.

67. "The High Price of Integration," *Phylon* 13 (1st quarter 1952): 7; "From *Native Son* to *Invisible Man*," *Phylon* 14 (1st quarter 1953):34.

68. "A Critical Retrospect of the Literature of the Negro for 1947," *Phylon* 9 (1st quarter 1948):3–4; "Reason and Race," *Phylon* 7 (1st quarter 1947): 17, 19.

69. Locke, "Dawn Patrol," p. 11; "Wisdom *de Profundis*," *Phylon* 11 (1st quarter 1950):11.

70. "Self Criticism: The Third Dimension in Culture," *Phylon* 11 (4th quarter 1950):392–94.

71. "Race and the Negro Writer," Ibid., p. 371.

72. Langston Hughes and the Editors, "Some Practical Observations: A Colloquy," Ibid., p. 311.

73. Mozell C. Hill and M. Carl Holman, "Preface," Ibid., p. 296.

74. "Inventory at Mid-Century," *Phylon* 12 (1st quarter 1951):5. Robert Bone lent credence to Locke's views, for he claimed later that the special issue in its "majority sentiment both reflected and helped to create the dominant mood of the period." Bone, *Negro Novel in America*, p. 165.

75. "Which Way for the Negro Writer?" *Masses & Mainstream* 4 (March 1951): 53, 57, 60, 56.

76. "Faith Without Works in Negro Literature," *Phylon* 12 (4th quarter 1951): 380–81. *Phylon* editors had earlier criticized *Mainstream*, one of the immediate precursors of *Masses & Mainstream*. The initial editorial in *Masses & Mainstream* had urged writers "to fight anti-Negro, anti-Semitic, anti-labor and anti-Communist influences in life and letters today . . . we combat such degraded influences as Trotskyite nihilism in the literary field; we fight the literary anti-Sovieteers who constitute an auxiliary legion of the warmakers." The commentator in *Phylon* replied: "It is to be regretted that the journal's maiden editorial does so much violence to one's intelligence, makes one unprepared for the choice materials the magazine incorporates in its first issue." "Mainstream," *Phylon* 8 (2nd quarter 1947):182.

77. "Integration and Race Literature," *Phylon* 17 (2nd quarter 1956):144, 142.
78. Cruse, *Crisis of the Negro Intellectual*, pp. 213, 215, 208. Cruse declared that there was "nothing wrong with the art of protest or political agitprop" if it remained *"in its place"* (p. 216). In a footnote on the same page, he alluded to James Baldwin, who had criticized protest literature in "Everybody's Protest Novel," an essay asserting that such a novel "argues an insuperable confusion, since literature and sociology are not one and the same." "Everybody's Protest Novel," *Zero* (Spring 1949): pp. 54–58.
79. Cruse, *Crisis of the Negro Intellectual*, p. 219.
80. "Letter to the Editor," *Harlem Quarterly* 1 (Fall–Winter 1950): 61; "Are Negroes Winning Their Fight For Civil Rights?" *Harlem Quarterly* 1 (Winter 1949–50):22.
81. "H. Q. Scope," *Harlem Quarterly* 1 (Spring 1950):55.
82. Cruse, *Crisis of the Negro Intellectual*, p. 214; "Prospectus of Harlem Quarterly," *Harlem Quarterly* 1 (Winter 1949–50):1.
83. "The Last Volume," *Harlem Quarterly* 1 (Winter 1949–50):36–41; "Within the Haze," *Harlem Quarterly* 1 (Fall–Winter 1950):33.
84. "How to Be a Bad Writer," *Harlem Quarterly* 1 (Spring 1950):13.
85. "Voices," Ibid., p. 52.
86. Ibid., pp. 51, 50.
87. "Miss Samantha Wilson," *Voices* (Winter 1950): pp. 16–17.
88. "An Interview With Frank Marshall Davis," *Black World* 23 (January 1974): 46.
89. Statement by the January Club, *Shadows* 1 (Spring 1934):2. Information in a letter to the authors from Harvey M. Williamson, a founding member of the January Club, October 26, 1975.
90. "Introduction," *Free Lance* 1 (1952):1.
91. "The Music Teacher," Ibid., p. 8.
92. "Lisbon," *Free Lance* 1 (1953):28; "Notes on Negro Poets," *Free Lance* 2 (1954):16.
93. "Perspectives," *Black World* 21 (October 1972):49; "Black Art & Artists in Cleveland," *Free Lance* 22 (January 1973):26, 25.
94. Susan Edmiston and Linda D. Cirino, *Literary New York: A History and Guide* (Boston: Houghton Mifflin, 1976), p. 137.
95. Table of Contents, *Yugen* 1 (1958):1. Theodore R. Hudson, in his study of Jones, indicated that *Yugen* "was not widely circulated." As a result, copies of the journal are now viewed as "collectors' items," with issue one bringing five dollars even when not in "mint condition." Issue four, he explained, "is simply not available." *From LeRoi Jones to Amiri Baraka: The Literary Works* (Durham: Duke University Press, 1973), p. 15.

Chapter 6

1. "The New Directions of the Negro Writer," *Crisis* 70 (April 1963):205; "The New 'New Negro'; Emerging American," *Phylon* 24 (Winter 1963):361.
2. *"Negro Digest* Fans are a Persistent Breed," *Negro Digest* 10 (June 1961):3.
3. *Negro Digest* 11 (August 1962):45.
4. "Perspectives," *Negro Digest* 10 (September 1961):50; "Letters to the Editor," *Negro Digest* 13 (November 1963):97.
5. "Negroes With Pens," *Mainstream* 16 (July 1963):5. *Phylon* is best classified not as a "college review" but as a scholarly and interdisciplinary journal open

to a small amount of creative writing and critical discussion of literature. *Dasein* fits the label of "college review" much better. The quarterly magazine, which appeared regularly from 1961 to 1969 and only occasionally in later years, served as an outlet primarily for a group of Washington writers known as the Howard Poets. Included in the group were Percy Johnston and Walter De Legall; Sterling Brown, Arthur Davis, and Owen Dodson, among others, served as advisors to the magazine.

6. Berger, "Negroes With Pens," p. 5.

7. The Editors, "Foreword," *Umbra* 1 (Winter 1963):3–4.

8. Charles N. Glaab and A. Theodore Brown, *A History of Urban America* (New York: Macmillan, 1967), pp. 305–6.

9. Gerald, *Negro Digest* 19 (November 1969):29, 24.

10. The Editors, *Soulbook* 1 (Winter 1964), introductory page; Gerald, p. 24.

11. "Letters to the Editor," *Liberator* 6 (June 1966):20.

12. "Towards a Black Communication System," *Soulbook* 3 (Fall–Winter 1970): 44, 43; "On Spiritualism and the Revolutionary Spirit," *Journal of Black Poetry* 1 (Fall–Winter 1971):89.

13. For a discussion of one independent black press and its development, see Dudley Randall, "Broadside Press: A Personal Chronicle," in *The Black Seventies*, ed. Floyd B. Barbour (Boston: Porter Sargent, 1970), pp. 139–48.

14. "Perspectives," *Negro Digest* 19 (November 1969):50; "The Black Studies Boondoggle: A New Cop-Out on the Black Struggle?" *Liberator* 10 (September 1970):7–8.

15. "The Black Writer's Role," *Liberator* 6 (June 1966):8.

16. Ahmed Alhamisi, "On Spiritualism and the Revolutionary Spirit," pp. 88, 93.

17. "Is *Ebony* a Negro Magazine?" pt. 1, *Liberator* 5 (October 1965):5; "Is *Ebony* a Negro Magazine?" pt. 2, *Liberator* 5 (November 1965):18–19.

18. "Report on the 'Essence' Magazine Affair," *Journal of Black Poetry* 1 (Winter–Spring 1970):108.

19. "Some Notes (an editorial)," *Journal of Black Poetry* 1 (Summer 1972):3.

20. *The Black Aesthetic* (New York: Doubleday, 1971), p. xxiii.

21. Don Lee, among others, found it difficult to arrive at a detailed definition of the black aesthetic: "a blk/aesthetic does exist, but how does one define it? I suggest, at this time, that we not try." "Black Poetry: Which Direction?" *Negro Digest* 17 (Sept.–Oct. 1968):31.

22. The Black Writer's Role: Richard Wright," *Liberator* 5 (December 1965):20; "The Black Writer's Role: Ralph Ellison," *Liberator* 6 (January 1966):11.

23. "Perspectives," *Negro Digest* 17 (January 1968):9.

24. "Black Poetry: Which Direction?" pp. 29–30.

25. Gerald, p. 28.

26. "Statement," *Journal of Black Poetry* 1 (Spring 1967):14; "Black Poetry: Which Direction?" p. 28.

27. LeRoi Jones and Larry Neal, ed., *Black Fire: An Anthology of Afro-American Writing* (New York: William Morrow, 1968), p. 656.

28. "The Black Contribution to American Letters: Part II, The Writer as Activist—1960 and After," in *The Black American Reference Book*, ed. Mabel M. Smythe (Englewood Cliffs, New Jersey: Prentice-Hall, 1976), pp. 776–77, 770.

29. "Uncool Motherfuckers," *Nommo* 1 (Fall 1969):34; "Black Revolutionary Language," *Liberator* 9 (November 1969):8–10.

30. *Liberator* 3 (January 1963):2; "Letters to the Editor," *Liberator* 9 (August 1969):22.

31. *The Crisis of the Negro Intellectual* (New York: William Morrow, 1967), p. 407.

32. Cruse, *Crisis of the Negro Intellectual*, p. 254. Richard Moore was also a regular contributor to *Freedomways*, another quarterly magazine established in New York City during 1961 and a rival of *Liberator*. *Freedomways*, which is still published, is historically important partly because it dramatized the clash between Marxism and black nationalism and because it served as the swan song for one of the dominating black writers of the century. While the magazine was not an organ of the Communist Party, its supporters were black and white Marxists, many of whom were members of the party. The editor, Shirley Graham, was a Communist, as was her husband, W. E. B. Du Bois. She and one of her associate editors, W. Alphaeus Hunton, had been on the editorial board of *Freedom*. The managing editor, Esther Jackson, was married to James E. Jackson, described by Cruse as "the leading Negro theoretician in the Communist Party" (pp. 242–43). As years went on, the editorial board changed, as did the names of contributors. The Marxist orientation of the magazine continued, however. Thus, the journal largely steered clear of the new nationalistic literature and discussions of the black aesthetic, even though it occasionally published some of the emerging young poets.

   Du Bois made his last bow as a magazine contributor in *Freedomways*. He contributed the lead article, "The Negro People and the United States," to the first issue, published in the spring of 1961. The Winter 1962 issue carried his "Ghana Calls," a poem which shows that the ninety-three year old man, who had emigrated to Ghana, had found a home at long last. He died one year later, his passing acknowledged in *Freedomways*. The journal paid Du Bois a final tribute with a special issue dedicated to him in the winter of 1965.

33. Cruse, *Crisis of the Negro Intellectual*, pp. 405, 406–7.

34. "Dream and Reality," *Liberator* 3 (October 1963):2.

35. "Watts, L.A.,—The Nation's Shame," *Liberator* 5 (September 1965):3; "Rev. King & Vietnam," *Liberator* 7 (May 1967):3.

36. "The Eve of Revolution," *Liberator* 7 (September 1967):3.

37. Cruse, *Crisis of the Negro Intellectual*, p. 413.

38. Neal, "Richard Wright," p. 20.

39. Ibid., p. 22.

40. Neal, "Ralph Ellison," pp. 11, 10. For the statement ascribed to Ellison, see "Editorial Comment," *Negro Quarterly* 1 (Winter–Spring 1943):30.

41. "The Black Writer's Role: James Baldwin," *Liberator* 6 (April 1966):18.

42. "Development of LeRoi Jones," *Liberator* 6 (January 1966):4.

43. "The Revolutionary Theatre," *Liberator* 5 (July 1965):4.

44. *Black Mass*, *Liberator* 6 (June 1966):16, 17.

45. "Black Art," *Liberator* 6 (January 1966): 18; *Drumvoices: The Mission of Afro-American Poetry* (Garden City, New York: Doubleday, 1976), p. 356.

46. *Liberator* 3 (January 1963):2.

47. Cruse, *Crisis of the Negro Intellectual*, p. 406.

48. Dingane, rev. of *Dynamite Voices*, by Don L. Lee, *Journal of Black Poetry* 1 (Summer 1973):88. Goncalves sometimes used the name, Dingane.

49. "The Crises in Black Culture," *Journal of Black Poetry* 1 (Spring 1968):5.

50. Dingane, rev. of *Dynamite Voices*, p. 88.

51. The Editors, *Soulbook* 1 (Winter 1964): introductory pages.

52. *Soulbook* 1 (Spring 1965):78.

53. "That Boy Le Roi," *Soulbook* 1 (Spring 1965):111–13, (rpt. New York *Post*, January 15, 1965, p. 38).

54. "A Reply," *Soulbook* 1 (Spring 1965):113–14. Saunders Redding shared Hughes's understanding of LeRoi Jones, saying that he "takes off ... from an emotional base that would do no credit to a tantrum-pitching six-year-old. He is like a child who, having stubbed his toe on a rock, kicks and screams at the rock as if he expects it to get up and go away." "Since Richard Wright," *African Forum* 1 (Spring 1966):23–24.

    David Llorens responded to Redding as Hamilton had to Hughes. "Saunders Redding is today one of the meanest critics—save the white detractors—of black writing, of young black writers," he asseverated: "his scathing attacks on LeRoi Jones appear peculiarly pathological." "What Contemporary Black Writers Are Saying," *Nommo* 1 (Winter 1969):26.

55. "A Letter to Boy Wilkins," *Soulbook* 2 (Winter–Spring 1967):130.

56. "Editorial," and "Revolutionary Black Artist," *Black Dialogue* 1 (Winter 1966):3–4, 15–16.

57. "A Letter to Ed Spriggs: Concerning LeRoi Jones and Others," *Black Dialogue* 3 (Winter 1967–68):3–4.

58. "Black Dialogue," and "Editorial," *Black Dialogue* 4 (Spring 1969):2, 3–4.

59. Gerald, p. 27.

60. Dingane, rev. of *Dynamite Voices*, p. 88.

61. *Kitabu Cha Jua* (Summer 1974): table of contents. None of the issues of the magazine carries a volume number.

62. "Notes on the Authors," *Journal of Black Poetry* 1 (Summer 1966):17; Dingane, rev. of *Dynamite Voices*, p. 89. Imamu Amiri Baraka will be used hereafter in this chapter instead of LeRoi Jones, even though some of the works cited may be signed by Jones. From Theodore Hudson's study of the writer, one can conclude that Jones began the process of changing his name approximately in 1966 and that he completed the procedure by 1970. Amiri, derived from Ameer, later came to be the middle name. According to Hudson, Imamu signifies "spiritual leader" and Baraka means "blessed prince." *From LeRoi Jones to Amiri Baraka: The Literary Works* (Durham: Duke University Press, 1973), pp. 34–35.

63. "When State Magicians Fail: An Interview with Ishmael Reed," *Journal of Black Poetry* 1 (Summer–Fall 1969):75, 74, 73.

64. "An Afterword," *Journal of Black Poetry* 1 (Summer–Fall 1969):76, 77.

65. Dingane, rev. of *Dynamite Voices*, pp. 91, 87, 86, 90, 87.

66. "My Child," *Journal of Black Poetry* 1 (Summer–Fall 1969):16; "On Seeing Pharoah Sanders Blowing," *Journal of Black Poetry* 1 (Fall 1967):5.

67. Jones, "Statement," p. 14; "The Fire Must Be Permitted To Burn Full Up," *Journal of Black Poetry* 1 (Summer–Fall 1969):64, 65.

68. Neal, "The Black Contribution to American Letters," p. 777.

69. "Perspectives," *Negro Digest* 17 (December 1967): 93; Neal, "The Black Contribution to American Letters," p. 777.

70. Gerald, pp. 25–26; "Perspectives," *Negro Digest* 16 (March 1967):83.

71. "Toward a Definition: Black Poetry of the Sixties (After LeRoi Jones)," in *The Black Aesthetic*, pp. 238–239; "Harlem My Harlem," *Black World* 20 (November 1970):93; Neal, "The Black Contribution to American Letters," p. 778.

72. "Ivory Towerist vs. Activist: The Role of the Negro Writer in an Era of

Struggle," and "A Poet Apologizes to His Critics," *Negro Digest* 13 (June 1964):62–66, 68.

73. "The Negro Writer in the U.S.: Assembly at Asilomar," *Negro Digest* 13 (September 1964):46.

74. "Perspectives," *Negro Digest* 16 (May 1967):49; Darwin T. Turner, "A Rebuttal: The Literary Presumptions of Mr. Bone," *Negro Digest* 16 (August 1967):54, editorial statement preceding article; "The Critics *Will* Learn," *Negro Digest* 18 (November 1968):53.

75. "Books Noted," *Negro Digest* 14 (August 1965):51–52.

76. "Perspectives," *Negro Digest* 14 (October 1965):49–50, 83.

77. Neal, "The Black Contribution to American Letters," p. 778.

78. "The Task of the Negro Writer as Artist: A Symposium," *Negro Digest* 14 (April 1965):54.

79. Ibid., pp. 60, 59, 75, 65, 58.

80. "A Survey: Black Writers Views on Literary Lions and Values," *Negro Digest* 17 (January 1968):10, 48.

81. Ibid., p. 16.

82. Ibid., pp. 19, 12, 16, 17. With a brief notation in the 1965 symposium, Fuller had acknowledged the absence of any statement by either James Baldwin or Ralph Ellison. He thought Baldwin had never received his communication, since he was then in Europe and difficult to contact. Fuller had sent a letter to Ellison at his home address in New York. When no response was forthcoming, Fuller asked Random House for permission to quote a passage from *Shadow and Act*. Random House, in turn, asked Ellison if the material could be reprinted in *Negro Digest*. "The reply came back by wire," Fuller remembered, "REGRET ANSWER IS NEGATIVE." "A Note on the Symposium," Ibid., p. 83.

83. Ibid., p. 14.

84. Ibid., pp. 12, 33, 84.

85. Ibid., p. 83.

86. "All In A Name," *Negro Digest* 19 (March 1970):98; "If I Call U Negro, You'll Act That Way!" *Black World* 19 (October 1970):45.

87. "Introduction," *Black Review* (1971–1972): p. 6.

88. "Did I Dream Them Times: Or What Happened?" *Black World* 21 (May 1972):67; "On Images and Control: The National Black Writers Convention," *Black World* 24 (January 1975):90–91.

89. " 'Why I Changed My Ideology': Black Nationalism and Socialist Revolution," *Black World* 24 (July 1975):33, 36, 30, 42.

90. "Division and Confusion: What Happened To The Black Movement," *Black World* 25 (January 1976):28, 26, 25, 24.

91. "Renaissance Personality: An Interview with George Schuyler," *Black World* 25 (February 1976):75, 76; "Perspectives," *Black World* 24 (November 1975): 49. The wider range of Fuller's literary midwifry among black writers during the 1960s can be seen in his involvement in OBAC. Organized in 1967, the Organization of Black American Culture began as a local community art center in the south side of Chicago. "The interest then," wrote Fuller several years later, "was primarily political; art for the sake of Black empowerment was the principle." "Foreword," *Nommo* 1 (Summer 1972):2. The group originally launched a variety of community-oriented projects during the first year, but only one—the Writers' Workshop—sustained that initial interest and support. Two years later, with a grant from the Illinois Art Council, OBAC

brought out *Nommo*, the title being a Bantu word meaning "life force." Planned as a quarterly, the literary journal appeared only three times from early 1969 to the summer of 1972. The magazine had neither an editor nor an editorial board, but Fuller served as advisor to the periodical as well as to the writers' group. The OBAC Writers' Workshop attempted to provide support for the aspiring writers by giving them both criticism of their work and, through *Nommo*, an outlet for their efforts. In the final selection of contributions to *Nommo*, radical literary politics prevailed, as affirmed in a "Statement of Purposes," carried in the fall 1969 issue of the journal. The group committed itself, so the statement declared, to "the conscious development and articulation of a Black Aesthetic...." This concern pervaded most of the writing—primarily poetry—which appeared in *Nommo* and was advanced by the better-known members of OBAC, such as Don Lee, Carolyn Rodgers, and Johari Amiri (Jewel C. Latimore).

92. "Slogan's End," *Liberator* 11 (March 1971):3.
93. "A New Reality Is Better Than A New Movie!" *Kitabu Cha Jua* 1 (Summer 1975):27; "Today," Ibid., p. 28; "The Decline of Black Nationalism & What Can Be Done About It," Ibid., p. 37.
94. "From the Publisher," *Black Creation* 6 (Annual 1974–75):3.
95. "Arts Organizations in the Deep South: A Report," Ibid., p. 76.
96. Neal, "The Black Contribution to American Letters," pp. 783–84.
97. "Seeking a New Image: Writers Converge at Fisk University," *Negro Digest* 15 (June 1966): 57.
98. "Black Poetry: Which Direction?" p. 31.

Epilogue

1. "Foreword," *Fire* 1 (November 1926):2.
2. *Negro Digest* 19 (November 1969):29; "Editorials," *Voice of the Negro* 1 (January 1904):38.

Selected Bibliography

I Primary Sources

A. PERIODICALS
Abbott's Monthly, 1930–33
African, 1938
African Forum, 1965–67
Alexander's Magazine, 1905–07
American Life Magazine, 1926–28
Anglo-African Magazine, 1859
Arts Quarterly, 1937–39
BANC: Black, Afro-American, Negro, Colored, 1970–71
Black Creation, 1970–75
Black Dialogue, 1964–70
Black Opals, 1927–28
Black Orpheus, 1957–76
Black Review, 1971–72
Black World, 1970–76
Bronzeman, 1929–33
Caroline Magazine, 1927–29
Challenge and *New Challenge*, 1934–37
Champion, 1916–17
Colored American Magazine, 1900–09
Common Ground, 1940–50
Competitor, 1920–21
Crisis, 1910–76
Dasein, 1961–69
Dawn, 1935
Fire, 1926
Freedomways, 1961–76
Free Lance, 1953–76
Half-Century Magazine, 1916–25
Harlem, 1928

Harlem Quarterly, 1949–50
Horizon, 1907–10
Kitabu Cha Jua, 1974–76
Journal of Black Poetry, 1966–73
Liberator, 1961–71
Midwest Journal, 1948–56
McGirt's Magazine, 1903–07
Messenger, 1917–28
Metropolitan, 1935
Mirror, 1935
Negro Digest, 1942–51, 1961–70
Negro Quarterly, 1942–44
Negro Story, 1944–46
Negro World Digest, 1940
New Era, 1916
New Vistas, 1945–46
Nommo, 1969–72
Opportunity, 1923–49
Palms, 1926
Phase II, Journal of Black Art Renaissance, 1970–71
Phylon, 1940–76
Pulse, 1943–48
Race, 1935–36
Reflexus, 1925
Renaissance 2: A Journal of Afro-American Studies, 1971–73
Saturday Evening Quill, 1928–30
Soulbook, 1964–76
Spokesman, 1925–26
Stylus, 1916–41
Survey Graphic, 1925
Umbra, 1963–75
Urbanite, 1961
Voice of the Negro, 1904–07
Voices, 1950
WATU: Journal of Black Poetry/Art, 1971

B. MANUSCRIPT COLLECTIONS

New Haven. Yale University Library. James Weldon Johnson Memorial Collection.
New York. New York Public Library. Schomburg Collection of Black History, Literature and Art.
Washington, D.C. Howard University Library. Alain Locke Papers.
Washington, D.C. Library of Congress. Booker T. Washington Papers.
Washington, D.C. Library of Congress. National Association for the Advancement of Colored People Papers.
Washington, D.C. Library of Congress. National Urban League Papers.

C. BOOKS

Aptheker, Herbert, ed. *The Correspondence of W. E. B. Du Bois.* 3 vols. Amherst: University of Massachusetts Press, 1973–78.

Barbour, Floyd B., ed. *The Black Seventies.* Boston: Porter Sargent Publishers, 1970.

Brown, William Wells. *The Black Man: His Antecedents, His Genius, and His Achievements.* Boston: Robert F. Wallout, 1865.

Du Bois, W. E. B. *The Autobiography of W. E. B. Du Bois.* Edited by Herbert Aptheker. New York: International Publishers, 1968.

Gayle, Addison, ed. *The Black Aesthetic.* New York: Doubleday, 1971.

Hopkins, Pauline. *Contending Forces: A Romance Illustrative of Negro Life North and South.* 1900. Reprint. Miami: Mnemosyne, 1969.

Hughes, Langston. *The Big Sea.* 1940. Reprint. New York: Hill and Wang, 1963.

Hurston, Zora Neale. *Dust Tracks on the Road.* 1942. Reprint. Philadelphia: Arno, 1969.

Johnson, Charles S., ed. *Ebony and Topaz: A Collectanea.* New York: National Urban League, 1927.

Johnson, Fenton. *Tales of Darkest America.* Chicago: Favorite Magazine, 1920.

Johnson, James Weldon. *Along This Way.* New York: Viking, 1933.

————. *Negro Americans, What Now?* New York: Viking, 1934.

Jones, LeRoi, and Neal, Larry, eds. *Black Fire: An Anthology of Afro-American Writing.* New York: William Morrow, 1968.

Lee, Don, ed. *Dynamite Voices: Black Poets of the 1960s.* Detroit: Broadside, 1971.

Locke, Alain, ed. *The New Negro.* 1925. Reprint. New York: Atheneum, 1970.

McKay, Claude, *A Long Way from Home.* New York: Lee Furman, 1937.

Major, Clarence. *The New Black Poetry.* New York: International Publishers, 1969.

Ovington, Mary White. *The Walls Came Tumbling Down.* New York: Harcourt and Brace, 1947.

Schuyler, George S. *Black and Conservative.* New Rochelle, New York: Arlington House, 1966.

Thurman, Wallace. *Infants of the Spring.* New York: Macaulay, 1932.

Stewart, Donald O. *Fighting Words.* New York: Harcourt and Brace, 1940.

D. ARTICLES

Baldwin, James. "Everybody's Protest Novel." *Zero* 1 (1949):54–58.

Berger, Art. "Negroes with Pens." *Mainstream* 16 (1963):1–6.

Brawley, Benjamin. "The Negro Literary Renaissance." *Southern Workman* 56 (1937):177–84.

Brown, Lloyd C. "Which Way for the Negro Writer." *Masses & Mainstream* 4 (1951):53–57.

Du Bois, W. E. B. "Editing 'The Crisis.'" *Crisis* 58 (1951):147–51, 213.

Ferguson, Dutton. "Twenty-Six Years of Opportunity." *Opportunity* 27 (1949):4–7.

Herndon, Calvin. "Umbra Poets." *Mainstream* 16 (1963):7–13.

Hughes, Langston. "The Twenties: Harlem and Its Negritude." *African Forum* 1 (1966):11–20.

Locke, Alain. "Beauty Instead of Ashes." *Nation* 126 (1928):432–34.

————. "Fire: A Negro Magazine." *Survey* 58 ((1927):563.

Schuyler, George S. "Forty Years of 'The Crisis.'" *Crisis* 58 (1951):163–64.

Streator, George. "Working on 'The Crisis,'" *Crisis* 58 (1951):159–63.

Starkey, Marion L. "Jessie Fauset." *Southern Workman* 61 (1932):217–21.

"The Colored Magazine in America." *Crisis* 5 (1912):33–35.

"The Stylus." *Howard University Record* 19 (1925):372.

Thurman, Wallace. "Negro Artists and the Negro." *New Republic* 52 (1927):37–39.

———. "Negro Poets and Their Poetry." *Bookman* 67 (1928):555–61.

Wilkins, Roy. "The Crisis, 1934–49." *Crisis* 58 (1951): 154–56.

II Secondary Sources

A. BOOKS

Bone, Robert. *The Negro Novel in America*. New Haven: Yale University Press, 1958.

Bontemps, Arna, ed. *The Harlem Renaissance Remembered*. New York: Dodd, Mead and Company, 1972.

Broderick, Francis L. *W. E. B. Du Bois: Negro Leader in Time of Crisis*. Stanford: Stanford University Press, 1959.

Bronz, Stephen H. *The Roots of Negro Racial Consciousness; The 1920s: Three Harlem Renaissance Authors*. New York: Libra, 1964.

Buni, Andrew. *Robert L. Vann of the Pittsburgh Courier*. Pittsburgh: University of Pittsburgh Press, 1974.

Butcher, Margaret. *The Negro in American Culture*. New York: Knopf, 1956.

Chambers, Clarke. *Paul U. Kellogg and the Survey*. Minneapolis: University of Minnesota Press, 1971.

Cooper, Wayne F., ed. *The Passion of Claude McKay*. New York: Schocken Books, 1973.

Cruse, Harold. *The Crisis of the Negro Intellectual*. New York: William Morrow, 1967.

Dann, Martin E., ed. *The Black Press, 1827–1890*. New York: Putnam's Sons, 1971.

Davis, Arthur P. *From the Dark Tower*. Washington, D.C.: Howard University Press, 1974.

Davis, Arthur P., Brown, Sterling A., and Lee, Ullysses, eds. *The Negro Caravan*. 1941. Reprint. New York: Arno, 1969.

Detweiler, Frederick G. *The Negro Press in the United States*. Chicago: University of Chicago Press, 1922.

Edmiston, Susan, and Cirino, Linda D. *Literary New York: A History and Guide*. Boston: Houghton Mifflin, 1976.

Ellison, Ralph. *Shadow and Act*. New York: Random, 1964.

Emanuel, James A. *Langston Hughes*. New York: Twayne, 1967.

Fabre, Michel. *The Unfinished Quest of Richard Wright*. New York: William Morrow, 1973.

Ferguson, Blance E. *Countee Cullen and the Negro Renaissance*. New York: Dodd, Mead, 1966.

Ford, Nick A. *The Contemporary Negro Novel*. Boston: Meador, 1936.

Franklin, John Hope. *From Slavery to Freedom*. 4th ed. New York: Alfred A. Knopf, 1974.

Fullinwider, S. P. *The Mind and Mood of Black America*. Homewood, Illinois: Dorsey, 1969.

Garland, Penn I. *The Afro-American Press and Its Editors*. Springfield, Massachusetts: Wiley, 1891.

Glaab, Charles N., and Brown, A. Theodore. *A History of Urban America*. 2nd ed. New York: Macmillan, 1976.

Gloster, Hugh M. *Negro Voices in American Fiction.* Chapel Hill: University of North Carolina Press, 1948.

Hemenway, Robert E. *Zora Neale Hurston.* Urbana: University of Illinois Press, 1977.

Henderson, Stephen. *Understanding the New Black Poetry.* New York: William Morrow, 1973.

Hoffman, Frederick J., Allen, Charles, and Ulrich, Carolyn R. *The Little Magazine.* Princeton: Princeton University Press, 1946.

Hudson, Theodore. *From LeRoi Jones to Amiri Baraka: The Literary Works.* Durham: Duke University Press, 1973.

Huggins, Nathan I. *Harlem Renaissance.* New York: Oxford, 1971.

Johnson, James Weldon. *Black Manhattan.* New York: Knopf, 1930.

Kostelanetz, Richard. *The End of Intelligent Writing: Literary Politics in America.* New York: Sheed and Ward, 1973.

Logan, Rayford W., Holmes, Eugene C., and Edwards, G. Franklin, eds. *The New Negro Thirty Years Afterward.* Washington, D.C.: Howard University Press, 1955.

Ottley, Roi. *The Lonely Warrior: The Life and Times of Robert S. Abbott.* Chicago: Regnery, 1955.

Osofsky, Gilbert. *Harlem: The Making of a Ghetto; Negro New York, 1890–1930.* New York: Harper and Row, 1966.

Parris, Guichard, and Brooks, Lester. *Blacks in the City.* Boston: Little, Brown and Company, 1971.

Peterson, Theodore. *Magazines in the Twentieth Century.* Urbana: University of Illinois Press, 1956.

Redmond, Eugene B. *Drumvoices: The Mission of Afro-American Poetry.* Garden City, New York: Doubleday, 1976.

Rudwick, Elliott M. *W. E. B. Du Bois: A Study in Minority Group Leadership.* New York: Atheneum, 1969.

Rush, Theressa G., Myers, Carol F., and Arata, Esther S. *Black American Writers.* 2 vols. Metuchen, New Jersey: Scarecrow Press, 1975.

Thornbrough, Emma Lou. *T. Thomas Fortune: Militant Journalist.* Chicago: University of Chicago Press, 1972.

Wagner, Jean. *Black Poets of the United States.* Urbana: University of Illinois Press, 1973.

Young, James. *Black Writers of the Thirties.* Baton Rouge: Louisiana State University Press, 1973.

B. ARTICLES

Blassingame, John W. "The Afro-Americans: Mythology to Reality." *The Reinterpretation of American History and Culture,* edited by William H. Cartwright and Richard L. Watson, Jr. Washington, D.C.: National Council for the Social Studies, 1973.

Braithwaite, William Stanley. "Negro America's First Magazine." *Negro Digest 6* (1947):21–26.

Burks, Mary Fair. "The First Black Literary Magazine in American Letters." *College Language Association Journal* 19 (1976):318–21.

Chapman, Abraham. "The Harlem Renaissance in Literary History." *College Language Association Journal* 11 (1967):38–58.

Daniel, Walter C. " 'Challenge Magazine': An Experiment That Failed." *College Language Association Journal* 19 (1976):494–503.

Ivy, James. "First Negro Congress of Writers and Artists." *Crisis* 63 (1956):593–600.

Johnson, Charles S. "The Rise of the Negro Magazine." *Journal of Negro History* 13 (1928):7–21.

Meier, August. "Booker T. Washington and the Negro Press: With Special Reference to the *Colored American Magazine*." *Journal of Negro History* 38 (1953):67–90.

Neal, Larry P. "The Writer as Activist—1960 and After." *The Black American Reference Book*, edited by Mabel H. Smythe. Englewood Cliffs, New Jersey: Prentice-Hall, 1976.

Parker, John W. "Benjamin Brawley and the American Cultural Tradition." *Phylon* 16 (1955):183–91.

Partington, Paul G. "The Moon Illustrated Weekly–The Precursor of the *Crisis*." *Journal of Negro History* 48 (1963):206–16.

Rudwick, Elliott M. "W. E. B. Du Bois in the Role of *Crisis* Editor." *Journal of Negro History* 43 (1958):214–40.

Shockley, Ann A. "Pauline Elizabeth Hopkins: Biographical Excursion into Obscurity." *Phylon* 33 (1972):22–26.

C. DISSERTATIONS

Burks, Mary Fair. "A Survey of Black Literary Magazines in the United States: 1859–1940." Ph.D. dissertation, Columbia University, 1975.

Crane, Claire B. "Alain Locke and the Negro Renaissance." Ph.D. dissertation, University of California, San Diego, 1971.

Kornweibel, Theodore J. "The *Messenger* Magazine: 1917–1928." Ph.D. dissertation, Yale University, 1971.

Weiss, Nancy J. " 'Not Alms, But Opportunity:' A History of the National Urban League, 1910–1940." Ph.D. dissertation, Harvard University, 1969.

Index